People and Places in Newmachar Past and Present

PEOPLE AND PLACES

IN

NEWMACHAR

PAST AND PRESENT

Roy Bridges

Parish of New Machar Community Council
Newmachar, Aberdeenshire
2 0 0 1

This work is published by
The Parish of New Machar Community Council
as part of its commemoration of the year 2001

ISBN
0-9540701-0-0

A6 71 E
1274375

Printed by
Woods of Perth Ltd
113-119 Glover Street
Perth

Preface

Traditionally in Scotland, the turn of the year is an occasion to reflect on the year just past, and to muse on the significance of events for the year which is about to begin. When we stand at the threshold of the third millennium (even though there may be a dispute about exactly when that point may arise), how much more inspiring is it to cast one's thoughts over that longer time-span. Newmachar Community Council, when it was looking for some contribution to make to the Millennium celebrations that might not be entirely ephemeral, welcomed gladly the proposal that this publication be prepared and published. It was thought particularly appropriate because in the last twenty years or so, life in the Parish, responding to the economic and other changes to North-east Scotland which came with the discovery of oil and gas under the North Sea, has been transformed beyond all recognition.

A community that has lost sight of its roots is impoverished. We may better understand our problems, perhaps, if we have knowledge of how our community comes to be as it is and how our place evolved. For the many incomers, among whom I number myself, who have made their homes in our parish, a wealth of information lay locked up in memories and personal records. It is hoped that these reflections will both inform and entertain readers, and nurture a sense of our history, whether grand and aristocratic or ordinary and commonplace or somewhere in between. We all have our place, and this is ours. We have many reasons to be proud of it.

Robert Loughridge
Chairman
Newmachar Community Council.

CONTENTS

Preface by Robert Loughridge   v
Introduction and Acknowledgements   xi

I.   The Physical Background   1
II.   Prehistory to the Emergence of Scotland   4
III.   Early Medieval History: King Malcolm's Visit
        and the Bishop's Palace at Loch Goull   7
IV.   The Place Names of Newmachar   9
V.   Medieval Newmachar, the Black Death and
        the Emergence of Estates   12
VI.   Robert Gordon of Straloch (1580-1661)
        and Maps of Newmachar   18
VII.   Early Modern Newmachar: from the Creation of the Parish
        to the Old Statistical Account, 1609-1791   25
VIII.   Agriculture in Newmachar to c.1800   38
IX.   The Agricultural Revolution and Agriculture to the 1920s   42
X.   Water Power: the Mills of Newmachar   58
XI.   Transport 1: Roads, Garages and the Post Office   63
XII.   Transport 2: The Great North of Scotland Railway
        and its Successors   75
XIII.   The Church in the Life of the Community since 1804   85
XIV.   Civil Government c.1800 to 2001: Politics, Law and Order,
        the Poor Law and Local Government   104
XV.   Life in Greater and Lesser Houses in the Nineteenth
        and Twentieth Centuries   116
XVI.   Some Connections with the Wider World   128
XVII.   Education 1621-1918   136
XVIII. Education since 1918   143
XIX.   Contributions to the History of Newmachar by Pupils at
        New Machar School and Dyce Academy   149
XX.   Wars and Rumours of Wars   157
XXI.   Kingseat Hospital 1901-1995   163
XXII.   Newmachar's Social, Cultural and Sporting Activities   168
XXIII. The Twentieth-Century Economy: Agriculture and Farm Life
        since the 1920s   181
XXIV.   The Emergence of Shops and Businesses   202

Appendix: The 1821 and 1831 Censuses, Newmachar's Population
            and the extent of Newmachar Village   214
Sources: 1. Bibliography 2. Oral and Written Testimony   219

The Bridge of Steps

The Author: Roy Bridges is Emeritus Professor of History in the University of Aberdeen. He is a fellow of the Royal Geographical and Royal Historical Societies and currently a Vice-President of the Hakluyt Society. His interests are in the history of travel and exploration, especially in Africa, imperialism, African history and Scots overseas. Among many articles and books, his most recent works include writing and editing *Compassing the Vaste Globe of the Earth* (1996), *Imperialism, Decolonization and Africa* (2000) and a major contribution to the *Cambridge Companion to Travel Writing* (2002). Resident in the Northeast for forty years, he now lives in Newmachar in the former manse and is a member of the Community Council.

People and Places in Newmachar, Past and Present was commissioned by the Parish of New Machar Community Council as a means of marking the new millennium in 2001. The production of the book has been in considerable part funded by the 'Awards for All' scheme supported by the National Heritage Memorial Fund, the National Lottery Charities Board, the Scottish Arts Council and Sportscotland.

The cover picture shows the Free Church in Newmachar as it was in about 1920 with Disblair Road leading up to it. The watercolour was painted by Mrs Cecilia Kerr, who lived at the West Manse. It is reproduced by kind permission of Mrs Kerr's daughter, Mrs Marigold Nicol.

The Children with the Pram on p. vi is from a photograph taken for a postcard probably at some time in the 1890s when Mr Cooper, whose sign is on the shop (now Mace), was proprietor. Beside the shop can be seen the semi-separate building which was the Post Office. This was also a sorting office until the 1920s. One child has a can for collecting her family's supply of milk. The photograph is from Mr John Taylor's collection which he kindly made available.

The Bridge of Steps (892161) shown opposite is from a drawing by Mrs Joan Burnett and reproduced with her kind permission.

Large Group of Children in Summerhill

The date of this picture and the circumstances in which it was taken are uncertain. It seems likely to date from well before the end of the nineteenth century. Could it possibly be children from the Free Church School which would have been nearby on the left of the picture? This picture is from Mr John Taylor's collection.

Introduction

In the millennium since 1001 AD, Newmachar has received just two royal visits. King Malcolm came in 1058 and Queen Elizabeth, now the Queen Mother, in 1940. This rather low incidence of royal attention exemplifies a rather more general apparent lack of interest on the part of the outside world in the parish area and its people. Most of both the serious and the more popular written works on Aberdeen and Northeast history published during the last hundred years or so such as William Watt's *History* of 1900, or Robert Smith's *Discovering Aberdeenshire* of 1988 do not even mention Newmachar. The one standard published history of Aberdeenshire's parishes which does have an account is Alexander Smith's *A New History of Aberdeenshire*, published in 1875. It might have been better had Smith, too, left Newmachar alone; the account, which has unfortunately been put on the internet, abounds with errors. Two of the late and great Cuthbert Graham's 'This is my Country' series in the *Press and Journal*, cover Newmachar. These two newspaper features probably constitute the best existing published outline accounts of Newmachar's history. They appeared in February 1963 and March 1971.

Some amateur historians whose work has had very limited circulation have written about Newmachar's past. The Rev. D.R. Kerr gave a very scholarly account of the earlier history of the parish to a meeting of the Women's Rural Institute in 1931 but was never able to build on this. Also produced for the WRI was Mrs Catherine Imlah's 'A Short Outline of the History of the Parish of New Machar' of 1965; in its scope and approach this unpublished work showed a proper history was possible. Mrs Joan Burnett contributed no fewer than 84 articles on some parts of the area's history to the Community Council's newsletter in the 1980s and '90s.

Most outstanding among the unpublished works on Newmachar is a 1967 University of Aberdeen undergraduate geography thesis written by James Cowie, who was born and grew up in the parish. It constitutes by far the best account of the history of the parish which is properly seen as essentially an agricultural community.

Full details of existing works are provided in the Bibliography whilst indications of the relevant materials consulted on particular subjects are noted in each chapter. It should become apparent that there are some excellent archival sources relating to Newmachar which no-one has previously consulted. It is equally obvious that more such materials, especially estate records, will emerge if the effort is made to locate them. This study also hopes to demonstrate that another very important resource exists for the history of the parish and this is recollections which can be gathered from the inhabitants of the parish.

What *People and Places in Newmachar, Past and Present* aims to do is not only to give a voice to some of the present inhabitants through their contributions to this work but also to give a voice to their predecessors in previous centuries by using some of the historical materials which are available. Each chapter attempts to provide some sort of context for what was happening in Newmachar by reference to more general Scottish developments. The treatment is both broadly chronological and thematic, and there is inevitably more emphasis on nineteenth and twentieth-century history than that of earlier periods for which the materials are scarcer. The scope is indicated in the contents list showing the chapter titles.

I have incurred many debts in preparing this work. I am grateful first of all to the Parish of New Machar Community Council - to give it its correct title - for sponsoring this work and especially to the Chairman, Robert Loughridge, for his support and for agreeing to write a preface to this book. Mike Taylor, the Secretary and Glenda Gray, the Treasurer, have given much practical and moral support as have Mark Fraser, William Kennedy and Gordon Murray. Sandy Buchan and Fergus Hood have both also contributed directly to the content. I also acknowledge with gratitude the support of the Garioch Area Committee of Aberdeenshire Council in providing some financial help for the preparation of illustrations. Alison McLeod and Richard Belding helped over the surprisingly complex problem of recent population figures for Newmachar. The Area Manager, Mr Ian Fowell, and the former Committee Officer, Jan McRobbie, have been helpful and supportive as has Councillor Dr Martin Ford. At times, the Community Council must have wondered if their confidence was misplaced as the false millennium of January 2000 and the real one of January 2001 went by with no book published. My excuse must be not only other commitments but also the realisation of the scale of the work that was necessary if anything worthwhile was to be said about Newmachar. A book containing a collection of loosely-connected snippets of information could have been produced in a quarter of the time. For better or for worse, I have aimed at something a little more ambitious which might justify the Community Council's confidence and also, I hope, in a small way help them in their task of building Newmachar's awareness of itself as a living community. Even so, my claim is only to have sketched in the history and perhaps to have shown the possibilities for future research; I am only too conscious of whole classes of records I have not been able to consult.

I am especially indebted to all those who took the time and trouble to talk to me about their memories and their understanding of the past. Some are present residents of the parish; others are former inhabitants. Without exception, everyone received me kindly and hospitably with the result that my research, if not systematic, was extremely pleasant. It is inevitable that I shall have misunderstood or misinterpreted some of the information that I have been given. Where that is the case, I hope I may be forgiven. The list of informants and contributors will indicate their names. These have been the real makers and inspirers of this book. I am deeply grateful to them all. Many of the contributors and informants provided the originals of the photographs which appear here. I am most appreciative of the readiness with which they entrusted their pictures to me. John Taylor was particularly helpful.

Major Frances Irvine of Straloch, the heir of a long and important historical legacy in Newmachar, not only generously and unreservedly provided access to research materials in his possession but also encouraged me to persevere with the project. The Reverend Ian Dryden, Minister of the Parish from 1988 to 2001 and formerly a member of the Community Council, introduced me to the Council and its work. He has warmly supported this project and been a good friend. Miss Lil Irvine has provided more encouragement and reassurance than perhaps she has realised. Mrs Jean Emslie has also been most interested and helpful. For her support as well as permission to use some of her wonderful drawings of Newmachar, I am grateful to Mrs Joan Burnett.

Numerous other people have helped in various ways. I thank Allan Pirie and Louise Dunderdale of the Ellon Times; Mr Ian Proud for the copy of *Temple's Thanage of Fermartyn*; Dr Ian Shepherd, Miss Moira Greig and Mr Shaun Norman of Aberdeenshire's Archaeological Services; Mrs Sheila Spiers of the N.E. Family History Society for taking much extra trouble to provide me with her transcription of the epitaphs in New Machar Kirkyard; Mr Nicholas Bogdan for alerting me to relevant sources and relevant people. Dr John Durkan and Dr Evelyn Stell, both of the University of Glasgow, gave me invaluable aid in connection with Robert Gordon. The support of the staff from New Machar School and Dyce Academy will be apparent in Chapter IX. Mr Walter Baxter, formerly janitor, was also helpful in providing materials and information.

It would not have been possible to proceed with the project without the grant for a large part of the production costs from the 'Awards for All' organisation whose officials were courteous and helpful. Eminently practical advice from the Director of the organisation in Scotland, Mr Colin McLean, was especially valuable. In connection with the application for the award, the Community Council and I benefited from the supporting testimony of Dr Andrew Collins. The printing itself has been in the hands of Woods of Perth, who have been patient and efficient. I am especially grateful to Mr Harry Greig who has been a dispenser not only of excellent advice but also of friendly reassurance; it has been a pleasure to work with him.

The preparation of the illustrations for this book was made more difficult by my own rather clumsy attempts to scan the originals into my computer. Mr Kenneth Anderson of Scotscan Reprographics has done his best to retrieve my errors and I have much appreciated his kind and patient advice. Mrs Diana

Webster and her colleagues in the Map Library of the National Library of Scotland have been most helpful over Robert Gordon's map and its reproduction.

In undertaking the research for *People and Places*, I have been fortunate in having access to some splendid collections of materials looked after by experts who are also helpful. Aberdeen City Central Library provided the means to consult materials such as census records. Aberdeenshire's Library Headquarters at Oldmeldrum provided me with access to microfilms of all the available baptismal, marriage and death records relating to Newmachar and much other relevant material. I particularly benefited from the help of Mrs Dorothy Dewar and Mr David Catto.

The hitherto untapped records relating to Newmachar preserved now at the joint City/Aberdeenshire Archive at Old Aberdeen have been invaluable for this study. Judith Cripps and her colleagues, especially Iain Gray and Siobhan Convery, were unfailingly helpful.

It is above all upon the University of Aberdeen and its resources that I have relied for the attempts to provide Newmachar with a history. The Principal himself, Professor Duncan Rice, has been supportive and interested. Practical help came from the Computing Centre's Help organisation and I am especially grateful to Barry Morris. Neil Curtis and his colleagues at Marischal Museum, especially Hilary Murray, were helpful over materials and illustrations in their care. Many of my colleagues have been generous with their advice and help. Dr Jeffrey Stone's unrivalled knowledge of Scotland's cartographic heritage has been at my disposal. Dr David Ditchburn, Dr Richard Oram and Dr Grant Simpson gave advice on certain medieval questions. Dr Ian Olson enlightened me over Gavin Greig. Professor Michael Meston made available his edition of the 'Aberdeen Style Book' while Dr James Coull drew my attention to some key issues. I am particularly grateful to Donald Withrington who has patiently dealt with the questions of an amateur in Scottish history from the fount of his own wide knowledge and also pointed me towards some vital materials.

I have relied very heavily upon the University's Special Collections and Archives. The materials themselves are invaluable. This, of course, might be expected in a university which has been in existence for over 500 years. But the researcher's ability to profit from the materials depends upon the help and guidance received. Here I have been fortunate in having had the assistance and encouragement of Mrs Myrtle Anderson-Smith. Her knowledge of the University's local collections in particular and of the Northeast's historical heritage in general is in itself a wonderful resource. She has made all this knowledge available and very tactfully pointed an amateur in the field in the right directions. Her colleagues, especially Michelle Gait, cheerfully dealt with all my requests.

Despite the efforts of all these people many mistakes will remain and for these I take full responsibility.

My daughters, Sarah and Katharine, have given advice over archival, botanical and computing problems. My son, John, has helped over computing and related matters as well as providing the maps and the geological and geographical material in Chapter I. My other son, Alastair, has written on Thomas Reid and patiently read proofs. But my greatest debt, as ever, is to my wife, Jill. She herself researched some materials and first made me realise what might be possible. Jill has typed much of the work but, above all, she has alternately encouraged and cajoled. Without her the book would not have appeared.

Roy Bridges
November 2001

Note

1. Throughout the book I have used the term 'Newmachar' to indicate the area which is defined by the parish as it was in 2000 and as is shown by the map on the back cover and in Chapter IV. Of course, the name was non-existent before the parish was created in 1609; if any general designation was in use before, it would have been 'Monykebbock', at least for the southern part of the area. After 1609, the name should actually be 'New Machar', a form properly retained for the School and the Church. Until 1928, the village at the centre of the parish was 'Summerhill' but was then designated 'Newmachar' for postal purposes. Hence the village 'Newmachar' ought to be distinguished from the wider parish, 'New Machar'. In practice, 'Newmachar' now tends to be used indiscriminately and to avoid constant pedantic distinctions being made, I have followed the normal practice. Where necessary, I have made it clear if the village alone is being referred to.

2. National Grid references are frequently given in order to identify places. Since all but one or two are in the 100,000 metre grid square designated NJ, the letters are omitted. The references are the normal six-figure ones accurate to the nearest 100 metres.

Summerhill in the 1920s(?)
The Free Church tower can be seen and Mr McAllan (?) is washing the shop window.

The Station in its heyday
(Photograph by courtesy of Major Irvine)

Chapter I
The Physical Background

The parish of Newmachar covers approximately 38 km^2 of Lower Donside in a NW - SE orientation from Whiterashes (852240) to Parkhill (915135). (See map with Chap. IV.) The area has a gently undulating topography typical of the lowland areas of NE Scotland. The highest ground is in the north and east where most land is over 100m above sea level, reaching 186m (611ft) north of Newmachar village near Changehill (878226). The eastern and northern boundary of the parish is close to the watershed between streams which drain into the Elrick/Goval Burn and then the Don and those which drain towards the north east into the River Ythan or directly into the North Sea. The central and southern part of the parish around the valley of the Elrick/Goval Burn is at less than 100m (328ft) elevation, and at the southern margin the Goval Burn joins the Don (885142) at 40m(131ft) above sea level.

Most of the area is underlain by metamorphosed sediments of the Dalradian group which is over 500 million years old (Ma). The Dalradian is associated with the Caledonian Orogeny and is in turn intruded by the post-orogenic Younger Series of granites and basic igneous rocks. The northern limit of the main Aberdeen granite mass (400 - 460 Ma) intrudes the Dalradian rocks in the south western part of the parish. A large basic intrusion (489 Ma) is present just to the east of the parish boundary and lies in a NW-SE line from Beauty Hill (908206) to Belhelvie (948177). This intrusion has the best rock exposures seen in the vicinity of Newmachar. Some other areas, such as the rocky knolls running south from the Newmachar war memorial (883193) to Moneykebbock (868184), have outcrops near their surface. These include evidence of small granite intrusions. However, in common with most of the low-lying parts of NE Scotland, there is little surface exposure of the bedrocks across the parish. In fact, most of the bedrock in the parish is covered by grey-brown till. This unstratified material was deposited from ice sheets during or towards the end of the last major glaciation in Scotland (ending about 13000 years before present). Boulders within the till are mainly locally-derived granites and metamorphic rocks, sometimes having an orientation that reflects the ice movement from west to east.

Glacial meltwater deposits also cover much of the Newmachar area. These deposits can sometimes be identified by their hummocky topography (for instance to the SE of Straloch at Greendams, (870204) compared to the more even surfaces that tend to be covered by till. More extensive meltwater deposits are present near the Don around Parkhill and extend east towards the coast. This land surface is of the 'kame and kettle' type topography having hummocks of layered sand and gravel together with the Bishop's and Corby lochs (924145). In this part of the parish, the deposits do not follow the main pattern of

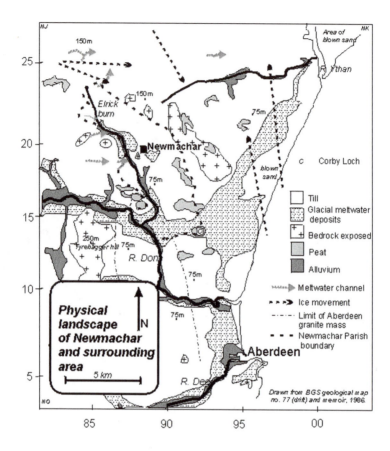

Physical landscape of Newmachar and surrounding area

N

5 km

drainage (the Elrick and present Don valleys). Although these valleys were major conduits for meltwater, sometimes as around Parkhill, subglacial water flow was diverted, and in this case flowed directly east to the coast. Other clear evidence for subglacial water channels in the area is shown by the dry valleys which are frequently discordant to the main drainage patterns. Some good examples are 200-400m long, W-E oriented valleys to the NW of the rocky knoll at Moneykebbock.

Minor recent alluvial deposits occur beside the Elrick Burn, but the most significant postglacial deposits are peat that formed between Corby Loch and Red Moss (915175) in areas locally deepened by glacial erosion. These peat deposits can reach 7.5 m thickness and some small scale extraction has taken place. The meltwater deposits in the parish have been extensively quarried for sand and gravel.

(Contributed by John Bridges, Natural History Museum, London)

The Corby, Lily and Bishop's Lochs

The three lochs in the south of the Parish were probably once one sheet of water. Despite the quarrying activities nearby, the lochs and their fringing reedbeds remain important wetland sites. There are pondweeds, bullrushes, sedges and reeds. 92 species of birds have been identified of which 56 breed there. Greylag geese roost here during their autumn migrations. Bishop's Loch is especially important in the early history of the parish as Chapter III will show.

(Peter Marren, *A Natural History of Aberdeen*, pp. 141-5 gives a full description of the natural features of the three lochs and of the earlier fruitless attempts to create a nature reserve.)

The Bishop's Loch after a drawing by Joan Burnett

Beauty Hill to Redmoss

The ridge of higher land just outside or along the eastern boundary of the Parish from Beauty Hill 167m (549ft) south to the Red Moss area at about 104m (332ft) provides us with some idea of what most the area may have looked like before the extensive peat cutting and the drainage improvements made by farmers in the early nineteenth century. (See Chapter IX.) Heather and hare's tail cotton grass and bog mosses prevail in the vegetation. Occasional outcrops of the bedrock add to the impression of an untamed landscape of great contrast to the now ordered farmers' fields on lower slopes. There is at least one small area of open water with reeds where a colony of black-headed gulls breed just over the boundary at 916175.

4

Chapter II
Prehistory to the Emergence of Scotland

Finds of prehistoric objects in Newmachar have nearly all been the accidental results of land drainage and farm improvement work in the nineteenth century. None of the objects is in sequence with others with the result that dating, either absolute or relative, is extremely difficult. Since also there is no context of settlement evidence, the objects tell us little about life styles. Often it is not even clear what their use was. Despite these shortcomings, the evidence does indicate that there was a continuous succession of inhabitants in the area from the very earliest period of the human occupation of northern Scotland.

Between about 9000 and 6000 BC as the ice sheet made its final retreat, **Mesolithic** (Middle Stone Age) hunters and gatherers came into the area. This is attested by finds of stone hand axes and some arrow heads in various parts of the parish and the nearby lower Don valley. The **Neolithic** era from about 4000 BC saw the introduction of agriculture and more permanent settlements. The number of people present should probably be counted in dozens rather than hundreds. They occupied much the same areas as later farmers were to find suitable — gentle to moderate slopes with well-drained soils. (Cowie, pp. 4-5, 7-9.) Probably dating from this period are barbed and tanged *arrowheads* like those found at Mameulah and Rannieshill and the *carved stone balls*, examples of which now in the University Museum, were found at Kinmundy, Parkhill and, the most interesting, Gaucyhillock Farm (879197). This one has six knobs and carved patterns on it. What these balls were for, no one knows but possibly they were symbols of power or prestige rather like the orbs of more recent monarchs.

By 2000 BC, some of the richer leaders were probably obtaining metal objects and in many ways the most important find in Newmachar, now also at the Museum, has been a hoard of three *bronze 'halberds'* the largest of which was 28.4 cm (11 in). These came to light during the building of a bridge over the stream at Newpark Farm (903156) in 1908. The blades were fixed to a haft at right angles but almost certainly would not have been strong enough to be used for actual fighting. Did a **Bronze Age** chief with a taste for conspicuous consumption live at Newpark?

However, the most striking and visible objects from the late Neolithic or early Bronze Age period are the *standing stones*. There are three, possibly four. Two, at Lochhills (915147) and Lochgreens (915154) seem to be collapsing. By far the most striking prehistoric monument in the parish is the 2.08m (6ft 10in) tall **Monykebbock Standing Stone** (872183). There is mystery about this object. No one can say precisely why such monoliths might have been erected. The site

24 Feb. 98   JMB

The Standing Stone at Moneykebbock, after a sketch by Joan Burnett

and surroundings make it highly unlikely that it was part of a stone circle of the type so common in the North East. Was it for ritual purposes or is it some sort of pointer to an important settlement? (The present owner of the field in which it stands does not know of any tradition connected with the stone although he himself has discovered possibly prehistoric animal bones in sands and gravels on the slope below. He points out also that it seems possible that there is another standing stone nearby not far from Chapel of Elrick (874182): Testimony of Mr R. Ingram.) What may be significant is the presence a hundred yards or so down the hill to the north of a mound which could be a round **burial cairn** (874183). On the other hand, the mound has never been excavated and might be simply one of the many kames in the area — in other words a glacially-created natural feature rather than man made.

Another oddity about the Monykebbock Standing Stone is that it is not mentioned in any of the early descriptions of the area by Robert Gordon in the 1640s, or Walter Macfarlane in the 1720s. Nor does General Roy's map of 1755 show it. Both Mr Stronach, who wrote the *Old Statistical Account* in 1791-2 and Mr Moir, author of the *New Statistical Account* in 1842 would have been able to see the feature very easily from the manse windows yet neither refers to it. There is just a suspicion that it may be an early nineteenth-century 'folly' rather than erected 4000 years ago. On the other hand, the first Ordnance Survey, which was made in 1868, clearly identifies the standing stone as an antiquity and it may be that it was not previously recognised as being something of historical importance. Even so, it is not until 1901 that there is definite testimony to its existence and a description. (*Proc. Soc. Antiquaries of Scotland,* **36**: 508.) It seems clear, incidentally, that stones have been added to the base in the last hundred years.

Perhaps from roughly the same period come two *short cist burials* found at Parkhill, one in 1867 the other in 1881 as gravel was being dug for the railway line's ballast. The skeletons are in the curled up position. In the 1881 cist there were the remains of a man about 25 years old, some boar bones and material which was possibly the remains of clothing plus the **beaker** illustrated here. This is the classic type of beaker normally associated with the first metal users and sometimes with incomers from what is now the other side of the North Sea in the Netherlands. Other pottery finds include the much cruder **Food vessels** like the one found at Straloch which also date from about 1500 BC.

For the succeeding **Iron Age**, there is relatively little to show in Newmachar. except some possible **crop marks** at Drumligair and Parkhill and **enclosures** at Lily Loch. Presumably the Iron Age inhabitants became better organised politically with the emergence of the supposed twelve tribes of the **Picts**. These matrilineal people must also have begun the process of creating a territorially-based kingdom. Yet not even their carved symbol stones are seen in Newmachar. Nor is there any sign of encounters with the Romans in 84 AD. There must have been Picts here, though, to whom missionaries were

sent in about 430 AD. (See Chap. IV.) The mound of stones which may be seen near Chapel of Elrick (875184) has been regarded by some as the site of the first **church**. However, most believe it was on a site about 500m away beside the burial ground (878179). Whether or no these Pictish inhabitants of Newmachar were fully Christian, to judge by the **silver chain** found at Parkhill in 1864, some of them had by about 750 become rather rich. How much of the Pictish way of life survived is arguable in what from 842 became the new Scottish kingdom of Alba.

(A good summary is R. Oram, *Scottish Prehistory*, Edinburgh, 1997. A useful digest on earliest humans in the region is by C.R. Wickham-Jones, *Scotland's First Settlers,* London, 1994. A more detailed guide to local sites is to be found in Ian Shepherd, *Aberdeen and North-East Scotland*, 2nd Ed, Edinburgh, 1996. Sally M. Forster, *Picts, Gaels and Scots*, London, 1996, is a useful introduction to the problem of the Picts.)

Chapter III
Early Medieval History: King Malcolm's Visit and the Bishop's 'Palace' at Loch Goull

We know almost as little of Newmachar in the two or three hundred years after the emergence of Alba as we do about the preceding years of Pictish history. There is no sign, for example, of any Viking impact. One can only speculate that as Aberdeen developed as a centre of economic, administrative and ecclesiastical activity, the Newmachar region was affected. The five or six estates which were to dominate the later medieval and early modern development of Newmachar have their shadowy beginnings in baronies (proto-feudal jurisdictions) and royal grants of land to the Church. The kings of Scotland were in fact consolidating their control although rules of succession were so uncertain that there was great instability at certain times. Hence the first royal visit to Newmachar in about 1057 or 1058 was when Malcolm Canmore was making his way north (see also Chaps. IV and XXI) to break Macbeth's power and kill him at Lumphanan.

One of Malcolm Canmore's sons, David I (1124 - 1153), began to make organisational changes which are usually summarised as being the introduction of the Anglo-Norman system of feudalism and the arrival of many Anglo-Norman families, although these families were not to affect Newmachar itself until after 1308. (See Chap. XX.) More important were the ecclesiastical developments David inaugurated.

The tradition of Christianity which St Colm or St Columba had introduced to Newmachar was of an organisation based on monasteries influencing those living around them. The Roman tradition of tighter organisation through formal territorial bishoprics was of long standing in Britain, but it was not until the reign of David I that Aberdeen was created as this kind of See with the installation of Bishop Nechtan in about 1130. Although the usual medieval forgeries complicate the story, there are charters which indicate that David granted the bishops revenues from lands at Kinmundy, Mameulah and the "three Govals". These charters were renewed or confirmed by Malcolm IV in 1153 and William the Lion in 1170. Mameulah and Kinmundy, at least, seem to have continued in church hands up to the sixteenth century though other parts of the area were obviously held by lay proprietors.

The physical presence of the church was presumably the chapel at Monykebbock originally founded by St Colm. (See Chap. IV.) Although there were other chapels all dedicated to St Mary — at Straloch, Clubsgoval and Loch Goull — the Monykebbock chapel must have been in effect, as Cuthbert Graham put it, "the cradle of the parish." In or about 1256 there is a change. The church building which served Newmachar up to 1639 is said to have been built then although 1256 is more likely to be the date when the Dean of St

Machar's Cathedral was instructed to ensure that a chaplain and clerk were maintained at Monykebbock. This would have been in the time of Bishop Peter de Ramsay or at the accession of Richard de Pottern.

Hugh de Bennum and the Bishop's Palace

Of course, what is now Newmachar was not a separate parish but part of the direct jurisdiction of the Cathedral. It is therefore not altogether surprising that a bishop's "palace" should be established on an island in Loch Goull (Goval), now known as Bishop's Loch, particularly if that area was part of the 1130 grant of lands. On an island, or a peninsula at low water, there are remains of two main buildings, one approximately 24.2 x 7.3m (80 x 24 ft) the other, St Mary's Chapel, 9.1 x 7.3m (30 x 24 ft). It is by no means clear when these buildings were erected or when they ceased to be used — 'before 1267' and up to the time of the building of the Chanonry in Old Aberdeen in 1329 (Aberdeenshire Sites and Monuments Record) or by Bishop Hugh de Bennum (Hugh de Benham) after he became bishop in 1272 and perhaps ceasing to be much used after he died. (Nicholas Bogdan.) What has intrigued later writers is that in 1282, Bennum 'suffocatus fuit in lacu de Goyle'. (Cartulary of Aberdeen c. 1400.) Some have translated this to mean that he was murdered by strangulation and others that he died of excess of catarrh. Speculation over this matter is complicated by claims that the lake referred to is really the loch which used to exist in Old Aberdeen where St Machar Drive now is. There is no real evidence for this assertion. The existence of the buildings and the traditions associated with them do make it reasonably certain at least that Bishop de Bennum used the island in Loch Goull and probably died there. (This very brief account of the story of Bishop de Bennum and his palace is based on an expert compilation of all the relevant writings, including Boece and Orem as well as modern authorities, by the historian and archaeologist Nicholas Bogdan of Barra Castle.)

Professional archaeological excavation of the site might clear up many of the mysteries surrounding De Bennum and his 'palace'. It seems likely that it was only a summer retreat rather than in effect the main residence of the bishop and that it was not in use for very long. In any case, the elaborated and romanticised story, although it continues to be repeated for its picturesque features, should not be regarded as having very much significance at all in the history of Newmachar; the centre of Christian activity remained at Monykebbock and by the end of the thirteenth century, powerful laymen were beginning to have an effect on the area as they developed holdings which were to turn into the later estates.

Chapter IV
The Place Names of Newmachar

The name used for the area of Scotland described in this book involves many
difficulties and ambiguities. Whatever it may have been called in the distant
past, through the medieval period it was generally referred to as **Monykebbock**
and there was a barony (i.e. a jurisdiction) of that name. However, when it
emerged officially as an ecclesiastical and civil parish in 1609, because it was
carved out of the large existing parish centred on the Cathedral of St Machar,
'Machar' became involved. The new parish was known variously as 'Upper
Parochin of St Machar', 'Upper Machar' or 'New Machar' although 'Money
kebbock' or some variant also continued to be used. **New Machar** prevailed and
the conflation into one word (e.g., 'Newmacher' appears in the 1696 Poll Tax
records) obviously soon followed.

Until 1928, the settlement at the centre of the parish was known as
'Summerhill' (a name preserved in the sheltered housing complex and one
other house) but to avoid confusion with Summerhill in Aberdeen,
'Newmachar' was substituted by the Post Office. The name was already in use,
it seems, possibly because the railway station nearby was always 'New Machar'
or 'Newmachar' but never 'Summerhill'. Technically, therefore, since 1928, the
name of the village has been 'Newmachar' and the whole parish, 'New Machar'.
In practice, **'Newmachar'** is now used indiscriminately and this book, perhaps
wrongly, follows the trend for reasons explained at the end of the introduction.

This is by no means the end of the complications. By 1609, everyone believed
that the original St Machar parish, and therefore also the new one, was named
after the saint. Machar was believed to have been a missionary sent to bring the
Gospel to the Picts of NE Scotland by his friend and mentor, St Columba (521-
597). Thus when Machar established a church in what we call Newmachar, he
named it after Columba and we have **'St Colm's'** or 'St Comb's' (variants of the
Irish name which is 'Columba' in Latin). However, some recent writers believe
that 'Machar' is actually derived from machair, a level piece of ground near
water, and merely describes the site of the cathedral by the Don. Christianity was
brought to the Picts earlier than Columba's time in about 431 by St Drostan's
three disciples, St Medan and St Fergus, commemorated nearby in Fintray and
Dyce, and St Colm, commemorated in Newmachar. (See e.g. Cuthbert Graham,
1963; F. Wyness, *City by the Grey North Sea*, Aberdeen, 1965, pp. 93-4.) On this
interpretation, Newmachar's St Colm is not Columba. Whether Colm was
Columba or an earlier saint, we can perhaps agree with Mr D.R. Kerr, the last
UFC minister of Newmachar, that the parish ought to have been named 'St
Colm's'. (Kerr, n.d.)

The place names within the parish, some of which are shown in the map
throw up almost as many difficulties as variant readings of Irish saints' names.

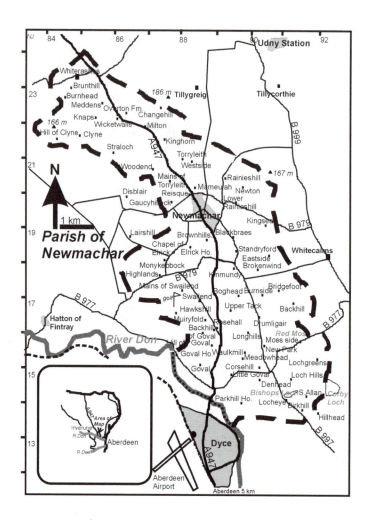

There may be Pictish roots but none is apparent in the Newmachar examples and little is known of the language anyway. Gaelic elements are more obvious but they have been modified by Scots and English. Most names were preserved as designations for natural features, fermtouns or estates and now for farms and houses. Over time, words become corrupted, clerks have used a variety of different spellings, while visiting mapmakers (and others) have been unable to understand the local accent. Modern linguists reject romantic interpretations of place names but cannot always offer clear guidance on the derivations. The following examples show just a few of the possibilities.

Beauty Hill	Yellow Hill (Kerr; but other authorities confess ignorance).
Betteral Well	'Better than ale': water from the well at Kingseat described by King Malcolm Canmore on his way to fight Macbeth in 1058.
Bishop's Loch	Where the Bishop of Aberdeen had his summer palace or retreat. But originally known as Loch Goull *qv*.
Boghole	soft or marshy area. Now Rosehall.
Broadtack	broad holding or tenancy.
Brokenwind	Broken *weind* = Broken wagons; or *wynin* =top corner of a field (with broken stones?).
Causewayend	where a track crossed a moss.
Changehill	Cheyne's Hill, person's name not where you changed horses.
Clyne	*clun* or meadow.
Corby Loch	*lochnacorb*, a common land moss.
Corseduick	crossing over a ridge.
Cunnighar	rabbit warrens — or a rabbit farm?
Disblair	South field.
Drumligair	the lodging place on the ridge (*drum*) ?
Elrick	*eileirg*: 'field of the fairies' is a romantic rendering, 'slope of a rocky hill' less appealing. More likely is 'cul de sac bounded by fallen trees', i.e, a place of ambush, especially a deer trap (Nicolaisen). It does not follow that there was a deer trap at Elrick in Newmachar which was probably named after the town of Elrick, the chief seat of the Burnett family, a branch of which came to Monykebbock.
Gaucyhillock	plump or portly hillock. (Look at it!)
Goval, Goull etc	*gabhail*: a tenancy or *gobhal*: a fork—in a stream or path?
Kaimhill	a gravelly hill.
Kinghorn	denhead or boghead.
Kingseat	the place where King Malcolm sat down and rested in 1058; a stone on which he allegedly sat was in the original Kingseat Farm — NOT the present Kingseat farm. (See Chap XXI.)
Kinmundy	ceann na *mointeich*: end of the mossy tract (i.e. the north end of Redmoss?) or at the head of the hill.
Locheye	outlet of a loch (in this case, Bishop's Loch, presumably).
Mameulah	no convincing derivation has been given.
Monykebbock	(and many variants) moine a moss + cabag a cheese [why?] but *cabaichle*, an eroded gully, seems more likely.
Rainnieshill	and variants: derived from the surname Rennie.
Reisque, Reisk	and variants: neither moor nor moss but wasteland with 'hard' grass (Alexander).
Straloch	i.e., Strathloch: a black (*loch*) strath or open valley.
Summerhill	No origin seems to be known.
Swailend	*swell* or *swile*: a marsh or drainage cuttings.
Whiterashes	White rushes viz. *aira caespitosa*.

(Based on Alexander, *Place Names* and other works.)

Chapter V
Medieval Newmachar, the Black Death and the
Emergence of the Estates

From about 1000 AD up to the time of the Reformation in 1560, some of the basic characteristics of the Newmachar area must have been developed. Yet there is not much more information about this period than about the preceding thousand years. The number of people who lived in what is now the parish can only be guessed at and the kinds of lives they led have to be inferred from evidence relating to other areas. A handful of people of more consequence — the holders of baronies or other superiorities — have their names recorded in charters but even these records are fragmentary and often extremely difficult to interpret. What is clear is that by the end of the medieval period, lordships of one kind and another had emerged and these were in the hands of a very small number of families.

Population and Pestilences

With almost no direct evidence to rely upon, demographic historians tend to work on the assumption that the rural population of Scotland in 1300 must have been roughly the same as it was to be in the eighteenth century. On this assumption, one may take Dr Webster's estimate for Newmachar in 1755 which was 1191, the 1801 Census showing 925 and the perhaps more reliable 1821 Census which counted 1133 souls (see Appendix) and guess that early medieval Newmachar had a population of about 1000 people. Although the present population is three times larger, most of that is concentrated in the village of Newmachar (Summerhill) which did not exist in 1300. Hence the population in the medieval period was greater than the present-day rural population of the parish.

One of the great unanswerable questions is whether there was a significant loss of population during the fourteenth century. The Black Death reached Scotland in 1349 but little is known about its precise incidence and effects. One of the principal informants is the chronicler John of Fordoun who says that one third of mankind died because of the bubonic plague. John of Fordoun was very likely a priest attached to St Machar's Cathedral and so, although he wrote later than the events he reports, one may assume he had acquired some knowledge of what happened in the vicinity of Aberdeen. Even so, there is no direct evidence at all that Newmachar was affected by the 1349 epidemic. Nor, for that matter, do we know whether the later outbreaks of 1361, 1379-80, 1392, 1401-3, 1430-2 or 1439-55 had any impact. It is a fair assumption, nevertheless, that the late medieval population of Newmachar, like that of many other parts of Europe declined or at least failed to increase. If that is so, land may have become cheaper and easier to acquire and peasants more easily able to escape from serfdom.

The Land and Way of Life

As well as reporting the Black Death, John of Fordoun said that the landscape of upland Scotland was 'hideous'. Whether he would have had in mind an area like Newmachar is difficult to say. Certainly the medieval countryside would have looked very different from the ordered pattern of fields with occasional substantial houses and steadings which we see around us today. That pattern has been imposed during the last 200 years or so. In 1300, the higher ground probably remained as mosses covered with gorse and coarse vegetation while the lower valley of the Elrick/Goval Burn would have been too wet to use for cultivation. This left the slopes between for use with ridged strips or 'rigs' 10 to 15 yards wide running up and down the slopes with the ditches between providing a crude form of drainage. It is possible to see the remnants of what may have been these medieval rigs in one or two places, e.g. near Drumligair Wood (908166).

The most intensively-used rigs, the 'infield', were manured regularly while those in the 'outfield' were less used or perhaps used for a few years until their yields dropped to unacceptable levels. Yields were very low by modern standards in any case; oats might yield as little as only three or four times the seed. As well as oats, barley or bere (for ale and bread), kale, peas and beans were probably grown. Oxen were kept for ploughing although hand cultivation would be usual. Cattle and sheep gave poor yields of milk, meat and wool. Most cattle would, in fact, be slaughtered at Martinmas in November. Those retained would probably be kept under the same roof as the humans.

The houses of the peasants would today be regarded as hovels: made of wattle and mud with turf roofs, they would have been dark, smoky and unhygienic. Although there probably were some individual farms, the great majority of people would have lived in small clusters of perhaps half a dozen houses — the 'fermtouns'. Those living in a fermtoun would farm co-operatively. Each group of rigs would be ploughed, sowed and harvested together with the same crop even though each rig was held by a different family. In practice, it seems that the number of rigs any one peasant might hold could vary a great deal so that some were substantial farmers and others on the edge of destitution. Perhaps it was those with less land and fewer cattle who tended to take ancillary jobs such as smithing. Land was measured in oxgangs, i.e. how many ploughing units there were. Kinmundy, for example, seems to have been extensive enough to have needed eight plough teams.

There must have been fifteen to twenty fermtouns in Newmachar, including Goval, Monykebbock, Rosehall, Kinmundy, Mameulah, Whiterashes and so on. The farming routine as practised in such places was probably traditional, difficult to change and not all that responsive to market forces. On the other hand, as Aberdeen grew, wool for export and peats for heating may well have been supplied from areas like Newmachar.

The Feudal System

The farming system so far described was essentially collective and capable of working to its traditional rhythms without any need for outside direction or interference. Of course, however, there was interference. Superimposed upon the peasant communes, if one may call them that, were systems of social control and economic exaction which profoundly affected the lives of ordinary people. Newmachar was part of the Thanage of Formartine in the early medieval period. Just who the thanes were and what sort of authority they wielded is not clear. Presumably they had the king's authority to obtain whatever military service or economic resources seemed necessary from the inhabitants of the region. During the reigns of David I and Malcolm IV in the twelfth century, a feudal system not unlike that already introduced into England by the Normans was established in Scotland. Not only was this a new system, but it was also introduced with new families of Anglo-Norman extraction granted lordships by the monarchs. Lordships, some of them designated as earldoms, were present at one level, perhaps replacing thanages. However, at a lower level was the more basic unit which became known as the barony.

In strict feudal theory, a barony was a knight's fee, in other words, the means of maintaining one knight for service with his lord — who might be the king if the holder of the barony were a tenant-in-chief or a lesser lord if he were a sub-tenant. In practice, and perhaps from the very beginning in Scotland, a barony was an heritable tenure for which a money rent, rather than military service, was paid to the lord, be it the king or one of his tenants. And a barony might be split up in various ways. In fact, most lordships or 'manors', as they were sometimes called, were not actually baronies, because they did not have the full range of legal privileges.

In Newmachar, it seems clear that the earliest and most important lordship was a barony. This was Monykebbock. Its jurisdiction probably extended over pretty well the whole of the southern half of the present parish. Like other baronies, Monykebbock would have encompassed several fermtouns. The inhabitants, although collective farmers, were in feudal terms serfs, that is bondmen who held their rigs at the discretion of the holder of the barony. In return for their holdings, the bondmen were bound to provide labour services for the lord on the land he directly farmed — the demesne or 'mains'.

The bondmen were also required to mill their corn in the lord's mill and to be subject to his judgements in both civil and criminal matters.

In practice, by 1400 and perhaps partly because of labour scarcities caused by the Black Death, the peasants would have been freemen who leased their land in return for money payments. Even so, leases were very short and continuing restrictions like the need to use the lord's mill meant that life for the majority of people was by no means secure and prosperous. Holding a barony gave the legal right to maintain a doocot as at Elrick or Disblair; depradations of their crops by the lord's pigeons were not welcomed by the ordinary inhabitants who were subject to harsh penalties if they killed the birds.

Disblair doocot

From about 1450, the number of landowners seems to have increased, perhaps because land had become cheaper. An important factor for Newmachar must have been the proximity of Aberdeen; merchant burgesses and lawyers began to seek the security and social position which went with having landed property. Before the fifteenth century, a 'baron' was simply someone who held a barony; there was no peerage system with graded ranks of nobility in Scotland. By 1450, however, honorific titles were being bestowed and this tended to emphasise the widening gulf between the lords and the rest of the population. The Newmachar area was no different from others in this respect. It would seem that baronies and other forms of lordships were possessed by a relatively small number of families who tended to intermarry with one another, who promoted their own family interest where they could and who would take all the advantage they could of any family connection with one of the handful of great magnates in Scotland. Local jurisdiction, even if it was small-scale consisting, say, of control over only two or three fermtouns, might thus be linked to larger groupings of family or regional power. The Flemings of Monykebbock seem to have had a marriage connection to the Earl of Mar.

If the peasants lived in hovels, presumably their overlords lived in more substantial houses but nothing is known of any in Newmachar. No secular building earlier than the late eighteenth century has survived in recognisable form although it is known that an earlier house existed, for example, on the site of the present Straloch House.

Leading Families and the Emergence of Estates
It would be wrong to imagine the medieval lordships as equivalent to the great estates which became such important economic units and engines of agricultural change in the nineteenth century. They were the means of extracting an

economic surplus from peasant agriculture rather than organisations promoting capitalist production. A high proportion of the land in Newmachar served the needs of the bishops of Aberdeen. Nevertheless, the lordships are the basis on which the later estates developed and they established the positions of families who were to have considerable importance for the area.

The evidence about the lordships in Newmachar is very sparse or non-existent before the fifteenth century and what is available for the later medieval period is patchy, difficult to understand and difficult to fit together. Nevertheless, something may be said about the lordships which existed.

Monykebbock/Elrick

Before the designation 'New Machar' emerged in the seventeenth century, Monykebbock or some variant was the name most commonly given to the whole area. This was no doubt because it was a barony and was clearly associated with the area's church, St Colm's, and its burial ground. Nevertheless, it is not until 1343 that 'Monycabbo' emerges as a landholding in official records. David II then granted the barony to one Donald Strathechin. At some time in the next half century it must have passed into the hands of the Fleming family who, as noted above, let it out for a time to Alexander Stewart, Earl of Mar from 1406. The crown seems to have retaken Monykebbock in 1435 and had it managed by Ranald Cheyne of Straloch (*qv*, below) but it returned to Fleming hands in the 1490s. By this time, various parts of the barony had been detached or separately mortgaged with the Earl of Huntly having an interest in 1492 which comprised Elrick, Tillymaud and part of Little Goval. In 1528, the barony was in the hands of Walter Ogilvie but by 1553 was controlled by the Innes family. It is clear that Elrick had now become the effective centre of the barony. Was a late medieval house built on the same site as the present mansion? For what it is worth, the symbol on Robert Gordon's map suggests it was. (See Chap. VI.)

Kinmundy

Kinmundy is mentioned as early as the reign of King Malcolm (1153-65) as having been granted to the Bishop of Aberdeen. The charter may actually have been a later forgery but Kinmundy was in Church hands in 1549 when the scandalous behaviour of Bishop William Gordon, which included getting into debt, forced its leasing to laymen. It was split into two and the yearly rent for each half was fixed as 2½ marks (£1 13s. 4d) in cash, half a sheep, a goose, one eighth of a mart (an ox or cow), 3 firlots (about 24 gallons) of bere meal and the same quantity of oats plus some lime, slate and salt. In 1580 James VI granted Kinmundy — then referred to as a barony — to John Gordon of Pitlurg and it was there, possibly, that his second son, the famous Robert was born in 1580.

(See Chap. VI.) However, it is typical of the difficulty with the evidence that records exist to show that the Gordon family owned Kinmundy from 1506. This Kinmundy is almost certainly the estate south of Mintlaw (NK008436). Another complication is that the prominent Aberdeen family, the Menzies, acquired Kinmundy in Newmachar at some time before the 1640s and held it for long afterwards. If they owned it in 1580, as some accounts suggest, then Robert Gordon was not born there.

Mameulah/Rainieshill
Like Kinmundy, Mameulah is said to have been part of King Malcolm's grant to the Bishops of Aberdeen in about 1153. Again like Kinmundy, it had to be leased out in 1549 — in this case to one Nigel Pook. But soon the Harvey family acquired all or part of it. This is possibly the family which was to have a long and important connection with Newmachar in the seventeenth century.

Clubsgoval (later Parkhill) and Boghole (Rosehall)
Once more part of the alleged 1153 grant to the Church, Clubsgoval, including Lochhills passed into lay hands in 1543 and 1550, the lessee being Henry Moultry. Boghole went to Thomas Menzies who later, according to some accounts, also bought Kinmundy — from the Gordons?

Straloch
Compared with the confusions associated with the other holdings in the area, Straloch's ownership appears comparatively straightforward. Not itself a barony, it was in the hands of the Cheyne family from 1249 until 1606. Whiterashes was added to the holding in 1590. The Gordons of Pitlurg (an estate and castle two miles south of Keith) acquired Straloch in 1606. As we have seen, they may already have had interests in Newmachar at Kinmundy. John Gordon died in 1619 and was succeeded by his brother Robert (1580-1661) who chose to live permanently at Straloch rather than the family seat of Pitlurg. Straloch was to remain in Gordon hands until 1766.

By the beginning of the early modern period, half a dozen families dominated Newmachar. They controlled properties we can begin to call estates which were to be central to the life of the parish for over 300 years.

(The authorities consulted for the details on Straloch and the other estates include the *Registers of the Great Seal of Scotland*; Joseph Robertson, *Illustrations of the Topography and Antiquities of Aberdeen and Banff*, (Spalding Club, 1857); John Henderson, *Aberdeenshire Epitaphs and Inscriptions*, (Aberdeen, 1907); William Temple, *The Thanage of Fermartyn*, (Aberdeen, 1894). The sketch of the old Disblair Doocot is by Joan Burnett.)

Chapter VI
Robert Gordon of Straloch 1580-1661
and Maps of Newmachar

Robert Gordon is the most distinguished person associated with Newmachar. A real 'Renaissance man', besides being Laird of Straloch, he was a scholar, a musician, and respected as a mediator in the civil wars of the 1630s and '40s. Above all, he was and is admired as a pioneer cartographer. It is generally assumed that Gordon was actually born in Newmachar, at Kinmundy. It seems to the writer at least highly possible that his birth took place at the Kinmundy which is just south of Mintlaw and that it was to this estate that James VI's grant of baronial rights to Sir John Gordon in 1580 relates, Kinmundy in Newmachar then being in the hands of the Menzies family. (See Chap. V., above and 'Straloch Papers', Spalding Club, *Miscellany*, 2 vols. 1841, Vol 1: 8, 28.)

Robert Gordon

Robert Gordon's birth, wherever it took place, was on September 14th 1580. His parents were Sir John Gordon of Pitlurg (1547-1600) and his wife, Isobel Forbes (1548-1622). On Sir John's death, the eldest son, John, succeeded. According to some accounts, John bought Straloch from James Cheyne in 1606 but Robert either purchased it from him or was allowed to live there after his marriage to Katharine, a daughter of Alexander Irvine of Lynturk, in 1608. In any event, John died without children in 1619 and so Robert now inherited all the properties. Rather than live at Pitlurg, he chose to remain at Straloch for the rest of his life. He died there in 1661 and was buried in the kirkyard of New Machar Church. He had no fewer than eleven sons and six daughters.

Robert Gordon at Straloch: Politics and Scholarship
Gordon's education had included tuition at the new Marischal College and University founded in Aberdeen by George Keith, 4th Earl Marischal, in 1593. In fact, Gordon was the very first graduate. Compared with King's College, Marischal put more emphasis on protestant theology and on mathematics and other practical subjects which might be useful to the commercially-minded burgesses of Aberdeen. Perhaps this partly explains Gordon's later interests in geography and maps. Even more of a formative influence seems to have been the period he spent in Paris from 1598 to 1600 where he met distinguished Scotsmen studying or working there as well as French scholars.

It would be interesting to know how Robert Gordon managed Straloch but there seems to be no information on this. Nor is it clear when and how his cartographical work began. All one can say is that he must have found that his interests began to coincide with perceived needs: both Renaissance scholars trying better to understand the world and contemporary governments trying more efficiently to rule their realms wanted maps. As for politics, the leader of an important family group connected with several others was bound to become involved in the complicated series of political struggles which took place in Scotland after 1638. His instinct was to mediate rather than take up a strong commitment. He seems to have been respected on all sides but his principal efforts were devoted to saving his kinsmen, the earls of Huntly, from the consequences of their maintaining Catholic sympathies and lacking astuteness in politics. He mediated between the then Marquis of Huntly and the famous Earl of Montrose in 1639, and then tried to save Huntly from the 'insatiable malice' of the Covenanters over the next few years. Possibly it was Gordon who advised Huntly to retreat from the encounter with the Covenanters' Army at Monykebbock in 1647. (See Chap. XX.). A particularly tricky problem arose after the execution of Huntly when there were disputes between Huntly's sons and a son-in-law, Lord Argyll, who was anti-Royalist.

Music
Robert Gordon was interested in music, more particularly songs and their accompaniments for lute. What is even more striking is that he collected Scottish songs of the period which are thus preserved and can be performed today.

The principal evidence for Gordon's work in the field is a manuscript music book of 92 leaves, 'An Playing Booke for the lute... Notted and Collected by Robert Gordon...in the Year of our Lord 1627.' Apparently it contained 78 songs with the tablature (musical notation) for the lute. Unfortunately, the book itself is lost and only a partial copy by an Edinburgh antiquarian, George Graham, is available. The original had somehow come into the possession of Professor Skene of Marischal College who passed it on to the musicologist, Charles Burney; on Burney's death in 1814, it was sold to James Chalmers, who made it possible for Graham to see and partially copy it. But when Chalmers died, the book was sold to a now unknown person and has not been seen since by any scholar or musician.

Almost certainly Robert Gordon would have played the music he collected on his lute. This adds a new perspective to the life of this remarkable man.

Description of Aberdeen and Banff
The respect in which all held Robert Gordon was no doubt because of his personal qualities but there seems also to have been recognition that he was an

eminent scholar. His writing was as often in elegant Latin as in English, including the uncompleted 'History of Scots Affairs' and several memoirs to go with Blaeu's Atlas. One of these was his *Description of the Shires of Aberdeen and Banff*. The general observations are full of interest. He is aware of the usefulness of lime for soil fertility and the benefits that spreading peat ash could bring. Oddly, he seems to say nothing directly of Straloch or Newmachar but there are remarks on the area from the Ythan to the Don:

> nothing of note presents itself save the numerous castles and mansions of gentlemen of lower rank, many of whom are called barons; or, where they are not found, the cottages of the peasantry occupy almost the whole countryside. Of idle lands there is little or none.

Gordon noted that the gentlemen now disdained trade and so to make money had to enlist as mercenary soldiers in continental wars — as did one of his own sons. Local patriotism is in evidence as well as a gentle criticism of Highlanders:

> the inhabitants surpass in gentler temperament, in subdued judgement, and in culture of mind and manners, all their neighbours, but particularly those who live to the north and west of these shires.

One suspects that the qualities which Gordon admired in people of the Northeast were ones he himself exemplified. Such good qualities, he claimed, were a product of the influence of the University of Aberdeen and the experience of foreign travel.

In 1646 and again in 1649 the Scottish Estates (Parliament) agreed that so that he might 'the mor friely attend and perfyt that work...of helping and correcting the severall cairtes of this kingdome', he should be relieved of the burdens of taxes and having troops quartered at Straloch. It would be to the 'honor of this nation' that he complete his work.

Robert Gordon and his Maps

Robert Gordon possessed an astrolabe which is now in the Scottish National Museum and he was clearly aware of the classical geographer Ptolemy's latitudes but there is no evidence that Gordon was a practical mapmaker in this sense.

· A Request from the King

Trustie and weill beloved   We greitt yow weill Haveing laitly sein certane cairttis of divers schyres of this our ancient kingdome sent heir from Amsterdam   To be correctit and helpeitt in the defectis thairof   And being informed of your sufficiencie in that airtt   And of your Love   bothe to Learneing and to the creditt of your natioune We have thairfoir thoucht fitt heirby earnestly to intreitt yow to taik so mutche paines   As to reveis the saidis cairtis   And to helpe thame in sutch thingis as yow find deficient thairintill,   That they may be sent back by the director of our chancellerie to holland, Quhilk as the samyne will be honorabill for your selff   So schall it do us guid and acceptable service   And if occasioun present we schall not be vnmyndfull thairof   ffrom our paleice of Halyruidhous the aucht day of October 1641.
(Letter from Charles I to the Laird of Straloch)

In fact, as the extract from one of his maps here shows, his work tended to be somewhat haphazard as to scale, distance and precise position and lack any adequate representation of physical features. Perhaps, strictly speaking, he was a chorographer — one who describes the places in a region. Such descriptions were needed: until his maps were published in Volume V of Johannes Blaeu's *Atlas Novus* of 1654, there were no remotely adequate maps of Scotland. Simply assembling the information for one was an enormous task.

That task had actually been started by the Rev. Timothy Pont (1560-1614) who travelled all over Scotland between 1583 and 1596. The results were never published but were purchased by the government. Sir John Scot of Scotstarvet (1585-1670), who had connections with the Amsterdam publishing house of Blaeu, tried to arrange for the printing of Pont's maps. But finding they were incomplete or of poor legibility, he turned to Robert Gordon for help in the late

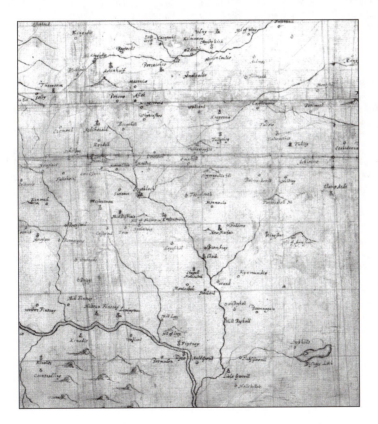

Extract from one of Robert Gordon's Manuscript Maps
showing the Newmachar Area
(Reproduced by kind permission of the National Library of Scotland)

The places in or adjacent to Newmachar Parish are listed below with their modern equivalents and their grid reference numbers. The places on Gordon's map are taken roughly in order from west to east and north to south. Asterisks indicate places which appear in the Atlas Novus of 1654.

Achenhuif*	Auchenhuive	842251	Hill with cross	*St Mary's Chapel*	
					841253
Ardiheraull*(?)	*Windywalls*				
(now deserted)		843232	Brunthill	*Brunthill*	848230
Whiterashes	*Whiterashes*	854235	Knaperna	*Knapperna*	87241
Tulieve	*Tillyeve*	896228	Kendal	*Old Kendal*	839225
Tullygreig Hill	*(hill at)*	878226	Tillygreig*	*Tillygreig*	886229
Tulicorthie	*Tillycorthie*	909230	Tulity	*Tillery*	910226
Clun-hill	*Hill of Clyne*	843219	Overtoun	*Overton*	864223
Overhill	*Changehill*	873224	Achloon	*Auchloon*	922223
Ova Clun	*Hill of Clyne Fm*	843215	Nether Clun	*Clyne*	852156
Knapps(?)	*Knaps*	855222	Slugmagullie Hill	*Whitlam*	885215
Bal-na kettil	*Balnakettle*	897219	Hilbray	*Hillbrae*	906215
Westortoun*	*Wester Blair*	202842	Sutitoun	*Sittyton*	852207
Strathloch*	*Straloch*	861211	Torryleith	*Torryleith*	877204
Mamoula	*Mameulah*	884202	Tarkastell M(ons)*	*Beauty Hill*	908206
Mid Disblair*	*Middleton*	848198	Hill of Middleton	*(hill at)*	856199
?Eastretoun*	*Mill of Cavil*				
	(note symbol)	874195	Calsayend	*Causewayend*	875166
Toun	*Cairnton*	856194	Spouthuis(?)	*Disblair House*	863195
New Machair*	*New Machar*				
	(Church)	887195	Boddoms	*Boddoms*	
			now Pinkie (Whyte's Garage)		894188
Kingseat	*Kingseat*	902193	Hill of Kingseat	*(hill at)*	913192
Lairshill	*Lairshill*	865187	Broombray	*Broombrae*	880189
Elrik*	*Elrick*	883184	Chapell of Monicabok		
				Monykebbock Chapel	878179
Kynmundie*	*Kinmundy*	896176	Monicabok*	*Monykebbock*	875181
Swalend*	*Swailend*	884168	Ward	*Ord*	882178
Over Bogholl*	*Rosehall*	892163	Drumnagair	*Drumligair*	902165
Mill Bogholl	*Waulkmill(?)*	897156	Auld Guervil*	*Goval*	885151
Clubsguervil*	*Clubsgoval*				
	or Parkhill	897140	Lochhills	*Loch-Hills*	912146

1630s and prevailed upon the King to add his entreaty. (See above.) With the considerable aid of his son, James, the parson of Rothiemay, Gordon set to work and despite the disorders in the country, was able in 1648 to deliver the material for 49 maps of Scotland. This was to make the country for a time one of the best-mapped in the world. Some of the maps in the *Atlas Novus* were predominantly based on Pont drafts, some on Gordon's alone but most were a mixture. Since most of Pont's originals (including whatever he had drawn covering Newmachar) have now been lost, one usually cannot state precisely how each map was produced. Dr Jeffrey Stone, the leading expert on Scotland's maps, says that 'clarity of execution and fine penmanship characterise Gordon's work' and he identifies about ten of the *Atlas* maps as based on Gordon's work alone. It is certain that the data for Map No. 30 in the *Atlas* — the depiction of Aberdeen and Banff — was prepared by Gordon. It therefore relates to the 1640s rather than to Pont's surveys of the the 1580s. Gordon's original drafts are extant and part of the material on which the Aberdeen and Banff map was based is shown here. However, to add further complications to the story, the map in the *Atlas* is different in detail from what is seen here. This may indicate a later revision or simply lack of space for all the places.

The Newmachar Example

Problems over scale and the inconsistent use of symbols are immediately obvious drawbacks to the example shown. Nevertheless, the great historical value of this map is that all the centres of any population in about 1640 can be identified. There are great houses and a couple of churches but most of the names will represent fermtouns. Approximately 50 names are shown in the area which is the parish. If one assumes something like 20 to 25 people per settlement, this means a total population at something a little over a thousand. Nearly all the places still exist with the names for the most part recognisably the same. If a present-day settlement is not on the map, e.g. Kinghorn Farm, it is a reasonable presumption but not a certainty that it did not exist in 1640. Clearly, however, Summerhill (Newmachar village) was not in being.

Later Maps of Newmachar

Robert Gordon's maps were not superseded for almost a hundred years. General Roy's map of 1750 marked an advance in accuracy but provided no better information than Gordon on places. Route Guides like that by Taylor and Skinner in 1776 indicate the main road (what is now the B997) but only the gentlemen's houses, Parkhill, Rosehall, Kinmundy, Elrick and Straloch. There is still not yet a village around the Church. Thomson's map of 1826 has many inaccuracies but shows relief and indicates that the turnpike, now the A947, was in existence. But there is still no village. However, by this time, estate owners were beginning to commission large-scale maps of their holdings. The Straloch Map of 1835, the surveys by David Walker of Swailend of 1819 and of the Rainnieshill estate in 1841 (which includes Summerhill) are superb pieces of work. So, too, was the Elrick survey by Walker and Beattie in 1835 but it is now unavailable. Estate maps continued to be produced as valuable management tools but in 1867-8 came the first Ordnance Survey maps. The 25 inch, and 6 inch sheets were followed in the succeeding 100 years by the 1 inch, 2½ inch and then the current 1:50,000 sheets which everyone now takes for granted. Each issue is a useful historical tool but none is so fundamentally important as

Robert Gordon's maps. The existence of detailed Ordnance Survey maps helps us to realise the sheer magnitude of his achievement in assembling so much information on Scotland; most of us would be unable accurately to map the flowerbeds in our gardens.

Sources consulted include the McDonald Collection of Maps in Aberdeen University; Jan Blaeu, *Theatrum Orbis Terrarum sive Atlas Novus*, 5 vols, Amsterdam, 1654-5; Spalding Club, *Miscellany*, ed. John Stuart, 2 vols, Aberdeen, 1841, Vol 1: Preface, 29-38, The 'Straloch Papers' Vol 1: 1-58; 'Robert Gordon's Description of Aberdeen and Banff, 1649', *Geographical Collections Relating to Scotland made by Walter Macfarlane*, ed. Arthur Marshall, 3 vols, Edinburgh, 1906-8, Vol 2: 268-70, 295-302. See also 'Praefecturarum Aberdonensis et Banfiensis..nova descriptio, auctore Roberto Gordonio' *Collections for a History*...ed. Joseph Robertson, Spalding Club, Aberdeen, 1843; J C Stone, *Illustrated Maps of Scotland for Blaeu's Atlas Novus*, London, 1989; J C Stone, *The Pont Manuscript Maps of Scotland*, Tring, 1989. The section on music is based entirely upon Evelyn Stell, 'Sources of Scottish Instrumental Music 1603-1707', Ph.D. Thesis, University of Glasgow, 2 vols, 2000, Vol 1: 191-197. The CD numbered CCD CMF 005 has some of the Straloch music. (Information supplied by Dr Stell.)

The picture of Robert Gordon is from a copy of the painting by the contemporary portraitist, Jameson, owned by the University of Aberdeen and on display in the Marischal Museum. The reproduction is printed here by permission of the University.

Chapter VII
Early Modern Newmachar:
from the Creation of the Parish to the Old Statistical Account,
1609-1791

On 9th May 1609 Newmachar was 'decerned' as a parish. Although it had had some sort of existence as an area centred on the Chapel at Monykebbock, it was now a recognised civil and ecclesiastical entity. Various designations came into use (see Chap. IV) but 'New Machar' became the usual name until 1928.

The Creation of the Parish

Nothing is known of the arrangements made by the medieval Bishops of Aberdeen for St Colm's Chapel at Monykebbock to be served by a priest. A journey of about eight miles over muddy tracks from the Cathedral to Monykebbock may not have been a welcome chore. Not until after the Reformation do the names of those now given the task appear in the records. 'Alexander Garioche redar of Monegabow' is mentioned in the Chronicle of Aberdeen (Spalding Club Miscellany, 2 vols, Aberdeen 1842, Vol 2: 29-70, p. 50) but it seems he had ceased to officiate in 1574 with Beroald Innes and Alexander Forsyth named in 1576 and then Robert Williamson from 1578-80. After this there is no record of what arrangements for worship were made even when the parish came into being in 1609 although the responsibility continued to lie with the Cathedral authorities. Possibly nothing was done because of the greed and dilatoriness of the officials of King's College. David Rait had become Dean of the Cathedral and Minister of the St Machar parish as well as Principal of the College and it was part of his responsibility as Dean to provide for Newmachar. Then in 1618, a new bishop arrived, Patrick Forbes (1564-1635). The Bishop soon carried out a visitation of the University. As a result, Rait was ordered to give up his parish ministry and supply 500 merks from College resources to cover the cost of providing for a replacement and another 500 merks (£333 6s-8d) for a Newmachar ministry. It took a second visitation by Bishop Forbes in 1623 before Rait eventually complied in 1626. The College chose James Hervey (variously Hervie, Hervye, Harvie or Harvey). Newmachar should be grateful for the great zeal and determination of Bishop Forbes who made the parish a reality. (D. Stevenson, King's College Aberdeen 1560-1641, Aberdeen, 1990, pp. 63-70.)

James Hervey, the First Minister

(This section is based largely on information supplied by David James Harvey of Fonthill Road, Aberdeen. Mr Harvey has kindly provided some of the results of his own researches on his ancestor James Hervey and other members of the family.)

The Hervey family was already a distinguished one by the sixteenth century. It was James Hervey of Boyndis (near Inverurie) and his wife Agneta Leslie who began to acquire property in Newmachar. In 1564 they obtained Tillymaud and a third of Monykebbock including Chapel Croft which was destined to become the home of the minister James Hervey and probably that of his successors. By 1583, Hervey of Boyndis and his wife had purchased the whole Monykebbock barony including Elrick. Kinmundy followed in 1590 for a time.

As he graduated M.A. from King's College in 1617, James Hervey the minister must have been born around the turn of the century. He became Humanist (teacher of Latin) there in 1624 but was given the Newmachar charge on 13th August 1626. Hervey obviously continued his close association with the ecclesiastical politics of Aberdeen and was chosen to represent the Presbytery and the 'Aberdeen Doctors' at the General Assembly of 1638. He is said to have picked up a throat infection on the way to Edinburgh and was unable to speak. This may be a polite fiction covering the fact that, as an anti-Covenant figure, he was not allowed to do so. (See James Gordon, 'History of Scots Affairs', *Collections for a History of ...Aberdeen and Banff*, ed. Joseph Robertson, Spalding Club, 1843, p. 154.) Shortly after this, Hervey was invited to become minister at Keith but it seems he preferred to remain in Newmachar where he was minister until 1649 and possibly a resident even after that.

It is not clear how James Hervey the minister fitted into the rest of the Hervey family associated with Newmachar. The *Fasti Ecclesiae Scoticanae* says that James Hervey's wife was Helen Neilson but this seems to be a confusion with James Hervie who was owner of Mameulah for which he enjoyed a rental value of 550 merks in 1667. On the other hand, there are uncertainties about the end of Hervey's ministry. Is it possible that his anti-Covenant views led to his removal from the ministry and that he lived on in Newmachar as a landowner like other members of the Hervey family? But difficulties over chronology and stated relationships seem to make this unlikely. Gilbert Hervie, burgess and merchant of Aberdeen, owned Mameulah and Elrick at the time of his death in 1656 and the James of Mameulah in 1667 is more likely to have been his son or grandson.

Hervey's Ministry and its End

The first available volume of Kirk Session Records for Newmachar begins in January 1642 and covers the normal disciplinary matters. A vagabond is obliged to make 'publick repentance'. Robert Forbes and James Sangster — a regular sinner — and his brother also have to sit on the stool of repentance. However, the records also show that grants of money are made to the poor. In September 1647, there was a service of thanksgiving for the end of an outbreak of plague. The pages which might have explained the end of Hervey's ministry have disappeared and the next entry relates to 2nd September 1649 when his successor, James Chalmers, officiated as minister for the first time. Chalmers instructed the Elders in their duties and heard them take their oaths. This first recorded list of Elders for Newmachar is interesting as a list of men and the places where they lived or farmed but it contains several puzzles. There is a James Hervie from Bogholl and a James Hervie as Church Officer. It seems inconceivable that an ex-minister would stay on as Church Officer. Yet after all, the world had been turned upside down in other ways in 1649 with the execution of King Charles I. (Kirk Session Records, Ms 2544, Aberdeen University.)

Newmachar Church Elders, 2nd Sep 1649.
From the Kirk Session Records

Alexander Frazer	in Little Govell
Arthur Dilgairdno	in Lochhills
Robert Cheyne	in Old Govell
James Harvie	in Bogholl
Andrew Forbes	in Bogholl
George Logie	in Kinmundie
William Cruickshank	in Monicabock
Andrew Mar	in Elricke
William Mill [?]	in Mameulay
William Blischal [?]	in Straloch
James Montgomerie	in Torri Leyth
George Gray	in Swailend
John Abel	in Mid Clune
Andrew Skeyne	in Uppertoun of Straloch
George Burnet	in Brownhills

Thomas Mil clerk to the Sessione and James Hervie Church Officer
James Simpson door keeper
                James Chalmers Minister
(Ms 2544 Aberdeen University)

The Church Building and the Manse
During the first thirteen years of his ministry James Hervey presumably continued to use St Colm's Chapel at Monykebbock. As a carving on a still existing gatepost confirms, a new church was built on a different site in 1639 and Hervey began to preach there in 1641. Why the particular site — which is where the present church stands — was chosen can only be guessed at. It must have been more central for the whole parish, it was on the main north-south road and, lying between the valleys of the Elrick and Pinkie Burns, it was on higher and thus perhaps better-drained land at 101m (332 ft) in elevation. Who gifted the land for the Kirk and the surrounding burial ground and glebe land is not clear. The building itself was a 'plain rectangular structure' with round windows at either end. (Information from Rev. Ian Dryden.) It was to remain in being until 1791. Probably the manse continued to be Chapel Croft at Monykebbock but there is no certain evidence. (Information from Mr Donald Ingram.)

Later Ministers
James Chalmers, 1649-1652, George Melvill, 1654-1663, and Alexander Leask, 1665-1669, were the immediately succeeding ministers of whom little is known. James Garden, 1672-1675, later became Professor of Divinity at King's College while George Seaton, 1687-1704, had two sons both of whom became priests in the Episcopal Church. William Mitchell, 1706-1716, and John Bisset, 1717-1728, were the next ministers. Bisset became a person of some note in his later career as the minister of the East Church of St Nicholas in Aberdeen and he

kept a diary of the events of the '45. (See Chap. XX.) Bisset's most notable act in Newmachar occurred not during his own ministry but at the end of that of his successor, the interesting figure of Thomas Ray, 1729-1736. Ray was disliked because he was imposed on the parish by King's College and because of his scandalous behaviour. One would like to know more of this because the specimen charge levelled against him was merely that of 'powdering his periwig on the Sabbath'. Though found not guilty of this crime, he was deposed in 1736 for other reasons which are not recorded. (*The State of the Care of the Parish of New-Machar and Mr Thomas Ray*, Edinburgh, c. 1730 which I have not been able to examine.)   As the next call was being moderated, Bisset now took the opportunity to return to Newmachar to preach a vehement denunciation of the patronage system for appointing ministers. This resulted in the hostile reception the next man was to receive. (D.R.Kerr, 'The Parish of Newmachar', n.d., p. 12.) It is said that Mr George Moir, who was to go out at the Disruption in 1843, (see Chap. XIII), had the text of Bisset's sermon among his papers. (Guesses at Truth, Newmachar United Free Church, 1913, pp. 3-4.)   Notwithstanding Bisset's sermon, King's College managed to present a minister who turned out to be not only good for Newmachar but also one of the greatest figures of the Scottish Enlightenment, Thomas Reid, 1737-1752.

A Philosopher in Newmachar: Thomas Reid

In the first half of the eighteenth century one of Scotland's greatest men, the philosopher Thomas Reid (1710-1796), lived in the parish of Newmachar. Reid was born in a small village near Banchory where his father was minister. As a young man he studied and worked as librarian at Aberdeen's Marischal College; his time there provided him with a broad education in the arts and natural sciences. In

1737 Reid was appointed minister in the parish of Newmachar. Having secured this position through the patronage of King's College in Aberdeen, Reid was greeted with hostility by at least some of his new parishioners: it is said that on his arrival he was ducked in a pond and was obliged to deliver his first sermon with an armed guard in attendance. But Reid's good nature quickly won him and his family the respect and affection of the parishioners.

During his ministry in Newmachar Reid engaged in the intellectual labours that provided the foundations for the system he later advanced in his philosophical works.

Reid's philosophy sprang from his reaction to the writings of his great contemporary, David Hume. Hume had argued that all human knowledge consists only of distinct ideas and impressions in our minds - and that we cannot have direct knowledge of the subjects of our ideas and impressions. Reid was among the few men of his time who understood the significance of Hume's work: that it seemed to deny the possibility of absolute knowledge and values. In his greatest work, *An Inquiry into the Human Mind on the Principles of Common Sense* (1764), Reid says of Hume that he "hath built a system of scepticism that leaves no ground to believe any one thing rather than its contrary.

His reasoning appeared to me to be just; there was, therefore, a necessity to call into question the principles on which it was founded, or to admit the conclusion."

Reid argued in the *Inquiry* that there exist laws governing human judgements that cannot be explained only by Hume's system of ideas: something permanent and external to our ideas - which Reid held to be divine in nature, though fully intelligible through reason - was required to provide a full account of human understanding. He gave the following example: when we smell a rose the sensation we have of its scent leads us to believe, through the operation of the laws governing human judgement, in the existence of the rose as something real and external to our own mere idea of the rose. We can be confident that our judgement is well-founded, that our senses have not deceived us, because we know that there are permanent laws governing our judgements across all fields of life: for example the common assumptions about human nature which underlie different languages.

Reid's arguments proceed from an examination of the five senses; and he is often known as the founder of the common sense of school of philosophy. His contribution to the development of eighteenth century philosophy was considerable. Moreover his interest in the relationship between the operation of the senses and human knowledge provided an important starting point for the new discipline of psychology which grew up in the nineteenth century.

In 1752 Reid left Newmachar to become professor of philosophy at King's College in Aberdeen, where he worked on his *Inquiry*. In 1764 he succeeded another leading figure of the Scottish enlightenment, Adam Smith, as professor of moral philosophy at the University of Glasgow. Yet it seems just to conclude that his experience of the lives of the people of Newmachar, eking a hard living from the fields of the parish, contributed as much to the development of his view of human nature - broad and tolerant, while grounded in certainty - as did his time in these two great universities.

(Alastair Bridges)

****

Reid was followed by John Maxwell, 1752-1773. During his ministry an important change took place. Then as now impecunious, in 1769 King's College sold its right to present ministers to Newmachar to the Earl of Fife. The Earl paid just under £250 for the right which, as his factor pointed out, was 'a pretty thing in the family' — no doubt as a provision for any illegitimate sons. (*Lord Fife and his Factor*, ed. A. and H. Tayler, London, 1925, pp. 51-3.) Robert Lumsden was

Possessions of the Church Noted in Kirk Session Records

When Mr Stronach was admitted to Newmachar in June 1782, there was £4. 11.0 in the box and £80 was out to John Lumsden of Cushny. The Kirk's treasures included two silver and three pewter cups; two metal tasses [goblets]; two pewter plates; one large communion tablecloth and one small; a table napkin; a Bible given by Dr Fordyce of Elrick; one pewter basin; one towel for baptisms; a 'pick' of six chairs, eight forms, four tables for sacrament, three mortcloths and a chord.

(Margaret Begbie.)

Minister from 1774-1781 and then the Earl presented William Stronach, 1782-1804. A new manse, much nearer the Church was built for him in 1781, he had the Church itself completely rebuilt in 1791 and at roughly the same time wrote the Newmachar entry for the *Old Statistical Account*. (See below.) Sadly for Mr Stronach, his young wife, Harriet Reid, died in 1796 at the age of 28. Her grave may be seen today just near the south wall of the Church — which was then the front of the Church.

Life in the Parish: (i) the Lairds and their 'Mannours'

Developments in the ownership of the various lordships may be followed by means of charters and other legal documents which have been preserved and, in many cases, printed. The Scottish Government's attempts to collect taxes in a more efficient manner during the seventeenth century through the machinery of the estates meant the creation of valuation rolls which can yield information about the estates and their owners. Walter Macfarlane's 'Geographical Collections' of 1748 include a section on 'New Macar' which is undated but may have been compiled in the 1720s. This refers to six lordships or what he calls 'mannours' and tells us about ownership but frustratingly little beyond. Certainly, information is more abundant than for the previous centuries. Nevertheless, changes in ownership and sizes of holdings are often bewildering as families flourished or failed and properties were split up or augmented.

Monykebbock/Elrick

As noted above, the Hervey family had owned various parts or all of Elrick but in 1663 it was acquired by John Burnett, a member of a prosperous Aberdeen family. He died in 1675 and the estate then passed through many hands as brother succeeded brother on at least three occasions. Another John Burnett (1745-1822) made money at the East India Company post of Bencoolen in Sumatra. Doubtless this helped to pay for the splendid Elrick House but while John Burnett was away, he must have leased the estate to a Dr Fordyce who took a part in the life of the parish for several years. According to Mr Kerr (Kerr, pp. 14-15), this must have been Sir William Fordyce (1724-1792). One of the sons of a Provost of Aberdeen, he served in the Army, became for a time a fashionable doctor in London, was knighted and became Lord Rector of Marischal College. The work which earned him fame was *The Great Importance and Proper Method of Cultivating and Curing Rhubarb in Britain for Medical Uses*. If the identification is correct, can one assume that he grew his rhubarb in the garden at Elrick?

Kinmundy

The Menzies family continued to hold Kinmundy until the 1740s and then, after an interval, it was purchased by the Earl of Aberdeen. It would seem that there was a manor house of some kind. Later, the estate would be divided into two.

Boddoms/Kingseat

These estates were owned by William Forbes of Tolquhon in 1705 but by 1792 had passed into the hands of Alexander Thomson of Banchory. Macfarlane does not refer to Kingseat as a separate 'mannour'.

Mameulah/Rainieshill

The Hervey/Harvey family continued as owners of Mameulah until 1706 when George Gordon, Professor of Hebrew at King's College, became the proprietor. It seems that the Harveys had run into financial difficulties and Gordon seized the chance to buy. However, he soon found himself in dispute with Mary, Elizabeth and Catherine Hervey. There was a complicated lawsuit which lasted from 1723 until 1748. The ladies claimed that their father Patrick's holding had somehow passed to his nephew, their cousin, William Harvey, who allowed Gordon to buy it. But William Harvey, said the ladies, was 'an idiot, or not many degrees from it'. Gordon was also their cousin and seems to have won in the end although by that time the estate had passed into the hands of Alexander Thomson. (Henderson, *Inscriptions*, p. 448.)

Straloch House

Straloch

The Pitlurg/Straloch branch of the Gordon family began to fall on hard times in the earlier part of the eighteenth century. Alexander Gordon represented Aberdeenshire in the first British parliament after the Union of 1707 but then got mixed up in John Law's disastrous Mississippi Scheme and lost so much money he had to sell Kinmundy and Pitlurg in 1724. The direct family line ended and James Gordon, a remote cousin, succeeded to Straloch. But Straloch itself was sold by about 1770 during the minority of James' grandson, John Gordon Cuming who was later to add Skene to his name. (See below.) John Gordon Cuming Skene had a long career in the army, becoming a general. He is buried in the Straloch Mausoleum at Newmachar Church. The man who bought Straloch in about 1770 was John Ramsay of Melross and Barra (d.1785). He married Isabella Shepherd and began to build the handsome house which still stands. His daughter, Mary, married John Innes who then took the name Ramsay to become another John Ramsay of Barra and Straloch; he died in 1814.

Boghole (Rosehall)/Clubsgovil/Parkhill

Owned by William Thomson in 1667, Boghole passed to Henry Panton of Clubsgovil. Old Goval was owned by a John Kintie and Little Govil by Henry Panton's wife. All these properties were brought together with Parkhill by Andrew Skene in 1714. Later Skenes died without issue and in 1794 the whole estate, now the largest in Newmachar, was entailed upon General John Gordon Cumqing on condition that he took the name Skene. (The General's great grandmother had in fact been a Skene.) He took over the estate in 1815.

The Value of the 'Mannours'

For the most part, taxation was managed through the lairds whose lands — their 'mannours' — were valued for the purpose. The 1667 and 1674 valuations show that James Hervie of Mameulah and the owners of Kinmundy (the Menzies) were assessed at £336. 13s 4d. Francis Irvine of Hilton (in the parish of Old Machar) who owned Clubsgovil was worth £550 13s.4d but presumably this was mostly for his property outwith Newmachar. His daughter married Henry Panton who was assessed at £450 for Boghole and presumably other properties in a different parish. Elrick was worth £550 while James Sangster (the habitual sinner?) had property worth £100 but it is not clear where this was. Further information of this kind may be gleaned from the records left by the Jacobites when they raised money for the Old Pretender in 1715. By 1770, Straloch was valued at £800 and Parkhill at £927 9s 4d whereas Elrick remained at £550.

Life in the Parish: (ii) the Tenants and other Inhabitants

With greater or lesser degrees of efficiency, the Newmachar ministers and their Church officers recorded baptisms, marriages and deaths. With the aid of these records one can trace the names of many of the ordinary inhabitants of the parish from the late seventeenth century. More information can be obtained from the grave stones in the kirkyard. Robert Gordon's seems to be the earliest name there but doubtless many were interred in unmarked graves. It is also clear that the land near the original chapel at Monykebbock continued to be in use for burials — as indeed it was up to the 1970s.

In the hard times of the 1690s, the experiment of a poll tax — i.e. a tax on each individual — was attempted and so most people's names were recorded, not just those of the lairds. However, the 'List of Pollable Persons in the County of Aberdeen' made in 1696 does not include Straloch which was a detached part of the County of Banff. The lairds of Elrick and Boghole (Robert Burnett and Henry Panton) carried out the survey so that each person could be made to pay six shillings and six shillings more if he had a trade, plus one fortieth of his rent. Even John Black, 'criple in the hand' and a cottar at Little Goval had to pay the six shillings and his wife another six shillings. At least children were not assessed although some of those of the landowners seem to have been counted. The landowners paid various other kinds of extra sums. The details can be followed easily enough in the printed edition of the list *(List of Pollable Persons in the Shire of Aberdeen, 1696,* ed. John Stuart, 2 vols, 1844, Vol 2: 540, 551.) but the general picture which emerges is of the existence of about 22 fermtouns in this part of the parish. (See Chaps. V and VII.) 530 people are noted of whom 15 seem to be regarded as gentry — 8 of the Panton family, 2 Menzies, 2 unnamed from Kinmundy and 3, also unnamed, from Monykebbock. Then there is the Minister and his wife. 37 can be regarded as tradesmen: 6 millers and wrights, 16 weavers and tailors, 12 cobblers and 3 blacksmiths though one assumes that most of these would have cultivated some land. About 80 men or women seem to be servants. The remaining 400 are in one way or another apparently engaged in agriculture. (See also Chap. VIII.)

Besides the poll tax records, other evidence on ordinary life in Newmachar is rather scant. Alexander Keith's survey of 1732 tells one little although it is the first work to display any serious interest in the history and antiquities of the parish. Macfarlane's 'Geographical Collections', mentioned above, is the best, if still rather inadequate early eighteenth-century source. Besides talking about the 'mannours', this account notes the importance of peat sales to Aberdeen and the existence of five mills on the 'chief burn'. There is also reported to be a good inn near the Church, presumably at Reisque. Later, Dr Webster's survey of 1755, which was apparently based on returns from every parish minister in Scotland, estimates the population of Newmachar to be 1191 all of whom, incidentally, were protestants. (See Chap. XXV.)

The Management of the Parish

Various statutes of the Scottish parliament from 1424 provided for the management of local affairs. Parishes were defined as the smallest units of administration in 1617 just as Newmachar came into existence. However, there is little information on the overall management of the parish in the period under review. Clearly, the Church tried to exercise social control as well as providing religious and moral instruction. A school was certainly in existence by

Elrick House, built in the 1780s

the eighteenth century. (See Chap. XVII.) By this time, too, the work of Justices of the Peace had replaced the jurisdictions of baronies. The heritors (landowners) of the parish were recognised as carrying public burdens in respect of church, school and, the greatest problem of all, the relief of the poor. An Act of 1579 had established the key principle that authorities could 'taxe and stent haill the inhabitants within the parochin according to the estimation of their substance'. *(Lindsay, Scottish Poor Law p. 12.)* The authorities were the minister and kirk session meeting jointly with the heritors. Half the financial burden would fall on the heritors and half on their tenants. Powers were further defined in 1698 following the disastrous famine years of the 1690s when perhaps a fifth of Aberdeenshire's population died. There seems to be no direct information on the extent to which Newmachar was affected by these disasters, the births and death records being too scanty to make it possible to draw conclusions. (R. Tyson, 'Famine in Aberdeenshire, 1695-1699...', *From Lairds to Louns*, ed. D. Stevenson, Aberdeen, 1986, p. 41.)

Famine continued to threaten in the eighteenth century. The spring of 1782, for example, brought frequent rainstorms in Aberdeenshire with April being the wettest ever recorded until April 2000. Bad weather continued right through the summer with the result that crops failed. Newmachar did not escape these disasters. The situation is described thus:

Nationwide crop failure in 1782-3 is notable for the fact that, for the first time, there was government intervention. In Newmachar, the number of poor receiving the normal quarterly distribution of assistance was greatly increased and to these were added 'several poor families' who received interim supplies. In July 1783 the government supplied the parish with 12 bolls of pease and sold another 23 bolls to the Kirk Session 'at moderate price'. But the Session and the heritors had already used the poors' fund to purchase 15 bolls of pease at £1. 12s. per boll and meet the cost of drying, milling and carriage from Aberdeen (which they had to meet for the government's supplies, too). Very little cash was left and the Kirk Session had to call on the heritors who responded generously and 'bought a considerable quantity of pease for the support of their tenants'.

(Margaret Begbie)

The Transition to the Modern World: the Rev. William Stronach and the *Old Statistical Account*

In the 1790s Sir John Sinclair sent 160 queries to each minister of the Established Church so that Scotland's current condition and 'the means of its future improvement' might be determined. The results were printed in what has become known as *The Old Statistical Account*. Mr William Stronach responded for Newmachar in 1791-2. His is a comparatively short exposition but one packed with vital information.

The 1782-3 crisis was a recent memory and the population had actually fallen since then. Although the heritors and three other farmers had enclosed their 'mains' farms, most of the parish was still cultivating on the open field, runrig system. The majority of the tenants were still liable to provide various labour services for their lairds or for public purposes. There were no turnpike roads and no post office. On the other hand, Mr Stronach could point to signs of progress. The people were 'tolerably industrious' and usually kept away from the six ale houses on the road through the parish. The new church building in 1791, the new manse and new mansions, together with the trend towards agricultural enclosure, were all signs that Newmachar was a parish in a state of transition from old ways originating in the medieval period to new attitudes, ideas and arrangements.

The Parish Church much as it would have looked in 1791, the year of its construction and the time when the Rev. William Stronach was writing his account of Newmachar for the Old Statistical Account. Mr Stronach said that the Church was built 'on a very good plan'.

In 1597, there had been a 'witch panic' in and around Aberdeen with the result that at least thirty women and one man were burnt at the stake. Although there is no evidence of witches or accusations actually in the Newmachar area, witches were apprehended in Dyce and Fintray while John Duguid and Alexander Cobban from Mill of Auchenhuive served as members of juries which found women guilty. ('Trials for Witchcraft, 1596-7', *Miscellany of the Spalding Club*, ed. John Stuart, Vol I (1841) 82-193, pp. 154, 183.) By 1797, this sort of thing would have been impossible. No doubt there was much credulity and neighbourly back-biting of the kind which made witchcraft allegations possible but there were more civilised ways of settling disputes — or combating the Devil. At least the standard of living was rising and the 1782 crisis had been weathered without major loss of life. Mr Stronach noted that gentlemen were beginning to pay attention to the improvement of their estates and this included freeing their tenants from 'that servitude, under which they in former times groaned.' He hoped that as a result, the lower class would gain 'a sort of independence natural to creatures of God, and to free-born citizens.'

Politically, Newmachar was as firmly part of the British state as any other area of Scotland. What was to prove even more important for its future was its growing integration with the wider British economy which was not only industrialising but had become global in the reach of its trade. Newmachar was and remained mainly agricultural and so it is in agriculture that the transition is most clearly seen. The next two chapters deal with agriculture from 1600 to the 1920s.

A Note on Sources

The Scottish Record Office collections of parish records on births, baptisms and burials are available in microfilm form at the Aberdeenshire Library Service Resources Centre at Old Meldrum. Besides the published works mentioned above, see William Temple, *The Thanage of Fermartyn*, Aberdeen, 1894, pp. 288-329; Alexander Keith, 'A View of the Diocese of Aberdeen', *Collections for a History of the Shires of Aberdeen and Banff*, Spalding Club, 1843, pp. 235-6; 'The Aberdeen Style Book' ed M.C. Meston, *Stairs Society*, 2000 which includes the 1674 Valuation; *The Valuation for the County of Aberdeen for 1667*, ed. A. and H. Tayler, Spalding Club, 1933, pp. 32-3; *A Directory of Land Ownership in Scotland*, ed. Loretta Templeton,

Scottish Record Society, New series, V (1976); *The Jacobite Cess Roll for the County of Aberdeen* in 1715, ed. A. and H. Tayler, Spalding Club, 1932, pp. 235-7; *Geographical Collections Relating to Scotland made by Walter Macfarlane*, ed. A. Mitchell, 3 vols, Edinburgh, 1906-8, Vol 1: 84-5; William Stronach, 'The Parish of New-Machar', *The Statistical Account of Scotland*, Vol VI (1792) pp. 465-476; a more accessible version is the second edition, Vol XV, ed. Donald Withrington, 1982, pp. 349-360.

Chapter VIII
Agriculture in Newmachar to c. 1800

Even as recently as 1800, the landscape of Newmachar would have been unrecognisable to modern eyes. The village did not exist and a very high percentage of the land throughout the parish was unused. Fields as discrete areas of land enclosed by a fence or dyke were rare. There were only about 1,200 cattle — not much more than the number of people — and only some 300 sheep. Nevertheless, Newmachar was an important agricultural area usually producing enough for its own needs and even exporting produce to Aberdeen. The agriculture was organised on a system going back hundreds if not thousands of years although superimposed upon it (see Chap. V) was a more recent system of manorial control.

The Agricultural System

Fermtouns were the basic settlements. The touns and their associated agricultural practices were probably not very different in 1650 from what they had been in the medieval period. (See Chap. V.) Each toun can be shown to be sited usually on a south-facing slope of moderate steepness (2°— 4°). Both the more exposed higher land and the valley bottoms, ill-drained and subject to frost pockets, were avoided. The precise location might be determined by the kame and kettle physiography (Chap. I), the nature of the soil — usually a sandy loam developed from the glacial till — and the location of springs which develop at the junction of the till and the bedrock. (Cowie, pp. 5, 8-9 and Fig. 3.)

In an elegant exercise in historical geography, James Cowie was able to relate such physical realities to the evidence available on the fermtouns and their inhabitants in the Newmachar section of the 1696 'List of Pollable Persons within the Shire of Aberdeen'. He goes on to say:

Each fermtoun had its infields and outfields worked by tenants holding land from the laird, and a number of sub-tenants and cottars who often combined their agricultural work with a trade. In all, every settlement combined from eight to forty people including tenants, sub-tenants, servants, cottars and tradesmen, each with their families, the number giving an indication of the relative importance of a fermtoun... Another common feature was the home farm or 'maynes', equivalent to the English demesne, attached to each estate from which the laird drew his food requirements. The latter were also met by tenants, who paid rent in kind as well as in services and money.

Frequently, the less important estates of the parish were run by tenants who paid rent to absentee lairds residing in other parishes, where they probably had more important landed interests. Such was the case with the proprietor of the Rennieshill and Kingseat estate, who resided in Forgue parish...while the proprietor of Mameulah resided in Old Machar parish. (Cowie, p. 8.)

The inhabitants of the fermtouns would probably have lived in mud and wattle buildings which could easily be reconstructed if they fell down or if declining soil fertility indicated the desirability of moving. Each fermtoun's infield, outfield and common grazing areas would be arranged according to environmental conditions and chance.

On the infield, which was more or less continuously cultivated, there was a system of rotation with, probably, bere or barley for one year, oats for two and then peas for one year. Kail was also grown. The fields would be regularly manured and, increasingly from the seventeenth century, treated with lime, supplies of which could be obtained from near Kinmundy. The outfield would have been manured only for comparatively brief periods during the summer when cattle were on the shielings. Oats or other crops might be grown for up to four or five years and then the land would be left as 'faugh' or fallow for an equal period. Within each cultivated area of the infield or outfield, each tenant would have a large or small number of strips — rigs — usually running up and down the slope. The earth in each ridge tended to be piled up as a result of ploughing which thus also created furrows which served as the means of drainage. Among the rigs, there might be those owned by the laird on which the tenants would be obliged to work as a condition of holding their own land. As pointed out by James Cowie, however, by 1696, the lairds' lands were separated off from the other land and enclosed.

Although as the list of persons in Brownhills below shows, there were herders, the number of cattle kept was probably relatively small. Only in the eighteenth century did the practice of growing turnips for winter feed begin, which meant that fewer animals needed to be slaughtered young. The most important beasts were the teams of oxen kept for ploughing, rather than cattle for milk or meat. In the 1790s, according to the *Old Statistical Account* of Newmachar written by

Mr Stronach, there were no fewer than 68 ploughs in the parish and as late as that date still over 250 oxen were being used to pull the ploughs. Farmers continued to sell their animals as calves to provide veal for the Aberdeen market rather than keep them for beef or milk production. In the 1600-1800 period, the inhabitants of Newmachar themselves probably ate very little meat; protein came from leguminous crops and cheese made from the milk of cows or ewes grazed on the shielings in the summer months. Perhaps the occasional pigeon or rabbit provided variety but in

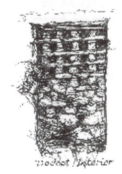

fact, the diet was based mainly on oatmeal and peasemeal and must have been very monotonous. And right to the end of the eighteenth century, there was the ever-present possibility of actual starvation if the crops failed.

Rural Industry

In addition to its agricultural base, Newmachar in the 1600-1800 period would have seen much activity in what may be termed rural industries. A largely self-sufficient population, needed not only food, but also shoes, clothes and the tools for their agricultural work. Hence the presence in the 1696 Poll Tax List of weavers, tailors, cobblers and smiths. (Cowie, p. 10.) The largely arable economy also dictated the need for mills to produce flour from the grain or to crush the peas so that brose could be made. It follows that the mills of Newmachar are a vital part of the human landscape. (See Chap. X.)

Another fundamental need was, of course, warmth and so peat-cutting was a vital ancillary activity for the inhabitants of the fermtouns. Redmoss in the south-east part of the parish is the principal area where there is still peat (which continued to be cut into the 1970s) but 'mosses' were formerly much more extensive. (Cowie, pp. 9-10.) An important summer activity was cutting enough peat as fuel for the winter months and this could interfere with other demands on labour during that season.

The Fermtoun of Brounhills as it appears in the 1696 List of Pollable Persons

Margaret Harvie, widow, tennent, of valuatione 15s 6d with her own and two sones *in familia*, their generall poll is	£1	13	6
William Clerk, servant, fee £19 6s 8d, fortieth pairt with the generall poll	0	15	8
Margaret Clerk, servant, fee £10 13s 4d, fortieth pairt and generall	0	11	4
Marjorie M'Kie, servant, the lyke fee and generall poll	0	11	4
John Logan, herd, fee £3, fortieth pairt whereof and generall poll	0	7	6
Andrew Still, herd, the lyk fee and generall poll	0	7	6
James Harvie, shoemaker, a hooks land 1s 2d, with 6s for his trade and his oun and his wyfes generall poll	0	19	2
Geils and Helen Harvies, their generall poll is	0	12	0
Elspeth Hepburne ther, her generall poll is	0	6	0
John Johnstoun, taylor, for his trade 6s with his oun and his wyfes poll	0	18	0
Barbra Johnstoun, their daughter *in familia*, her poll	0	6	0
	£7	8	0

The Beginnings of Change in the Eighteenth Century

By about 1750, the landscape pattern in Newmachar was beginning to change in significant ways. Using the evidence of General Roy's Map of 1750, Cowie is able to identify four important developments. Firstly, although most of the farmed land was still managed on the runrig system, there were about half a dozen small areas of enclosed arable fields and an equally small number of enclosed pastures for cattle. In the latter, and this is the second development, what Mr Stronach called cattle of 'good size [and] beautiful shape' were being bred. His account also mentions the closely-connected new practice of turnip growing which meant there was winter feed for cattle. Arable farming, thirdly, was being extended into previously unused or perhaps seldom used lands as peat was cut away or rough land ploughed. Fourthly, areas of woodland were being developed, sometimes as shelter belts, but also around the great houses like Straloch. (Cowie, pp. 12-14 and Fig. 4.) The parkland trees must have been important not only for ornamental purposes but also for preserving game and, in the longer run, producing timber. From other sources we know that a fifth change was the increase in the number of stone-built houses for farming people. The increasing use of horses for ploughing (Stronach, p. 353) was yet another sign of changes in farming practice.

It is apparent that before the end of the eighteenth century, Newmachar was no longer simply a self-sufficient agricultural economy. Store cattle were becoming a feature of farming. Some animals might be driven to market in Aberdeen and the drove road to the city became more and more important. Surplus oats and barley were also sent outwith the parish for sale. Peat had long been sold in Aberdeen although this was now subject to competition with seaborne supplies of coal. Mr Stronach says that about five acres of land in the parish were producing flax for linen production. He notes that women knitted stockings as a form of domestic industry although they were running into difficulty.

The problem with stockings was that there was now a machine to make them. This and the flax growing was a sign that even a little-regarded parish like Newmachar was beginning by the 1790s to be affected by the economic changes which are generally referred to as the Industrial and Agricultural Revolutions.

James D. Cowie, 'The Landscape Evolution of the Parish of Newmachar, Aberdeenshire', Aberdeen University Geography Department Thesis, 1967. William Stronach, 'Parish of New-Machar', *The Statistical Account of Scotland*, 2nd ed., 349-360. In addition to Mr Cowie's dissertation and Mr Stronach's work, see John Burnett Pratt, *Buchan*, Aberdeen, 1858 and later editions; Alexander Fenton, *Country Life in Scotland*, Edinburgh, 1987 and *Scottish Country Life*, Edinburgh, 1976. The Brownhills Poll Tax list is extracted from *List of Pollable Persons in the Shire of Aberdeen*, ed. John Stuart, 2 vols, Aberdeen, 1844, Vol 2: 548. The sketch of the doo'cot interior at Disblair on the western edge of the parish is by Joan Burnett.

Chapter IX
The Agricultural Revolution and Agriculture to the 1920s

Signs of change in Newmachar's agricultural practice were in evidence before 1800 (Chap. VIII) although in the *Old Statistical Account*, Mr Stronach tells us unequivocally that, with the exception of the principal landowners' home farms and three others, the parish was open. In other words, nearly all agriculture was still organised on the runrig system. Rapid change came in the early nineteenth century. According to the Rev. George Moir, writing for the *New Statistical Account* in 1842, it was in the preceding ten years that the greatest changes had taken place. (*New Statistical Account* [hereafter, *NSA*], Vol XII, p. 1031.)

Fermtouns and co-operative agriculture came to an end. Estates became economic units in the sense that they controlled production by imposing certain requirements on tenant farmers. The tenants worked as individuals on consolidated holdings consisting of enclosed fields. Taking advantage of various improved techniques and better equipment as well as a paid labour force, they were farming for the market, not subsistence. The essential market for Newmachar and many other parts of Aberdeenshire became the Smithfield Market in London; in other words, cattle farming for beef production came to be the crucial activity. The tenant farmers employed farm servants who, in theory at least, ceased to be bound by any feudal regulations and became freemen able to sell their labour for the best available reward. Looked at less optimistically, the situation was that to sell their labour was the only thing they could do: the majority of the rural population now had no land which in any sense was their own. Agriculture had been made fully part of a capitalist mode of production and the peasantry had ceased to exist. The co-operative way of life characteristic of the Newmachar fermtouns, where people had possessed land and rights as well as obligations, had been radically altered. There was now a rural proletariat.

It is easy to produce this simple model of the social consequences of the agricultural revolution. In practice, of course, the situation was much more complicated than the model would suggest. By no means all farms became large capitalist concerns, for example, and some old methods of working and peasant attitudes persisted. Nevertheless, profound technical and social changes did take place and a new way of life was created dominated by the enclosed farms. This way of life was to last well into the twentieth century. Consequently, the testimonies of living members of the community can help us to understand the nature of the situation which the agricultural revolution created.

The Technical Changes in Agriculture
(i) Enclosure
'In no parish, perhaps, within the last ten years have improvements in agriculture been more vigorously and successfully carried out than this.' So

wrote Mr Moir in 1842. (*NSA*, p. 1031.) Unfortunately, he does not say precisely what he means. The specific measures he goes on to mention are clearly being undertaken in enclosed fields but he does not tell us whether this ten-year process included the enclosure process itself. Probably it did. Whether it was in the 1830s or a little earlier, we have no indication of whether it was something which provoked opposition. The 1830s were a period of considerable agrarian unrest in many parts of the country but the likelihood is that in Newmachar, the expansion of the cultivated area in the parish would have made it possible for practically every one who held land in a fermtoun to be given some sort of consolidated holding. Such small holdings might easily be swallowed up by larger farms at a later stage.

Mr Moir does not tell us which of the landowners led the way in forcing on enclosure and improved husbandry techniques. Was it Susan Innes, widow of John Ramsay at Straloch, or William Gordon Cuming Skene at Parkhill, perhaps? Interestingly, it is a tenant farmer whom he takes the trouble to mention as an improver. It was Mr William Harvey, 'the spirited and skilful tenant of Monykebbock' who had effected the 'greatest improvements in agriculture in the parish.' (*NSA*, p. 1032.) Perhaps he had a free hand because the laird of Elrick, Mr Peter Burnett, was habitually in Italy. William Harvey (1802-1879) is yet another member of the Harvey family whose activities had so often been important in the development of the parish. (See Chap. VII.)

Whenever and however precisely the revolution took place, enclosure was basic. The estate of Rainnieshill serves to illustrate the results. Although the estate was small compared with Parkhill or Elrick, all but one of its farms were in the parish. There are about a dozen farms and various other holdings. As can be seen in the table, of the dozen farms proper, only four, Strypes/Westside, Upper Rainnieshill, Lower Rainnieshill and Mameulah were of any considerable size. The smaller farms in some cases took in more marginal land and, if Carter's interpretation is accepted, housed families which the larger farms could draw upon to supply labour. (Ian Carter, *Farm Life in Northeast Scotland 1840-1914*, Edinburgh, 1979, p. 176.) Leases were set for nineteen years. The owner of Rainnieshill in the 1830s and '40s, Alexander Thomson of Banchory, was encouraging tenants on the consolidated farms to build better steadings by repaying them their costs of doing so over a ten-year period. (*NSA*, p. 1032.) The repayment was effected by reductions in the rent which seems to have been a system very advantageous to the owner, especially if rents were increasing as they must have done as improvements proceeded. The table suggests rents did rise.

More generally, an idea of the way estates now began to regulate the activities of the tenant farmers may be gained from the rules produced in the name of the fifteen-year old laird for Straloch's tenants in 1846. (J. Ramsay, *General Conditions of Lease of Lands of Barra, Straloch...* n.p.s., 1846.) The regulations were not always popular with the tenant farmers who were usually obliged, as at Straloch, to allow shooting parties - and their prey - on to the farmland.

Sequestration by the laird under the 'Hypothec law' if rent fell into arrears was another problem but more important in Newmachar and elsewhere was the question of what allowances should be made at the end of a lease for any improvements which had been paid for by the tenant. (Carter, pp. 68-71.)

(ii) Clearing and Draining

'By draining, liming and other applications,' says Mr Moir, 'not only has a large addition been made to the arable land in the parish, but the soil in previous cultivation has been rendered much more productive.' (NSA, p. 1031.) This simple statement conceals the immense amount of work that was undertaken. Pick axes and even gunpowder might be used to move large rocks, the land was ploughed to expose more rocks for removal and perhaps cross-ploughed again. (James Farquharson's account of Alford for NSA p. 509ff. is extremely useful.) But the main work was done by hand with men using the *caschrom* to lift peat or get rid of stones. (A. Fenton, 'Tools and Tillage in Northern Scotland', *Fermfolk and Fisherfolk*, ed. J.S. Smith & D.S. Stevenson, Aberdeen, 1989, p. 83.) Of course, the stones were useful as ready materials for the dykes fencing the new fields.

In an area like Newmachar with its extensive coverage of boulder clay and a poorly-developed system of burns and rivers, drainage is very important. To improve it, farmers dug trenches and filled them with stones and brushwood. Later, and especially after 1846 when government land drainage grants became available, tile drains began to be set in the fields. As a result, more land could be treated as arable: the Rainnieshill Estate included no more than 2 acres of permanent pasture in 1891 (and so this is not shown in the table).

(iii) Cattle Farming

By 1837 over 7000 live cattle per year were being exported from Aberdeen, mostly to London. Ten years later the figure had more than doubled. (Carter, pp. 34-5.) This was made possible by the advent of regular steamship services which had begun from 1820. An important consequence was selective breeding of cattle to meet the needs of the Smithfield market:

> The cattle reared are either Aberdeenshire horned and dodded or crosses with the shorthorn and Hereford breeds. (Moir, NSA, p. 1031.)

Pure Aberdeenshire breed cattle actually fetched a higher price than crosses but crosses matured earlier and became bigger. (Ibid.) Getting the right balance, therefore, was a tricky matter which the Cruickshank brothers at Sittyton on the Straloch Estate were later to tackle. (See below.) Also on the Straloch Estate and actually in Newmachar, was Woodend Farm where Alexander Crombie became famous for breeding shorthorns. (Cowie, p. 18.) This herd and its reputation survived long into the twentieth century.

Newmachar farmers could now feed and fatten cattle on their own farms before selling them. Cattle fairs were held in Newmachar near the present Inn

Rainnieshill Estate 1869 - 1895

Farm	Grid ref.	Acreage in arable 1869	Acreage in arable 1891	Tenant in 1869	Tenant in 1891/95	Yearly rent or value, 1869	Yearly rent or value, 1895
Whitlam	887220	88	88	Robert Simpson	Peter Sangster	Not in Newmachar	)£113 - 5s - 3d
Strypes	888209	115		Robert Simpson	George Philip	£ 70 - 14s - 0d	)
Westside	887209	33	133	Andrew Duncan	John Rennie	£ 25 - 14s - 0d	)
Upper Rainnieshill	893205	135	135	George Godsman	William Murray	£135 - 0s - 0d	£ 90 - 10s - 6d
Newton	898202	101	94	George Thomson	David Gibb	£ 45 - 0s - 0d	£ 70 - 12s - 0d
Lower Rainnieshill	896196	128	128	John Youngson	William Burgess	£ 86 - 19s - 8d	£140 - 13s - 10d
Boddams later Pinkie	894188	45	51	William Murray	William Wood	£ 62 - 0s - 0d	+ Newbigging £ 70 - 10s - 3d
Mill of Boddams	895189	4	4	William Watson	William Johnstone	£ 16 - 0s - 0d	£ 41 - 0s - 6d
Newbigging	892188	6	4	David Murray	William Wood	£ 6 - 0s - 0d	
Greens	891190	56	56	James Duguid	William Murray	£ 67 - 18s - 0d	£ 70 - 7s - 6d
Inn Farm	884200	51	57	John Watt	William Wood	£ 72 - 16s - 4d*	£ 94 - 10s - 1d
Cunninghar	882195	53	53	John Keith	Alex Keith	£ 44 - 0s - 0d	£ 75 - 7s - 6d
Gaucyhillock	877197	78	78	Andrew Gibson	Miss M. Lumsden	£ 55 - 12s - 6d	£ 82 - 0s - 0d
Risque	883199	14	6	Robert Cheyne	W. Marnoch	£ 14 - 0s - 0d	£ 12 - 0s - 0d
(2crofts)				George Jamieson			
Newlands	882200	6	6	James Collins	James Collins	£	£ 13 - 2s - 3d
Mameulah	885202	183	183	Patrick Polson	Andrew Anderson	£183 - 16s - 0d	£232 - 7s - 11d
Miscellaneous		25					
Totals		**1168**	**1167**			**£931 - 6s - 10d**	**£1337 - 19s - 4d**

but they never became very successful; no doubt this was because it was relatively easy to take cattle to market in Aberdeen. (J.D. Marwick, *List of Markets and Fairs Now and Formerly Held in Scotland*, PP, C 51872, Appendix 73, 1890, p. 94.)

(iv) Dairying

The proximity of the growing city of Aberdeen encouraged the development of dairy herds in the later nineteenth century and a small farm like Corseduick (see below) could be successful in this field. This involved much labour in the dairy by the female members of the family and servants. It became necessary in the 1880s for the Parochial Council to enforce regulations about cleanliness in milking parlours. (See Chap. XIV.) As will be seen in Chapter XXIII, there were about 20 farms in the parish producing milk for the Aberdeen market by the 1950s.

The Economics of Dairying in 1881

In 1881, an official survey noted that most farms within easy reach of Aberdeen found it worthwhile to have a dairy herd. One productive cow cost about £25 when ready to calve and needed about 4-5 acres of land to support it. The rent per annum per acre would be about £1. Draff and other supplementary feedstuffs cost from 2s. to 3s 6d per week per cow. The cow might be expected to produce 1½ gallons of milk per day and the farmer would be paid 5d per Scotch pint for this — presumably, 5s. per cow per day. The report went on to calculate that the labour involved for, say, twenty cows would be 1 man, 2 women and one boy and that this would cost £100 per annum.

(Report by Mr G.J. Walker, PP. 1881, Vol XVI, C2778-2, p. 539.)

(v) Arable farming

Improving Newmachar tenant farmers abandoned the old infield/outfield system and the rotation which went with it. Most adopted a five- or seven-shift system:
1. Green crop, usually turnips or fallow
2. Oats or barley sown with grass seed
3. Grass for hay
4. Pasture   (and 5 & 6 in seven shift)
5 or 7. Oats
8. Oats

(*NSA* p. 1031; Cowie, p. 17.)

The oats and grasses would be new strains being developed by seed merchants. Oats like Scotch Birley which ripened earlier than traditional strains now became favoured. Using clover in hay crops became common. The application of lime and cattle manure now became more carefully controlled and by the middle of the nineteenth century, imported guano and bone meal were widely in use. It is clear that many of these improvements in arable practice were for the benefit of cattle production. Animals need not be slaughtered each November, as before, but could be fed through the winter on turnips and oat straw.

(vi) Equipment

Probably the most important changes in equipment and associated techniques involved ploughs. Wooden ploughs were replaced by iron ploughs with more than one share and coulter. They were increasingly drawn by horses which now became the most important source of motive power on farms. Small's plough iron with a curved mould board could do effective work with only two horses drawing it. (Fenton p.100.) The men who managed the horses correspondingly became the most important farm servants while the subsidiary trades of shoeing, harness making, etc. developed as vital adjuncts to farming. Although oxen continued to be used on smaller farms, sometimes in conjunction with one horse, the whole elaborate system of ox management with its own specialised vocabulary - on wyner, in fur, jouk! for example - began to disappear.

As far as collecting in the crop was concerned, one very simple but extremely significant development was the replacement of the sickle by the scythe. A man could reap two acres of oats in one ten-hour day with a scythe. (Fenton p. 113.) By the middle of the century reaping machines drawn by horses were coming into use. Threshing was also mechanised with the replacement of the hand-held flail; water, and eventually steam power began to be used. (See Chap. X.) Winnowing, formerly managed with the aid of flail, riddle and the wind, became a more controllable process with the use of power-driven fans.

Transport improvements in the form of better roads, especially the turnpike of 1801 and the railway of 1861 (see Chaps. XI and XII) were obviously vital for farms now geared to the market. But improvements on the farm were equally important: carts replaced sleds or the small capacity baskets ('currachs') slung on either side of a horse. However, within living memory, farmers were still using a puddock - a sort of sled for shifting harrows or big stones from one field to another. (Testimony of Mr Bert Sangster.) Peat cutting now became more controlled in the sense that some care was used to replace the top soil so that the area could be later used for grazing.

The list of technical innovations and improvements in the nineteenth century is almost endless. Nevertheless, farm work remained an extremely labour intensive business as the testimonies below make clear. The social changes which went with all the technical changes are not so easily described or interpreted.

Social Changes: 'Merrie Aberdeenshire'?
As estates became economic units, the lairds became businessmen as much as landowners — in a word, capitalists. The major tenant farmers, although circumscribed by estate regulations, e.g. on what they might grow and the extent to which they could sub-let land and beset by uncertainty about whether leases would be renewed after 19 years, became capitalists, too, with interests perhaps essentially not very different from those of the lairds. The position of smaller farmers and of the landless farm servants is more ambiguous. The 1831 census (Chap. XXV) shows 158 occupiers of land and only 76 labourers but the enclosure movement was then still not completed. The smaller farmer relying

on his own and his immediate family's labour might struggle to break in new land and produce a few cattle for sale to his more prosperous neighbours. Dairy farming could produce a not unreasonable living and he could hope to secure the lease of a larger property.

The farm servants, male and female, if one has to use class terminology at all, undoubtedly appear to be a rural proletariat — people who had only their labour to sell. The men lived in what were often called bothies but which were strictly 'chaumers'. In other words, there was accommodation for perhaps three or four men in a room in a steading or perhaps in the roof of a stable. In 1840 the wage was about £12 per year plus food which was provided by the farm kitchen. It might be argued that the labourers were not simply that and nothing more; everyone, it has been argued, was seen as part of a sort of extended family. Even so, life was extremely insecure in that employment contracts were for only six months. One had to go to the feein' market to secure a job. On the other hand, some men appear to have liked the opportunity to move around to different farms.

From the middle of the nineteenth century, most farm labourers who got married had the opportunity of living in a home of their own, albeit a tied cottage. As the testimonies which follow show, marriage could be a tremendous liberation especially for female farm servants, who were often at the beck and call of the farmer's wife and were worked very hard indeed.

Workmen had hierarchies of their own. The Horseman's Societies were especially important as a means of passing on knowledge and lore and maintaining hierarchy and prestige. More generally, story telling and bothy ballads enshrined and perpetuated a culture which was special to the Northeast of Scotland and in which everyone could share.

Clearly, there were many ambiguities about farm life in the nineteenth and twentieth centuries. Two very different positions can be taken about the situation. On the one hand it is possible to argue that there was a real community of interest in a society like that in Newmachar. Everyone went to the same school. Both master and man not only shared the distinctive Doric dialect of English but had the same interest in good fatstock prices in Smithfield. Gatherings of estate tenants and workers show there was a real sense of community not just a cash nexus. The births register indicates that Straloch tenants and workers named their children after the laird's family, apparently as a demonstration of real affection and respect. Service in the county militia could be another form of social bonding. There really were 'kindly relations'. Support for this approach might come if one looked at political and religious developments in Newmachar. The Great Disruption in the church of 1843 undoubtedly included elements of class division in many parts of Scotland. That does not seem to be the case in Newmachar with the largest landowner as well as many workers opting to 'go out'. Even during the years of the Great

Agricultural Depression of the 1880s, Newmachar seems to have presented a united front; there was no serious likelihood of either tenant farmers throwing over their lands or smaller farmers breaking ranks to join the farm servants in opposing capitalist landlords, large farmers and the associated large milling firms.

A very different way of looking at social relations is that offered by Ian Carter in his study of farm life in the Northeast. For him the ultimate reality is not an harmonious community but class interactions.   He points out that 'the conflation of sectional interests with general interests is an old trick.' (p. 183.). But Carter's principal contention is that the blurring of lines of class division by means of the 'kindly relations' was a result of the attempt of small farmers to avoid becoming proletariat. Among the farm servants, horseman societies were a levelling device to prevent the emergence of capitalists. Even more important in Carter's view is the fact that it suited the lairds, big farmers, and milling or meat companies to have an intermediate stratum of society, small farmers or crofters, essentially a peasant class. In Newmachar's case, it would be argued that these 'peasants' broke in ground which could later be bought cheaply by a big farmer and, by producing large families, acted as a reservoir of labour. He argues that the peasant class finally died out with the Great War.

How far we should accept one view of the nature of agricultural society in Newmachar rather than the other is a matter for debate. Some things are clear. The 'bothy nichts' approach is certainly to be discounted. To imagine that there was a sort of 'merrie Aberdeenshire' when everyone worked happily together and sang bothy ballads to one another by way of recreation is obviously absurd. Those who romanticise the rural past are invariably those who have managed to escape it to become lawyers, doctors, rulers of Empire or some such. To be a farm labourer was to work extremely hard for long hours in various kinds of bad weather and to be rewarded with very low wages. The small farmer or cottar, whether or no he was only a 'peasant', in truth had little chance of becoming a substantial farmer; there was a real chance of slipping into actual poverty as the records of Newmachar's Parochial Board show. His best hope might be that his children could break out of the system via the education system.

On the other hand, many tenant farmers worked themselves as hard as their men and were certainly not living lives of conspicuous luxury. As for the lairds, someone like Major Ramsay was a man who took his public duties extremely seriously, striving in the best way he knew to improve his estate and Aberdeenshire. Habits of conventional deference within an hierarchical society, which younger people living now find difficult to understand, may account for some of the respect shown for the lairds. Yet who is to say that there was not real mutual admiration and regard which could cross what appear to be formidable class barriers? Describing life in Whiterashes and on the Straloch Estate, George Davidson writes with real respect for the family and with what is surely genuine warmth of life as part of the community which was the estate. (George A Davidson, *Memories of Whiterashes*, Aberdeen 1983 passim.) Those who have provided information for this book are remarkable as individual people not as a members of an oppressed rural proletariat or a 'peasant fraction'. Overarching theories explain macro history but the historian must study the subject at the micro level, too.

****

Memories of Farms and Farm Life

No farm diaries or memoirs appear to exist relating to nineteenth-century farm life in Newmachar although it may well be that there are such things hidden in attics. However, there is information about Amos Cruickshank. In addition, there are the memories of older living members of the community who can look back to the early part of the twentieth century; they were part of a way of life that was not fundamentally different from that in the nineteenth century. The next great revolution was to come with the break up of the estates and then the arrival of tractors. (See Chap. XXIII.)

Ploughing with Clydesdales

(i) *The work of Amos Cruickshank*

'what is now known as the Cruickshank blood has done more for the shorthorns of Great Britain than any other sort or strain.'

Amos Cruickshank, 1808 - 1895, and his brother Anthony, 1812 - 1879, were two of the sons of John Cruickshank, 1770 - 1825, and his wife Sarah, 1782 - 1857, a prominent Quaker family most of whom are buried in the Kinmuck churchyard. Amos took the lease of Sittyton Farm on the Straloch Estate in

1837 and lived there with Anthony, whose chief occupation was running a hosiery business in Aberdeen. Anthony married Ann, 1808 - 87, and their son, John W. Cruickshank, 1842 - 1918, later became a prominent art historian and photographer associated with Elrick House. (See Chap. XV.)

Together Amos and Anthony began to form a herd of pure bred shorthorns. 'Reticent and taciturn', Amos was determined to produce the perfect herd and did not always agree with his brother about the qualities of the bulls which either bought. As Joan Burnett has written:

' . . . for 57 years Amos worked on a breeding policy for his cattle aimed at producing a strong, vigorous animal that would make good flesh and mature early. The local farmers bought his bulls and the good qualities of the strain spread; but it was a long time before the Cruickshanks achieved something near their ideal.

Searching England for a new stock bull, and not finding a suitable one, Amos wrote to a friend asking if he had such an animal. The friend replied that he had 'A good bull that might do until something better was found'. Amos might have him for 30 guineas. Amos bought the bull, Lancaster Comet, unseen and had him brought north. The animal did not survive the cold northern climate for long, but he did leave a son whom Amos called Champion of England. Though his owner did not consider the Champion perfect, nor prize-winning material, he had a strong constitution, vigour, and made rapid growth, qualities Amos was looking for.'

(*Newmachar News*, no. 40, 1985)

Amos made sure that his workers at Sittyton had a portion of the Bible read to them every evening and quietly insisted that everyone did a fair day's work. When a carter was seen to be proceeding rather too slowly, for example, Amos cut a twig of broom, handed it to the horseman and said quietly "Thee must quicken thy pace." The house at Sittyton was "solid and substantial" and Amos was interested in the flower garden as well as his cattle. But the cattle were his life: he knew and remembered all the cattle families.

In 1889 with his lease coming to an end and his health beginning to fail, Amos Cruickshank sold the whole herd to Argentina. Major Ramsay, the laird, asked Amos to live on at Sittyton as a yearly tenant which he did until his death.

(Based principally on Robert Bruce, "The late Mr Amos Cruickshank", *Trans. Highland Agricultural Society of Scotland*, 5th series VIII (1896) 214-224.)

(ii) Upper Tack: Mrs Margaret Mitchell, formerly Cowie

Mrs Mitchell's father was Peter Cowie who, as the photograph shows, served in the Glasgow Police force in the early 1900s. He bought the farm at Upper Tack sometime before 1914 and married a lady from the Strachan family, which is still established at Hillhead (919137). Mrs Cowie's mother, Grannie Strachan, is shown in the other photograph. The mainstay of Upper Tack farm became dairying and a milk delivery business.

As a child, Mrs Mitchell walked from Upper Tack to school each day and recalls using the tops of stone dykes as pathways when the snow was deep. Two brothers left farming for university and distinguished careers outwith Newmachar as a Russian linguist and a district officer in Zambia (Northern Rhodesia) but Mrs Mitchell had to remain on the farm and became responsible for the milk delivery business. Deliveries were made twice a day by horse and trap and later a van. Many farms relied on the unpaid labour of the family and

Constable Cowie

Granny Strachan

this could be particularly hard on girls. The dairying and the milk round continued until 1939. Jim Gray of Kinmundy took over the round.

(iii) Standryford: Mr Norman Duncan

The Duncan family is one of the oldest established in Newmachar. Duncans appear in the 1696 Poll Tax records at Rainnieshill ('List of Pollable Persons', p. 551) and eighteenth and nineteenth-century headstones in the graveyard testify to their later presence. Alexander Duncan was tenant of the Brokenwynd and Crosscausey farms from 1860 and up to 1895 but later must have taken over

Standryford from Arthur Singer.   Alexander was Mr Duncan's grandfather whom he remembers as a man with a large beard.

   Standryford was part of the North Kinmundy estate.   The laird was not seen; everything was done through the solicitors Davidson and Garden. Alexander Duncan was in the habit of going to market in Aberdeen by train.   He usually brought fish home from these trips to the city and is reputed to have thrown the packet from the train as it passed his home knowing that the fish would be cooked ready for his meal by the time he had walked back from the station. Interestingly, this story has also passed down through the Ingram family for one of Alexander Duncan's daughters, 'Lizzie', (the little girl shown in the gig with her brother) married Mr Charles Ingram.   Norman Duncan's father, Alec, took over farming at Standryford but continued to live at Longford (896186).   This was a croft house to which 'Auld Soddy' had retired when he ceased to run the

'Sod Inn', an ale house near the present Burnside (901171). (See also Chap. XI.)

   Standryford Farm was arable with cattle, with turnips, corn and oats being the main crops.   There was a mill (see Chap X) and, of course, horses.   But Mr Duncan's main memory of farm work at Standryford was that it involved much human physical labour. There were three horses until well after 1945 when a Ferguson tractor was obtained.   It was at this time that Mr Duncan's father bought the farm from the estate.   The horses were easily frightened by the trains and train drivers knew this and blew the whistle deliberately as they came out of the cutting to the north of the farm (896185).   But the railway was important for the farm: you went to the station to get coal or import calves from England.

(iv) The Horseman's Word: Mr James Imlah
Mr Imlah has provided information about his father, Mr Alec Imlah, who was a horseman and worked at various farms, eventually at Nether Kingseat, that is, the present Kingseat Farm. (See also Chap. XX.)   The Horseman Society had an initiation rite which involved cutting a nick in the novitiate's left hand - and drinking the bottle of whisky he had to bring along.   The 1939 war finally ended these societies.

(v) The Farmworker: Mr William Middleton
Mr Middleton was born in 1907 and moved round various schools as his father had jobs at different farms.   He himself began work at the age of 13½ at a wage

of £14 for six months; he had to learn to manoeuvre 10 gallon cans of milk and take them to the deck at the farm gates to be picked up by one of the early motor lorries. Milking of the herd began at 5 am. This was at Corthymuir, just over the border in Udny but later for four years he worked at Brokenwynd (897178) for Mr Charles Ingram. Every six months it was necessary to go the feein' market to secure a job. This system continued on into the 1930s.

Mr Middleton became a second horseman, never a first, because the era of horses was coming to an end and he had to move over to working with cattle.

Mr Middleton as a young farmworker; he is second from the right

During the 1930s wages fell so that by 1939 he was earning only £60 a year plus supplies of milk, potatoes and coal. Despite being in a 'reserved occupation' during the war, he experienced great danger through strafing by a German plane and then a bomb falling into a steading when he was nearby.

The system in the early part of his working life was that he lived in a bothy - in his case with two others - and took his food in the farmhouse. But relief from this came when he married and got a tied house. There was not much time for sport but one pastime was throwing the hammer - a real one - as a contest. In fact there were few holidays though one was given for George V's Silver Jubilee in 1935.

At the end of his career there were fewer jobs in agriculture and little chance of getting one's own farm and so Mr Middleton worked on the roads for 11 years up to 1972 having permanently moved into Newmachar from 1958. Mr Middleton's life has been full and interesting and he has no regrets.

(vi) **Mrs Middleton** was born near Newburgh as one of twins. She met her husband at a dance. Her early life involved living on various different farms and attending different schools as her farm worker father had to move between jobs. She left her last school at Barthol Chapel at 13½ and went into domestic service at various farms. This involved rising at 4 or 5 am to get breakfast ready for the men in the bothy. There was no day off except one Sunday every three weeks. Her first 6 month period of work in 1923 earned her £4, but she moved on to a situation where she received £6. Some farmers' wives who employed her were hard and greedy, and kept a girl's nose to the grindstone continually. Mrs Middleton was employed at various farms and expected to work hours which would now be regarded as altogether unacceptable.

Mrs Middleton married at the age of 20. This was a real liberation in that she could set up her own household. Mr and Mrs Middleton had a family of four daughters who were a great joy to them. Few consumer goods could be afforded in the 1930s but the wireless was an important acquisition.

(vii) Memories of Corseduick Farm, Mrs Elizabeth Walker, formerly Cooper

Corseduick Farm (Crossduick) (885192) was run by Mrs Walker's grandparents, Robert (1864-1925) and Elizabeth Brown née Cruickshank (1864-1937). Their son, born in 1898, was killed in France in July 1918. (See Chap XX.) Mrs Walker was born at Corseduick in 1916. The Browns bought the farm before

1914 from the Elrick Estate. The 1891 Census lists 3 houses at Corseduick, housing two general labourers, one mason plus one house uninhabited. The farm was made from more than one of these four houses originally at Corseduick. One was converted to become the wash house and steading. Mrs Walker's own sketch shows the farm as she remembers it.

The farm had four or five fields adjoining the glebe and Cunninghar fields. It was on the northern boundary of what had been the Elrick Estate. It was a mixed farm but dairying was the most important activity. Milk was sold from the farm: people came along with their pails to buy skimmed milk. Grannie Brown was renowned for making very good butter and cheese. The churn and pats are drawn by Mrs Walker. Granny also made honey. Mrs Walker remembers this childhood home as being comfortable and secure. Granny had a dais. There was

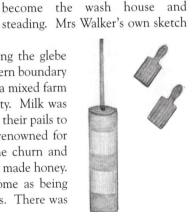

even a gramophone which played a roller type record. The cooking was done on the range which, as the sketch by Mrs Walker shows, had two binks and a sway. The water supply was from a well and this was obviously of crucial importance to the house and the dairy. The only time Mrs Walker remembers ever seeing her Granny angry was when a boy (who later became a vet) urinated at the well.

Not far away, one would see cattle being driven down the main road to market

at Kittybrewster, though there was a slaughter house at 1 Station Road.

This not unhappy childhood abruptly ended in 1923 when Mr Brown was killed following an accident with a horse and cart. The farm had to be sold and soon ceased to be a full scale dairy farm. Life became much more difficult for Mrs Walker and her mother, and ambitions to develop her interest in art were to be frustrated.

Her drawing from memory of Granny Brown's range at Corseduick is shown here.

(viii) Mr John Rennie of Westside (887209)

from information supplied by his grand-daughter, **Mrs Cecilia Penny**, formerly Rennie.

John Rennie, 1860-1929, originally from Longside, became the tenant of Strypes and Westside on the Rainnieshill Estate in the early 1890s. He had about 40 cows at Westside by 1900. These had to be milked sometimes as early as 2 am so that the milk could be taken into the city in churns carried on carts and later Rennie's Lorry. Rennie's Westside Dairy was set up in Aberdeen and expanded to become the Aberdeen Farmers' Dairy Company. The Westside dairy had four delivery carts with smart, matching dapple grey horses. Mr Rennie's sons had important and varied careers. John Rennie the younger, became a very distinguished engineer and founded the Rennie Tool Co. in Manchester but the others remained in or associated with farming. George Gall Rennie became a vet; James Rennie took over Westside and Alex took over Rainnieshill; Mr Lewis Rennie became tenant of Kinghorn Farm. (See Chap XXIII.)

(ix) Memories of Westside in the early 1900s
(Based on George Gall Rennie (1893-1963), *Son of the Soil*, Aberdeen 1958)

'Poaching expeditions in the Straloch woods, guddling for trout, and playing at 'Boers and British' with friends were remembered as childhood pursuits. No talking was allowed at the dinner table after grace had been said. The milk lorries set out from the farm in the early hours, milking having been started at 2 am, and would go even through snow and frost. They would also collect milk in ten gallon churns from other farms on the way to Aberdeen. Townsfolk demanded fresh milk each morning and so it had to reach the depot by 5 am ready for delivery. George Rennie began to take over the running of the farm as his father, John Rennie, concentrated on the dairy business in Aberdeen. However, the Great War intervened and returning wounded he was unable to resume farming and decided to train as a vet. Although serving in various parts of the world he did not work again in Newmachar but is buried in the cemetery.

(x) Memories of Mameulah and other farms: Mr John Mearns
Mr Mearns's father came from Whitecairns in 1923 to work as a cattleman for 24 years for Mr Hector at Middleton (856199) and then Mameulah (884202), taking over from the Andersons. There were 40 cows and one had to rise at 4.30 am to milk them at 5 am. Mr Mearns senior remained at Mameulah until it was sold to Mr Buchan in 1944. Then he worked as a gardener at Fintray House.

Mr Mearns himself was brought up at Mameulah cottages but left to work on farms at the age of 14 in 1931. He learned how to milk by hand and to handle horses and became 2nd horseman at Craigie where there were five horses, two ponies and an orra (spare) horse. The horses were Clydesdales and bred there. For a year and a half he was foreman but was then superseded when the son of the farmer returned. Disillusionment continued as he worked at various farms in the district, including Kingseat, 1932-36. Deciding that it was impossible to earn enough money in farming he became a mason from 1936. Having to live in a chaumer with three others was also a factor in his decision to leave farm work.

(xi) The Slaughterhouse in Newmachar
Testimony of Mr James Imlah.
Newton was a croft on the Rainnieshill Estate and Newton Cottage in the village was the slaughterhouse. Mr Imlah's grandfather, Alexander Imlah, born c.1860, was the slaughterman for many years. The animals were dispatched with a sledge hammer. The ring in the wall to which they were tied may still be seen. The meat produced was for the local butcher, Mr Dunn. (See Chap. XXIV.)

(The photograph of the horses and plough is Mr William Middleton's and was taken near Newmachar Inn. The photograph of Amos Cruickshank appeared in the publication cited. In all the other cases, the people providing testimonies supplied the related photographs or, in Mrs Walker's case, her own original drawings.)

Chapter X
Water Power and the Mills of Newmachar

A community which relies for its food on locally-grown grains and pulses will obviously need the means of grinding these crops into meal and flour that can be cooked and eaten. Presumably at one stage the people of the area would have hand ground their corn with querns but mechanical mills, even if only animal driven or with crude horizontal water wheels — the 'click-mills' — were in use in the medieval period. Certainly, by the sixteenth century, much more sophisticated mills with overshot water wheels were present in Newmachar.

As previous chapters have indicated (V & VII), the existence of a mill in a barony or other type of lordship was extremely important because profits from milling operations went to the lairds. Where *thirlage* prevailed — in other words, where tenants were obliged to use only the laird's mill — there could be resentment. In the sixteenth century, Elrick tenants certainly had to pay *multures*. A *multure* is a payment in kind or money of a proportion of the grain or pulses taken to the mill for grinding, or of sheaves for threshing. (Sale by Robert Innes to James Harvy and Agneta Leslie of the barony of Monycabok and the lands and mill of Elrick, 13 Nov 1564.) Just how many mills there were in the parish area in the 1500-1700 period is uncertain; even the 1696 Poll Tax records leave doubts. Only three millers are recorded and two of these are from Bogholl and the other nearby Clubsgovil. Clearly some of the other people listed must have been millers for there certainly continued to be a mill at Elrick and probably elsewhere.

Besides the water-driven mills, there may have been some animal driven ones. A prominent example is that of the mill beside the manse and presumably built with it in 1791. In and beside the modern *Mill House* on the site (882193), there are still traces of the animal's turning circle and the associated machinery. No doubt a mill was necessary to deal with the products of the glebe land and the payments in kind of the teinds allocated by the heritors to the minister for his living.

By the early part of the twentieth century, only *Elrick* and *Pinkie* remained as corn mills in Newmachar. (Testimony of Mr Archie Low.) *Multures* had disappeared, too, although as late as 1860, certain tenants were still paying money in lieu to the laird of Parkhill. (Valuation Roll, 1859-60.) During the later nineteenth century, local corn mills generally began to diminish in importance. There were two reasons for this. One was technological: roller mills were introduced in the 1870s and '80s and they needed to work continuously on large quantities of grain. This meant large plants, large firms and centralisation in cities. Secondly, such mills were needed more to deal with imported North American grains than domestic produce; even the milling industry in Aberdeen was undermined by that in Glasgow which had more immediate access to

Atlantic shipping routes. (Richard Perren, 'The Nineteenth Century Economy', *Aberdeen 1800-2000*, ed. W.H. Fraser & C.H. Lee, Aberdeen, 2000, p. 96.)

Corn mills were not the only kinds of mills to be found in Newmachar. Paradoxically, in fact, as corn mills became less important, the number of mills for other purposes increased and a very high proportion of the farms in the parish had a mill by 1900. The drainage works accompanying agricultural improvements involved clearing and straightening water courses and this could easily extend to the creation of dams and lades for mills. The most important reason for the increase was the growing use of machinery of various kinds on farms. Power was applied to threshing, bruising oats for the growing number of horses, and cutting turnips. A small dam and wheel could produce useful power. Examination of the estate maps and the six-inch scale first Ordnance Survey maps of about 1870 will show what a large proportion of the farms had sluices and mills. Nevertheless there were problems over water rights and water supply; a farmer downstream of a dam might well complain that he lacked water for his mill or his cattle.

(i) The Mills on the 'Chief Burn'

The account in Macfarlane's 'Geographical Collections' describing Newmachar in the early part of the eighteenth century (see Chap. VII) refers to the existence of five mills on the 'chief burn' which is presumably the Straloch/Elrick/Goval Burn. The mills are not named but perhaps they were *Woodend, Mill of Cavil, Old Mill, Elrick* and *Ord*. Five mills have used the power of this stream in living memory. These are *Kinghorn, Woodend, Mill of Cavil, Elrick* and the *Parkhill Pumping Station*. (Testimony of Mr Alexander Ingram of Elrick House.)

Kinghorn (formerly *Upper Kinghorn*) has a dam at 876215. A little further north, there is *Milton* (formerly *Mill Town*) (869218) on a different tributary of the Straloch Burn; presumably the corn mill was at *Mill Town*. *Woodend* (872207) is near the perhaps significantly-named *Greendams* (872204) which is on the Straloch Burn itself. There is rather less uncertainty about *Mill of Cavil* (874195); it was probably in use at the time of Robert Gordon's map (see Chap. VI) unless nearby *Oldmill* (875193) is actually the older site of the mill. In the nineteenth century, *Mill of Cavil* was certainly a corn mill, one of the three in the parish then capable of producing flour.

The present building at *Elrick Mill* (882185) is a nineteenth-century structure perhaps erected when a long lade which took water out of the Elrick Burn over half a mile upstream was constructed. Nevertheless, there was certainly a mill at Elrick in 1564 which is referred to in the charter noted above. In June 1693, the mill and estate were taken over by John Burnett. (*Register of the Great Seal of Scotland*, Vol 2, 1914, p. 213.) In the middle of the nineteenth century, the mill was still owned by a Burnett and the miller was John Walker. (Valuation Roll, 1859-60.) *Elrick Mill* remained operational in the early twentieth century when

Elrick Mill as it was in the 1950s

the miller was Mr W. Chalmers who had only one arm and was assisted by his sister, Peggy. (Testimony of Mrs Margaret Mitchell.)   A little downstream from Elrick House there used to be a dam but the absence of an obvious mill makes it seem likely that the ponded up water was there for ornamental purposes in the grounds of the house.

Much further downstream from Elrick there is the *Parkhill Pumping Station*. (888148).   This interesting but little-known complex was constructed as recently as 1898. Although built to resemble a local farmhouse, its function was to house turbines whose power was used to pump drinking water supplies for the village of Dyce across the Don to reservoirs at Overton and Kirkhill.   The turbines themselves were turned by the waters of the Goval Burn drawn into a lade over half a mile away on the other side of the A947. The lade feeds into the aqueduct above and behind the mill. Interestingly, the mill and its aqueduct are believed to be the first structures built in Scotland with reinforced concrete. (Information from Aberdeenshire Archaeological Service.) By the time they were last used, the turbines were being powered by electricity and the lade had become redundant.

The Parkhill Pumping Station

(ii) Mills on other streams

Kingseat (formerly *Nether Kingseat*) (902195), *Cockairn* (902187), *Buckie* (895162) and *Newpark* (903156) are all farms in the eastern part of the parish which appear to have had mills in the 1870s. However, by far the most important mill east of the Elrick Burn and ultimately most important overall was the *Pinkie Mill* (formerly *Boddoms*) (895189). This continued to be an operational corn mill well into the twentieth century. Its dam and sluice are still clearly to be seen. Did the smithy nearby also use its power? Early in the 1900s, the miller was Willie Duncan who lived on the upper floor of Derby Cottage on School Road. (Testimony of Mrs Margaret Mitchell.) Later on, in the 1930s, the miller was Mr Hopkins. Local people would go to the mill to buy oatmeal for their porridge. (Testimony of Mr Norman Duncan.) In the 1990s, local contractor Steve Wilson was engaged to rebuild the dam so that a fishpond for anglers could be created. (Testimony of Mr Steve Wilson.) Not far from the Pinkie Mill and on a tributary of the Pinkie Burn, there was in 1867 a saw mill (892193) with its dam just outside the present main cemetery.

Water on Farms: the Use of Pumps

Water supplies were essential for cattle and pumps were often used to bring it up from the water table. A local carpenter, Mr Cormack, was capable of using almost entirely wood technology to make very serviceable pumps. He hollowed out a tree trunk to make the outer casing which went into the ground. There was a wooden plunger with a leather valve to move up and down the trunk. The pump at Standryford Farm was such a wooden one.

Norman Duncan

The small scale of most of the farm mills can be seen from what remains of the mill at Strypes/Westhill (809208). The mill wheel was housed in a small stone building and got power from a small dam only about twenty yards away. Yet the mill was some hundreds of yards away and downhill from the farm buildings where its power was needed. The connection was made by means of a continuous cable. (Testimony of Mr Alexander Buchan, Westside.) Standryford (896184) was similar in this respect with its mill wheel being linked by cables to a building upstream which housed, unusually, rollers. This apparatus was out of use by 1926. (Testimony of Mr Norman Duncan.)

The set of mills on the tributary of the Goval Burn which flows in from the east near Little Goval are especially interesting. On 29th November 1565, James Harvy's possession of Monykebbock was confirmed as 'cum molendino fullonum, the walk mylne.' (*Register of the Great Seal of Scotland*, Vol IV, p. 363.) In other words, the parish then had a fulling mill for preparing wool cloth. There is no later reference to fulling being carried on at either *North* (897157 or *South* (899155) *Waulkmill*. Perhaps this early attempt at industrial diversification was undercapitalised but both *Waulkmills* did have mills as did *Upper Tack*. (See panel.) Not far from these mills there was a sawmill attached to the Parkhill Estate which was powered by water (901148).

Power and Water Supply Problems At Upper Tack (894166)

The mill at *Upper Tack* had an undershot wheel which was located near the back of the stable. Water came from a dam at the higher end of the adjoining field. The mill and its machinery were unfenced and highly dangerous. The mill fell out of use in part because damming the stream led to frequent arguments with the farmer at *Rosehall* (892163) who complained that insufficient water was being allowed to flow downstream to meet his needs. In addition, the neighbouring farmers found it convenient to come together to hire a steam traction engine for threshing etc. The difficulty was to get the machine under the railway to Upper Tack; its chimney had to be dismantled. (Margaret Mitchell, formerly Cowie, who was brought up at Upper Tack in the 1920s)

****

The mills of Newmachar are a fascinating reminder of the great importance of an early and very simple technology which remained in use well into the twentieth century. Steam power to a certain extent superseded water power but it was the coming of electricity which finally made Newmachar's water mills redundant.

The best general work on milling and millers is Enid Gauldie, *The Scottish Country Miller 1700-1900. A History of Water-Powered Meal Milling in Scotland*, Edinburgh, 1981.

Chapter XI
Transport 1: Roads, Garages and the Post Office

During the medieval and early modern periods, moving people and goods through the parish of Newmachar would have presented difficulties. Those who could afford horses might get along pretty well, as might those on foot - if rather more slowly. Horses or oxen could also be used to carry limited amounts of goods, mostly in panniers. Anything very heavy might be managed on a sled over short distances or even by wagon when the weather was dry. Some idea of the routes, tracks and pathways which were used may still be gained by examining paths and farm roads which are now off the main road networks.

Local Roads and Paths
Although life in 2001 tends for many people to be dominated by the A947, its heavy traffic and possible alternative routes into Aberdeen, certain tracks and paths which probably predate modern, tarred roads and even the turnpike remain of some local importance. For example, there was a path along the line of Summer Brae, the 'kirk roadie.' The upper end of the path still takes the walker up to the church. Around the base of the 'shannie' the road which led from the turnpike towards the manse and Monykebbock remains in use by walkers. Of real economic significance was the path which can still be walked for most of its route from the Gardener's Croft near Highlands (875177) southwards towards the Cothal Mills on the Don. Because it was used by the mill workers, it became knows as the 'Weavers' Road.' (Information from Mrs C Imlah.)

Former Roads and Tracks in the East and North of the Parish: Changehill and its connections.
(From investigations by Mr George Mitchell.)
Investigations based on consultation of Robert Gordon's Manuscript Map of 1637, General Roy's Map of 1750 and Thomson's 1826 sheet (see Chap. VI) as well as later maps, have enabled George Mitchell to identify roads and tracks which were once important but have now been superseded by more modern, made-up roads.
(i)   From Changehill itself, (873224) there is a road leading eastwards over the high point at Slugmagullie Hill at 186m (611 ft) to Tillygreig (886229) and then on eastwards to (ii) the old Tarves road. This road is just to the east of the Newmachar parish boundary but provides an excellent example of the way the older trackways kept to higher ground. It runs parallel to the modern Tarves Road (B999) almost all the way from the Brig o' Balgownie to Tarves and beyond to Haddo House. It is best seen where it leads north from Shielhill (936128) via Hillhead, the hill and the farm on to the track seen at Whitecairns 500 yards to

the west of the present main road and on north past Hillbrae (906215), then past Bridgend (885259) and west of Udny Castle via Raitshill (864283) to Tarves and straight on to Haddo. (iii) An alternative route to this road may be found leading north from Changehill past Auchnashag (873229) and Burnside and then to Bridgend. To the west of Changehill, (iv) a track can be traced along the line of the parish boundary (which may be deliberately co-incidental with the track) north westwards past Overton Wood to emerge on the present A947 just north of Whiterashes near Kingsford Croft (851238).

****

There is a tradition that Changehill's name is not derived from Cheyne's Hill (see Chap. IV and VI) but *does* mean a place where you changed horses after travelling the trackways described above. The fact that there was stabling for about twelve horses at Changehill seems to support this idea as George Mitchell points out. However, the present writer believes that the stabling was probably connected with Major Ramsay's sporting activities on the Straloch estate, of which Changehill was formerly part. Whatever the truth about Changehill itself, there is no doubt that its connections show that there exists evidence of a network of older roads and tracks probably used by horsemen, pack horses and people on foot, mostly on higher ground. The turnpikes and metalled roads of the nineteenth and twentieth centuries have superseded but not always obliterated these older routeways.

To c. 1800: the 'Back Road'

Wheeled traffic must have been comparatively rare on the medieval and early modern trackways of Newmachar. By the 1790s, however, when Mr Stronach wrote his account, more and more carriages were trying to move through the parish and finding it very difficult, especially in winter. The 'deep spouting clay' of the road surfaces, as the Minister called it, was soon rutted and churned up in the winter.

Perhaps Mr Stronach exaggerated because he was 'sensible of the great advantage of good roads'. Understandably, many of his parishioners were not: they were reluctant to turn out to provide labour services on the roads. When they did appear they performed in 'an awkward and slovenly manner.' (*OSA*, p. 358.) The system for the upkeep of roads had been established by Acts of the Scottish Parliament of 1669 and 1686. All owning property must pay 10 shillings per £100 value per annum towards the cost of road and bridge repairs and everyone else provided labour on six days of the year or five if they were prepared to do it all in one period of the summer. The Commissioners of Supply and J.P.s appointed an overseer and called out labour by a notice read out in church. Labour might be commuted at the rate of 3d per day - which many would have found it difficult to pay - so that skilled road men could be hired at the rate of 9d per day which Mr Stronach felt was the sensible alternative.

The main road through the parish was that from Bridge of Don through Scotstoun, passing just west of Bishop's Loch, past Drumligair, Standryford and on to the church. Its route was on relatively high and better drained land. It seems to have been a long established route although Mr Stronach implies that it was made into a usable road by the military earlier in the eighteenth century. Certainly it was in use as a post road. Both General Roy's map of 1747-55 and Taylor and Skinner's route map of 1776 show it clearly as the principal road of the parish.

The 'back road' as contemporary inhabitants of Newmachar tend to call it, has remained important. During the nineteenth century it was a cheaper alternative to the turnpike road (the present A947). Right up to the 1930s, Mr Alec Duncan of Standryford and his cattle dealer brother William were still driving their cattle on the hoof to Aberdeen for sale by this route; it was a more convenient means by which to reach the cattle mart on King Street which they used. (Testimony of Mr Norman Duncan.)

The Sod Inn

At least one of the six ale houses mentioned by Mr Stronach must have been the 'Sod Inn' at Kinmundy (the present Burnside (901171). The Valuation Roll shows it as in being in 1859. Called the Sod Inn presumably because it had a turf roof, it was run within living memory by 'Auld Soddy' who retired to the Longford croft by about 1920. The Sod Inn must have been at a convenient stopping place at the top of a hill for cattle drovers and the 'carriers and travellers' mentioned by the OSA. (Testimony of Mr Norman Duncan and OSA.) As pointed out by Mr George Mitchell of Changehill, Thomson's map of 1826 appears to show a similar inn at Kinghorn.

Today, the 'back road' is much used as an alternative route for commuters into Aberdeen. It is worth noting that Mr Moir, author of *The New Statistical Account* of 1842 erroneously refers to it as the 'old turnpike'. It was never this but always a 'commutation road' - that is a road maintained by using the revenue obtained by commuting labour services into money. Mr Moir's mistake has misled later writers.

1800 - 1865: The Turnpike

By the 1790s it was becoming clear that the existing system of building and maintaining roads with more or less unwilling statute labour or the revenue from the commutation of these services was not working. Somehow, roads good enough to take increased numbers of wheeled vehicles must be built and maintained. More and more people now expected to be able to travel at some speed in the comfort of stage coaches.

The solution was to set up trusts composed of investors who would arrange the building of a road and hope to recoup their investment from tolls paid by road users.　After much parliamentary difficulty, the 1795 Aberdeenshire Turnpike Act became law.　But it could not become effective until the Commutation Bill, to deal with the other roads, was passed in 1800.　John Burnett of Elrick and John Ramsay of Barra (see Chap. VII) were prominent members of the Trust.　The Deeside, Inverurie, Ellon and Skene roads were soon begun but it was not until April 1802 that Sutherland and Glass were awarded the contract to begin work on a road from Oldmeldrum to Aberdeen roughly along the line of the present A947.　Eventually, by 1807, the road extended from Aberdeen to Banff.　For the southern section there were toll gates at Parkhill, Straloch and Oldmeldrum - that is roughly six-mile intervals.　However, it seems that a toll bar was later also established in Summerhill. (1859 Valuation Roll.) There were 29 subscribers with Ramsay of Barra and Skene of Parkhill by far the most important, each producing £1100.　The road suffered from two problems. One was common to all such projects: travellers tried to find alternative routes on commutation roads so that they could avoid the tolls.　The second difficulty was that a bridge had to be built over the Don at Parkhill.　Even though it was only a wooden structure, it cost £2000.　This would make the capital difficult to recover. (John Patrick, *The Coming of Turnpikes to Aberdeenshire*, Aberdeen, n.d. pp. 7-9, 41-44.)

Ramsay of Barra (d. 1814) apparently took a close interest in the road, making sure tolls were paid and repairs carried out.　He began a tradition in the family of close involvement with road transport matters as the information below on his grandson shows.

Ramsay of Barra was not only an investor in the Turnpike to the extent of £1100 - a very large sum in 1802-3 - but also the leading light in the Board of Trustees for Aberdeenshire set up by the Commutation Act.　Newmachar became part of the Aberdeen district - one of the nine established.　Ramsay dominated this district too.　It would decide how much to rate the heritors and how much to demand for commuted labour services in order to provide funds for the upkeep of roads other than the turnpike. (Aberdeenshire Archives: AC 2/1/1 Trustees Sederunt Book.)

Ramsay and his colleagues were concerned about routes of access to the turnpike but there was not always agreement about what was reasonable use of the moneys available.　In 1809, Ramsay objected to £147-9s-1d of commutation money being spent on the old Oldmeldrum road (ie the back road) arguing that it was a pointless road as it was parallel to the turnpike.　But Mr Skene of Parkhill had tenants along the line of the old road and was equally unhappy about Ramsay's plan to spend the money on the road from the Bridge of Steps (893160) north via Swailend, Monykebbock, Highlands, Lairshill to Disblair (862191) which would be of benefit to his Straloch property.　Eventually, both roads had money spent on them.　The sums involved were of the order of £167-5s-3d in 1806 - the amount received from the levied rate. (AC 2/5/1: Trustees Minutes for 6th District.)

The arguments continued long after Ramsay's death. By the 1840s and '50s only about £50 or £60 was being raised annually for road upkeep. Every now and then a bridge needed building or repairing and this was an expensive business; that over the Goval Burn on the Fintray Road (885147) cost £50 in 1829. (AC 2/5/1.) Fortunately, a travelling merchant who had nearly drowned there in a snowstorm put up most of the money. (*Guide to Donside*, Aberdeen, 1844, p. 14.)

By 1837, the Turnpike road itself to Oldmeldrum had cost £9022-19s-6d in total. £1450-10s-4d had been paid in interest but a further £1500 had been borrowed. The tolls were farmed out for £320 p.a. This and other revenue meant an income in 1836 of £563-1s-0d. Repairs, overseers' salary and interest payment came to £434-17s-3½d. (John Clark, *The State of the Turnpike Roads in the County of Aberdeen*, London, 1837.) This would seem a good rate of return but the capital cost would never be fully recovered. Meanwhile the wooden bridge at Parkhill became increasingly unsafe. It was finally replaced with a stone bridge in 1851. There are two arches of 52 ft span and the bridge is still in use. (*The Guide to Donside*, Aberdeen, 1855 edition, p. 18.)

The whole system of combining a few turnpikes with commutation roads was unsatisfactory and it was dealt a further blow with the arrival of the railway in 1861. In 1865 the Aberdeenshire Roads Act became law. The Turnpike Trusts were dissolved and tolls ceased to be levied at Parkhill and Straloch. Whatever the deficiencies of the turnpike system, there is no doubt that the turnpike road through the parish had an enormous effect, especially on the development of Summerhill as a centrally-placed village of importance. (See also Chap. XII.)

The Era of Aberdeen County Road Trustees, 1865-1890

The County Road Trustees organisation was in one sense a development of the 1800 arrangements but more importantly anticipated the County Council since there were some elected representatives. Newmachar was one of the five sub-divisions of the 6th District and from first to last was to be chaired and very effectively led by John Ramsay of Barra (1831-1895). Later, in 1875, the districts were reorganised but Major Ramsay continued to be dominant.

Major Ramsay and his colleagues became responsible for 185 miles of former commutation roads and 58 miles of the former turnpikes. They reckoned these and the bridges would cost £1572 to keep in repair each year and so levied a rate of 6d in the pound.

Newmachar was reckoned to have 8 miles of what were designated first-class roads. One snow plough was reserved for the Oldmeldrum Road - but horses to pull it would have to be obtained locally. Patrick Polson and later Andrew Anderson of Mameulah, Alexander Duncan of Brokenwynd, William Burgess of Rannieshill and George Harvey of Monykebbock were among those who became tenant trustees. They and the major landowners soon had to deal with the implications of new technologies. The trustees purchased a steam-powered stone breaker in 1876 and were willing to allow a telephone company to erect their poles along the roads in 1882. On the other hand, in 1877 they opposed allowing tramways to be constructed and began to worry about the impact of steam-powered vehicles on the road surfaces and bridges for which they were responsible. (AC 2/5/4 and 2/5/5 Minute Book of the Trustees of the 6th District.)

At the final meeting in January 1890 the trustees proposed a 'hearty vote of thanks to Colonel Ramsay for his past services.'

John Ramsay 1831-1895

John Ramsay III was born on 3rd December 1831, the son of John Ramsay II and his wife Susan Innes. His father died in October 1832. Twelve years later, his mother married Captain Nares, RN. The young John Ramsay thus inherited Straloch when he was less than one year old. He graduated from Cambridge and it seems he could have become a university don at Trinity College but decided he must return to Newmachar to take charge of the estates. He married Leonora Bond in 1858 but Mrs Ramsay died in a tragic accident in 1862. There was one child, Mary.

John Ramsay lived the life of a country gentleman at Straloch. He paid great attention to field sports and entertained house parties of distinguished figures as well as his literary and intellectual friends from Cambridge. At the same time he had a very highly-developed sense of public service. Hence his involvement in the Militia as an officer in the Royal Aberdeenshire Highlanders and his being appointed by Queen Victoria as Deputy Lieutenant of the County of Aberdeen. It was, however, above all in his concern with transport that his public service is most notable. He was a director of the Great North of Scotland Railway. Having served on the old Commutations Committee, he became chairman of the Sixth (Aberdeen) District Authority and the County Road Trustees.

John Ramsay was keen not only to keep the roads in good repair but also to build or realign them. Wherever he could, he built straight. Hence the roads between Oldmeldrum and Colpy, from Inverurie to Fintray or eastwards from Drumligair, probably owe their long straight stretches to Major Ramsay.

Perhaps few people now notice the plaque on the Persley Bridge (908094) which is used a great deal more by motorists than by pedestrians. The plaque commemorates the opening of the bridge on 20th November 1892 by John Ramsay in his position as Chairman of the Aberdeen District of the new

Aberdeen County Council. He died on 17th June 1895. (Information based on Henderson, pp. 451-2; Temple, p. 321 and testimony from Major Irvine who also kindly made the photograph available.)

After 1890: Aberdeen County Council and problems of road works and repairs
As early as June 1872, Major Ramsay and his colleagues were concerned about the effect on their roads of the passage of steam-powered locomotives or agricultural machines. They were extremely heavy and potentially destructive of bridges and road surfaces. The new County Council of the 1890s had this as perhaps their major problem. In September 1896, for example, it was decided not to allow locomotives to cross the bridge over the Pinkie Burn at the Kinmundy cross roads (the bridge is now hidden by the modern road at 891182). In the next year Messrs. Milne's traction engines were completely ruining the Kinmundy-Whitecairns road and in 1898, 467 yards of road were destroyed as a result of heavy loads of clay for the Dyce reservoir being carried through the parish.

There were also labour difficulties. The road menders wanted a paid half-holiday in 1897. This was refused but they were given one when Queen Victoria's jubilee came around. (Aberdeen County Council: Aberdeen District Committee Minutes, 1894-1897, AC 3/1/1, 3/1/2, 3/1/4.)

Road making
John Macadam's treatise of 1817 on road making sets out the best ways of making roads. The foundation must be firm and kept drained. Upper layers must be of pieces of rock artificially crushed so that they are angular and fit together. The small stones on the surface must form a slightly convex impervious surface. Drains and ditches on either side of the road are vital. **Mr Bert Sangster** attests to the importance of breaking the stones - his father was employed as a stone breaker. He himself as a road-man was taught to fill in gaps between larger stones in the foundations. The loose angular gravel was actually washed in with water. A horse-drawn roller was used to compact the surface. The standard road width was 16 feet.

Victorian science proved that roads properly constructed on such principles were proof against any loading on them by horses and carts. But steam locomotives and then in the early twentieth century motor cars and safety bicycles required smoother and dust free surfaces. Even so, it is clear that Newmachar's roads remained macadamed but not tarred until well into the 1920s as the photograph of the main village street shows. (See the photograph printed on p. xvi.) The first tar macadam stretch of road was from South to North Kinmundy and then on the main road at the cross roads near the smithy (895181). (Testimony of Mr Bert Sangster.)

The Post Office

The question of roads is closely linked to the question of the carrying of the letter post. Aberdeen Town Council was arranging postal services in the 1590s and Scotland had a post service from 1603 and its own Postmaster General in 1689, but a parish like Newmachar benefited very little. The few who wrote and received letters had to make special arrangements with servants and messengers. But by 1708 there were 34 post towns in Scotland and mail began to be carried along the 'back road' to places like Fyvie and Banff three times weekly. In the 1790s the importance of this road was that it was the post road (*OSA* p. 358) although the nearest post office was at Oldmeldrum. A special gig began to be used with the opening of the turnpike and Summerhill became a recognised receiving centre for mail in 1839. In October 1841, Summerhill was accorded a full post office with its own date stamps etc. By this time adhesive paper stamps had come into use. In 1908, the official name of the Post Office was changed to Newmachar. In the photograph on p. vi, the post office can be seen next to the shop. It was then still important enough to be a sorting office.

In 1908 the mail was still carried in a two-wheeled high gig driven by Bob Calder which arrived in the village at 6.30 am every day. It went on to Whiterashes at 7.00 am and then Oldmeldrum, returning to Aberdeen at about 1.00 pm. (Davidson, p. 30; Information from Mrs C. Imlah; W.L. Falconer, A Short History of Aberdeen in *The Northeast of Scotland Philatelic Miscellany* ed. J.C. Stone, Aberdeen, 1985, pp. 3-10; Bruce Archibald, *Postal Marks of Scotland to 1840* 2nd edition, Kilmacolm, 1998 p. 10; A.R.B. Haldane, *Three Centuries of Scottish Posts*, Edinburgh, 1987.)

Bicycles

It is not generally realised how important the 'safety' bicycles of the 1890s and early 1900s were in encouraging better roads, better road signs and, above all, in facilitating local trade and travel. **Mr H G Catto's** Raleigh cost him £6-10s-0d in the 1920s and got him into Aberdeen from Kingseat regularly for his 9 am class in Forensic Medicine at Marischal College. **Mr Bert Sangster** acquired a Hercules at about the same time for £5. **Mrs Peggy Findlay** had a bicycle bought for her by Aberdeen County Council so that she could get to school. **Mrs Margaret Mitchell** had also used a cycle to get to school from Upper Tack and even to drive the cows in for milking. If you could not obtain your own bicycle, one could be hired; **Mrs Cham Robb** remembers that you could hire one for 6d a day from the shop in Oldmeldrum.

Certain kinds of work were made easier by using a bicycle. The District Nurse, Nurse Macrae, used a bicycle on all her rounds until 1946 when a car was obtained for her. The Rev. Harold Ross did most of his parish visiting in the 1940s and '50s by bicycle. A familiar figure at one time, as **Mrs Ruth Taylor** recalls, was 'Onion Johnny' who plied his trade by bicycle between about 1950 and 1986. His real name was Henri Chapalain. For many, however, the bicycle was a means of relaxation - or getting to some of the local functions, especially Saturday night dances, as **Mrs Frances Taylor** recalled. She obtained a BSA sports model for £3 in 1937.

From Carriers to Motor Buses

Travelling salesmen and packmen went from farm to farm on foot up to the nineteenth century. But by the 1790s at least the post was being brought from Aberdeen by wheeled vehicles along the Scotstoun or 'back road.' There is no doubt that the establishment of the turnpike road did make a difference. By the 1840s there was a regular stage coach on the Aberdeen to Banff road, the *Earl of Fife*; this brought the post each day as well as carrying people. Carriers flourished. Even after the railway arrived in 1861, there was plenty of scope for carrying goods and people over short distances or to the railway station. Important as the railway was, one should not over emphasise it significance for Newmachar; the turnpike and the network of roads connected to it remained vital for local needs and for much of the longer-range traffic. In 1877 there was one Newmachar based carrier, George Chapman, who went to Aberdeen on Tuesdays and Fridays and had to compete with three Oldmeldrum firms.

In the early 1900s there were two carriers and even in the 1920s Peter Craigmyle and Adam McDonald continued to carry goods on horses and carts between Aberdeen and Oldmeldrum. Then Mr Willie Annand acquired a motor lorry and George Reid introduced a bus service. (Sources include C. Imlah, *History of Newmachar*, p. 28; S. Wood, *The Shaping of 19th Century Aberdeenshire*, 1985, p. 27; Davidson, p. 31; *Donside Guide*, 1844, p. 84; *Worrall's Directory* for 1877.)

Soon the services of the bus became vital to link people to Aberdeen. As the splendid photograph shows, the Aberdeen-Fyvie service featured uniformed

drivers. Mr Robert Edward Gray is the one shown standing by his vehicle in Newmachar. He later emigrated to Australia. (Photograph and information by the courtesy of his niece, Mrs Ann Edward Hay.) **Mr Catto** recalled that competition between the buses of Daniels of Whitecairns and G R Burnett meant that they literally raced each other along the road to Aberdeen.

By 1950 *The Third Statistical Account*, Aberdeenshire (p. 161) could claim that the main roads were in splendid condition and that there was an 'excellent bus service.' As Newmachar becomes more of a dormitory suburb for Aberdeen, that judgement is surprising to readers half a century later.

There may now be no need for blacksmiths to shoe workhorses but tractors, lorries and private motor cars must be provided for and looked after. Newmachar has a driving school, a taxi service, Swifts, and a car repair and servicing business at Swailend. Just to the south of the village, a car sales and repairs business, Newmachar Motors, has an annual turnover of well over £1m, while Kennedy's Transport is a considerable road haulage business. There is also a highly successful coach business which caters for work and school needs and, increasingly, for tourism.

Whyte's Coaches 1967 -

Mr Whyte senior, Bill Whyte, was a delivery driver at Kingseat Hospital, a driving instructor between shifts and also involved in a band, 'the Blue Star.' He had bought a mini-van to carry the band and its equipment around, but with an Aberdeen County Council contract to carry school pupils obtained a PSV 12-seater Bedford van in 1967 for £45! Two years later, Bill left Kingseat and with his wife, Nora, started a taxi business which they ran from near the old Pinkie Mill. (See Chap. X.) Then in 1970 they bought their first coach - this time for £400. Driving lessons continued but were eventually given up as the coach business developed. By 1977 there were four coaches, two minibuses and several taxis, and Ian Urquhart, their son-in-law, had joined the business. An Aberdeen firm was taken over and it became possible to concentrate exclusively on contract and private coach hire together with increasingly popular holiday tours organised by the company. In 1986 the purchase of land near the Pinkie Mill made it possible to set up a purpose-built coach garage and offices. In its silver jubilee year, 1992, the business had four partners, one mechanic, fourteen full-time and eight part-time drivers and no fewer than twenty luxury coaches. Since then the business has expanded further not least by the acquisition of McIntyre's Coaches of Old Aberdeen. Both Scottish and overseas tours are organised. Whyte's is now a much needed contributor to local employment opportunities in Newmachar. (Information based on *Welcome Aboard*, 2nd edition, 1992.)

Garages: Alexander and Adam Wildgoose

The story of the development of the garage in Newmachar is a classic illustration of responses to evolving transport technology. Alexander Wildgoose trained as

a blacksmith in the 1890s, becoming an employee and tenant of William Marnoch on the main road of the village. By 1918, he had set up business on his own account - principally as a bicycle dealer and repairer. (Valuation Rolls 1895, 1918.) Based at the site which is now occupied by Beekie's Neuk, he responded to each new development, for example, the recharging of the batteries needed for using the wireless in the early days of broadcasting. But the greatest transition he made was to turn his business into a motor garage and petrol station. Known as Endfield Garage

it was selling petrol at 1s 3½d per gallon in the early 1930s. Later run by his son, Adam Wildgoose, the garage remained a major feature of the centre of the village until the 1970s as the photograph shows. (Information and photo provided by Mrs Rita Burr.)

The Shop and Garage at Reisque
(Testimony of Mrs Sheila Bruce)

Mr Alexander Cheyne's shop at Reisque was acquired in about 1957 by Mr Esslemont who added selling petrol to his business. Mr James Bruce and his wife, Sheila, took over this enterprise in 1959. Mrs Bruce had local connections through her grandmother and uncle and aunt - the Lobbans, famous for their concert parties - who farmed Torryleith. Larger tanks were installed for the two pumps selling 2 star and 4 star petrol as more and more local people acquired cars. Although Andrew Wildgoose's garage continued to sell petrol, relations were good. James Bruce added repair work, especially for electrical goods, to the other services provided. In 1986, Mr and Mrs Bruce retired and Roy Poppe ran the garage for a year or two until Fergus Hood took full control in 1988.

The Crossroads Filling Station, Reisque
(An account by the owner, Fergus Hood)

This is a seven day a week operation, open thirteen hours daily, eleven on Sunday. A local business for local people, the main activity is selling unleaded petrol and ultra low sulphur diesel. The sale of four star leaded fuel was banned by the government at the end of 1999. A new fuel, lead replacement petrol, has been introduced which produces fewer exhaust emissions although this fuel is not suitable for all older cars. These measures we are told are part of the government's commitment to meeting the targets set at the Kyoto Summit.

During 1994 new electronic pumps linked to a computerised pump controller in the shop were installed. The effect was to generate more business for the site as customers could fill their own vehicles and this has allowed up to five vehicles to use the pumps at any one time.

The real challenge facing a business like this and many others is competition. Taxation in the form of duty and value added tax accounts for approx. 80% of the pump price. The cost of oil refining and delivery is 15%, leaving a gross margin of 5% to be shared between the retailer and the oil company. However, with the price of oil in August 2000 at $32.10 per barrel, the oil companies were making huge profits from the sale of crude oil and covering their costs on the sale of refined products such as petrol and diesel.

The future is uncertain and will depend on the price of oil and government policy on tax on fuel. We may find some relief from the introduction of auto gas or liquid petroleum gas (LPG). Crossroads Filling Station is now selling this fuel. The big advantage of auto gas is the price. At 38 pence a litre in 2000, this was less than half the price of petrol. There is very little tax on gas as it is seen as a 'clean' fuel by the government. The disadvantage is the cost of converting the petrol engine to accept the new fuel: this varies from £900 to £1500.

The new housing developments in Newmachar and the increasing volume of traffic on the A947 north have helped to boost sales for the business and encourage diversification. During 1999 a major redevelopment was made in the shop, transforming it into a mini market selling a good range of grocery, frozen and chilled goods, in addition to the established car accessories, newspapers, cigarettes and confectionery. Joining the Costcutters supermarket group has allowed access to a wide range of goods which can be sold on at very competitive prices.

I would conclude this brief history by predicting that the survival of small, local filling stations will depend on the ability of the management to adapt to the changing needs of the consumers.

****

The story of Newmachar's roads since 1800 is one of constant change. The process continues; even the route of the turnpike has been changed to meet the needs of modern traffic by the elimination of some of the bends on the A947. Another change is that what was once a major traffic artery has now become a foot and cycle way. This is the former railway.

Chapter XII
Transport 2: The Great North of Scotland Railway and its Successors

The railway in Newmachar lasted for hardly more than a hundred years. It is looked back to with nostalgia for the steam locomotives themselves and the way of life which went with the era of steam. There is also now a realisation that perhaps some of the commuting problems faced by 21st century Newmachar inhabitants could have been solved had the railway remained in being. Nevertheless the railway was closed in 1968 because it seemed uneconomic and marginal to the life of the commuters along its route. Ten of the bridges which had to be built are now regarded as objects of archaeological interest.

Nostalgia should not blind us to the fact that the railway was always perhaps to some degree marginal. It is certainly a mistake to assume, as some do, that the coming of the railway in 1861 created Summerhill - Newmachar village. The nucleus of the village was created when the church was sited there in 1639. A second church was added in 1843. This new Free Church established its school in Summerhill well before 1861 while the existing parochial school was, of course, adjacent to the established church building. The road network with the post road joining the Oldmeldrum road near an important route westwards towards Kintore and Inverurie was a key factor in its growth. The turnpike road, the establishment of the Post Office, a general store, blacksmith, joiner, a bakery and a souter were all developments which came well before the arrival of the railway. When it did come, the fact that the station was some distance away from the nucleus of the village was a considerable disadvantage, as Douglas Flett explains below.

Newmachar and the Railway
by Douglas Flett

Mr J D Flett lived at Newmachar station for ten years and became a professional railwayman. He has retained his interest in railway history - not just the technical details on which he is expert but also the wider social and economic background. He has kindly provided the following account which is printed here in full. Mr Flett also provided the photographs of the railwaymen at Newmachar in the 1920s.

The railway came to Newmachar in 1861 with the opening of the Formartine and Buchan Railway, forever after known as the "Buchan Line". The Buchan Line was absorbed by the Great North of Scotland Railway in 1866 which in turn became part of the London and North Eastern Railway in 1923 and finally part of the nationalised British Railways in 1948. The route eventually chosen, from Dyce to Peterhead via Mintlaw with a branch from Maud to Fraserburgh via Strichen, was the product of a number of rival schemes which had aroused much controversy in their time. The need for the line to climb from the Don at Parkhill to the summit just north of Newmachar with the minimum of heavy

The photograph of Newmachar as the best station on the GNSR routes dates from 1930. It shows Mr Mackenzie, the Stationmaster, and his daughter. His granddaughter, Mrs Frances Peace, provided this information. The actual photograph is in the possession of Mr Bert Sangster. The photograph of the station on p. xvi shows a 4-4-0 engine arriving.

engineering works necessitated a huge curve, which swept the railway away from the village via Kinmundy and Kingseat and as a consequence the station itself had to be sited a little under half a mile from the village on the minor road to Tillygrieg. This was not a convenient location. The second station in the parish, Parkhill, altogether a smaller affair, was at the junction of the present A947 and the road to Hatton of Fintray.

The railway did not have the impact on Newmachar which it had on other places such as Udny Station, Auchnagatt, Maud and Mintlaw where important settlements grew up round the new railway stations. The reason was probably that the completion of the Meldrum turnpike made possible a round trip from Newmachar to Aberdeen well within the day by horse-drawn vehicle. Certainly the GNSR never felt the need to expand the small goods yard or to construct a large goods shed of the stone and lime type found at Udny and some other stations on the Buchan line. This which would indicate that much of the day to day goods traffic to and from Aberdeen continued to pass by road. (See Chap XI) Furthermore, Newmachar's natural lines of communication lay towards Oldmeldrum and Turriff, something well recognised by the later bus operators, rather than the Buchan. Nonetheless the railway was important to Newmachar if only for the general impetus which it gave to the development of trade and agriculture. Most goods and passengers moving more than ten or twenty miles would have been rail-borne even if mass commuting did not develop until after the railway closed. George Davidson in his *Memories of Whiterashes* (1983) tells of cycling to Newmachar station every afternoon for a parcel of a dozen evening papers for sale in the Whiterashes shop at ½d each. Well into the 1950s a loon or quine from Newmachar village would make his or her sleepy way to the station to collect the papers off the first train from Aberdeen for Willie Reid's shop. A caal, weet job, files, in the winter.

Over the years the railway brought mails, newspapers, coal, draff from the Speyside distilleries for cattle feed, lime, fertiliser, livestock to and from the marts, to say nothing of the materials for the building of Kingseat hospital and took away the output of the local farms including milk in the traditional churns. In later years the products of a rapidly developing consumer society arrived in ever-increasing quantities from ever more distant factories: cartons of cigarettes and pipe tobacco, crates of jam in jars, beer in bottles, whisky in pigs, sugar, tea, Lyons cakes and just about everything else required to stock the local shops. After the Second World War there was a boom in mail order ("clubbie") shopping which brought a flood of parcels to join the other assorted small consignments, all of which were delivered round the countryside from the station by Sandy Hopkins of Goval in a vehicle emblazoned "A. Hopkins and Son, Contractors, Newmachar" - but generally known as Hoppy's Laary.

The railwaymen were of the same rural stock as the communities they served and the mobile nature of railway work came naturally to those accustomed to the twice yearly feeing markets. The railway provided opportunities for those who wished to leave the land and afforded prospects of promotion for the ambitious. Railwaymen were also members of a larger, linear community which encompassed the whole of the Great North of Scotland Railway system. The sense of community was cemented by the rapid spread of railway news and gossip by means of engine drivers, guards and other travelling staff.

The railwaymen, and their wives, who staffed Newmachar and Parkhill stations for a hundred years, were typical of the breed working in a disciplined, hierarchical structure which functioned according to strict rules and regulations laid down to ensure the safe and efficient operation of the railway. Prior to the incorporation of the GNSR in the LNER in 1923, the station staff would have totalled four at most - a stationmaster, junior clerk, signalman and porter-signalman. After 1923 the introduction of the 8 hour day, 48 hour week, would have required two full-time signalmen, bringing the total to five and in the process increasing the costs of operating the railway at a time when competition from road transport was becoming increasingly fierce. In the late 1930s the stationmasters' posts at Newmachar and at Parkhill were abolished and the stations placed under the management of more senior officials at Udny and Dyce respectively. Oddly enough the then stationmaster at Udny, Alex Milne, seized the opportunity to move into the vacant house at Newmachar which he reckoned superior to the one he was occupying at Udny. The staff at Newmachar around 1923 is recorded as: William Robertson, stationmaster; Alex Edmiston, clerk; Harvey Stewart and John Abel, signalmen; Alex Turriff, porter.

Perhaps the most notable product of the railway community at Newmachar was the eminent journalist George Fraser, born in 1895 while his father was signalman at the station and who was still writing his column for the *Press & Journal* a century later. Less well known was Percy Drummond, a porter for a time during and after the Second World War, who as the Reverend WP Drummond served as minister at Garthdee for many years.

Between the two World Wars road transport, including convenient, frequent and flexible bus services, developed rapidly. By the end of the Second World War Newmachar boasted an hourly bus service to and from Aberdeen and two daily carrier services provided by Willie Glennie and Masson & Pressley both of Oldmeldrum. The role of the railway gradually diminished until, in truth, it had outlived its usefulness and the station was closed in 1965 and the entire line in 1975. Parkhill was closed even earlier, in 1950. Long after the decline in traffic at Newmachar itself the line as a whole remained busy and the station remained important to the operation of the route because of its location near the summit of the severe gradient from Dyce and because of its signal box and crossing loop which allowed trains to overtake, or to pass each other while travelling in opposite directions on the otherwise single track.

As late as 1920 the growth of traffic had prompted the doubling of the line from Parkhill to Elrick signal box (near Rosehall) as the first step in doubling the track as far as Ellon. The post-war slump rapidly put paid to that ambition and the second track between Parkhill and Elrick was removed in 1925. It would, however, have been invaluable during the second World War and for some years afterwards when traffic was again very heavy. The last real vestige of the railway disappeared from Newmachar when the signal box was closed on 9th November, 1965. Appropriately, John Abel, who had been a signalman at Newmachar since shortly after the first World War, was still in service. As has been remarked about other endings it was indeed "The end of ane auld sang". But as with the Scottish Parliament, one wonders if the Buchan Line might yet be reborn in another form.

Key to photograph: left to right, John McKay, Telegraph Inspector; George Fowlie, Telegraph Linesman at Maud; Alex. Edmonstone, Station Clerk; Harvey Stewart, Signalman; John Abel, Signalman; Alex. Turriff, Porter; William Robertson, Stationmaster.

"A Walk on the Wild Side"

This is a further slightly abbreviated article by Douglas Flett. It is in a more light-hearted vein and describes a recent return visit to the line of rail through Newmachar. It was published in full in *Great North Review*, the Journal of the Great North of Scotland Railway Association, 37 No. 147 (2000) 232-239. These extracts are published with the kind permission of the Editor, Mr Keith Fenwick and the Association as well as of Mr Flett himself.

The cuttings both north and south of Newmachar had an evil reputation in the days of fierce snow storms, but many of the serious blockages took place in the much shallower, barely perceptible cutting just at the northern end of the Newmachar crossing loop where the jagged remains of sleeper snow fencing still try to defeat the snow fiend. On the down side and across the line from the snow fencing, the goods yard is mainly occupied by what appears to be a warehouse and storage area with a length of loading bank restored for use by motor vehicles.

A little further on, the site of the signal box is covered in dense vegetation. Like Udny, the box at Newmachar was manned by the same two men, Harvey Stewart and John Abel, from just after the first World War until well after WW2. Jock Abel was the fortunate possessor of a personality fit to charm the proverbial birds from the trees. He was the local mole catcher, rejoicing in the sobriquet "Moley", interior decorator, poultry keeper, domino champion and many other things besides. Above all, he was an inveterate practical joker who would devote much time and ingenuity to perpetuating hoaxes. Sandy Melvin the Ganger (foreman of the Permanent-way squad) was a frequent sufferer. Jock borrowed a shovel and barrow from Sandy's locked shed for mucking out his poultry shed by the goods yard, apparently being able to unlock any padlock without using a key. He neglected, perhaps deliberately, to remove the evidence from the borrowed tools. Sandy was breathing fire and asked Willie Milne, the Permanent-way Inspector, to call in the Railway Police. Willie, a splendid man liked by all, realised that things were getting out of hand and had a word with Johnny Flett, the Agent, who then had a few, somewhat stronger, words with Jock, who had the virtue of knowing when to stop and made sure that on all future occasions the shovel and barrow were returned in pristine condition to the Navvies' Hut. And quite how did Jock gain his illicit entry? Simple. No duplicate keys or lock picking. He just unscrewed the padlock hasp from the door and replaced it when finished.

Newmachar station building, much altered, is now a private house and there has been some building in the large gardens of the former railway houses. At the south end of the loop the brick base of the minor signal-box lies in a tumbled heap and immediately behind is the same old sleeper fence separating the back garden of the Station House from the railway. Much of my childhood was spent in that house but my most vivid memory is of the great snows of 1947. By no manner of means could my brother and I have reached Newmachar School, to us no hardship, even if the school was normally within sight of the house. Throughout that first day of a storm which has since entered the realms of folklore, our large kitchen became a haven of storm-delayed train and snowplough crews, Permanent-way men, signal linesmen, and assorted others came and went at irregular intervals and it was not long before the floor was awash with melted snow from their boots and clothes. These men were grateful for the opportunity to thaw out, have a hot drink and a bite to eat. Remember those were the days of food rationing even more stringent than during the recently ended war; nor were there fridges and freezers to store food. In any case the Hydro had not reached beyond Newmachar village, so there was no electricity supply and all cooking was done by paraffin stoves and fireside ovens. My mother was often driven to distraction by my father's sense of hospitality, which seemed to extend to providing a 'fly cup' or 'denner' to just about every wandering railwayman who appeared. My mother did her not inconsiderable best but one day in 1947 the food, to say nothing of tea and sugar, ran out and the cupboard was bare indeed, so the marooned multitude in the kitchen considered what should be done. The nearest shops were in Newmachar village, about half a mile away, and Johnny Bisset, a well-known Kittybrewster driver, volunteered to make the journey. Rather in the manner of Captain Oates taking leave of Scott's party on their fatal journey to the South Pole, he set off clad only in his uniform reefer jacket and dungarees with his cap pulled at the favoured piratical angle. Just as the group in the kitchen was beginning to debate the wisdom of sending out a search party the redoubtable Johnny reappeared coated in snow from head to foot and explained that he had found increasing difficulty making progress against the 'blin drift' while struggling through deep snow in places up to his chest. It seems that he had eventually met someone struggling in the opposite direction who had advised him to the effect 'Gang back far ye cam' fae ye bloody feel, ye'll niver reach Wullie Reid's the day.' How the food stocks were replenished escapes my memory but replenished they were. Maybe Charles Adlen, the Newmachar Porter-in-Charge, one time regular soldier and holder of His Majesty's Commission who was a burly and resourceful chap, did the trick. Charlie was a raconteur supreme with his yarns of derring-do in India and other exotic places. In the North West Frontier he would tell of throwing his hot shaving water out of his tent and hearing it crash on the ground, the temperature being so low that the water had frozen in mid air.

The earthworks of the runaway siding on the down side of the line at the south end of Newmachar crossing loop are still prominent. Despite the fact that the siding was provided just for safety reasons to 'catch' any runaway vehicles heading down the hill to Dyce, it was often used for the storage of surplus plant (ie rolling stock) and it was a delicate operation to hold over the catch points manually until the shunting was complete. The brakes on the vehicles had also to be applied and secured in case they ran back down the reverse incline.

The mind boggles at what would have happened had a runaway vehicle crashed into the already occupied siding, which was perched at a considerable height adjacent to the Newmachar-Kingseat road.

The last lap to Dyce beckoned.   On my way I found the base of the Newmachar down distant signal which brought back memories of my first job on the railway as a temporary summer porter at Newmachar, deputising for Charlie Alden while he was off collecting tickets at Aberdeen.   My first job on a Monday morning was to fill and trim a signal lamp and walk to the down distant, climb the ladder and exchange the new lamp for old.   Try that without letting go the ladder with both hands for the vital change-over moment.   An employer would be prosecuted nowadays for turning a seventeen year old loose on a job like that with training which amounted to the laconic sentence, 'Ye'll easy ken the signal, it's the second ane on your right han' side an' its pentit yalla on the far-awa' side.'

The land once occupied by the double track between Elrick and Parkhill is easily discernible, as are the double width bridges.   Also looking as if it will stand forever is the granite base of the hut which contained the levers for the small gantry of six signals used for practical eyesight tests for drivers who had failed the medical examination.   In steam engine days spectacles were not allowed and it was a serious matter for a driver to fail the sight test so he could, in certain circumstances, ask for a practical test.   These signals were used only for that purpose and were normally kept in the 'off' position and were ignored so far as the working of the line was concerned.   Did this same granite base serve as the base of the original Elrick signal box, I wonder?   At Parkhill, the station buildings and station house have vanished and have been replaced with a large bungalow. The new footbridge across the A947 is certainly pleasing to the eye as it follows a graceful curve over the road, in contrast to the old granite railway bridge over the Don which looks as sturdy as ever despite having withstood many a spate during the last 140 years.   It is difficult to be sure if the short remaining distance of the Way to Dyce station exactly follows the line of the old railway.

I think the most appropriate words to mark the end of my journey are contained in some lines written by the Portknockie poet, James Wood.   His words are particularly apposite because, to me, the old railway was surely about people rather than rivets.

> Gone are they all, the kindly folk,
> And here I stand, a generation after.
> Where all that now remains are echoings
> Of songs and voices and remembered laughter.

Some further information about the Buchan Line

The Dyce-Ellon line of the GNSR was opened to goods and passengers on 18th July 1861. After earlier abortive legislation, it was the Formartine and Buchan Railways Act of 1858 which authorised the building of the railway. The Stationmaster in 1877 was James Hunter. (*Worral's Directory*, Oldham, 1877, p. 161.) Parkhill Station was closed to passengers on 3rd April 1950 and to goods on 7th August 1961. Newmachar Station was closed to goods on 23rd March 1964 and to passengers on 4th October 1965. The line was completely closed and the track taken up after a final journey on 5th October 1979. The line itself was torn up within a fortnight. (*P & J, 6th October 1979*) Full details on the technical working of the GNSR eg. signalling at the Parkhill, Elrick and Newmachar boxes and the Tablet working introduced in 1894 are available from the GNSR Association.

The section of line between Parkhill and the Elrick signal box was converted to double track on 13th May 1920, but reduced to single track working again on 23rd August 1925. Both the Parkhill and Elrick signal boxes were used only during this five-year period. **Mr Bert Sangster**, when a boy, lived at Kinmundy cottage from 1918-22 and was very much aware of the doubling of the line. His recollection is that at least the second line itself remained in place during the 1930s. The oral tradition about the railway of which he was aware was that the big curve in the route was because the laird of Pitrichie (a shareholder?) had demanded that the line run as near Summerhill as possible. Pitrichie (855257) is just outside the parish to the north. This tradition, whether correct or not, emphasises the failure of the railway to serve the northern part of the parish and Newmachar's general orientation towards Oldmeldrum.

The GNSR carried out surveys of its traffic in 1871 and 1903. (GNSR Association Abstract No. 3, 1990.) In 1871 the whole line, 54 miles long, made a profit of £4,430.

Concession tickets were given to fish wives or merchants with one creel - providing they travelled on slow trains. See also the information on Mr Fowler, the Fishmonger. (See Chap. XXIV.)

For many years farmers in the area relied heavily on the railway to bring them draff or transport cattle, sheep and horses to Aberdeen. Store cattle might be brought in from far afield. **Mr Alexander Ingram** recalls cattle being brought from Wales. Each animal was put in a large sack up to its neck so that it naturally lay down in the wagon.

Kingseat Hospital depended on the railway for the very large supplies of coal needed to keep the villas warm. (See Chap. XXI.)

The railways were also significant for schools and schoolchildren. There were summer outings by train for New Machar School pupils. (Testimony of **Mr Bert Sangster and Mrs Ethel Begg.**) Pupils wishing to go on to a senior secondary school might go to Ellon Academy by train.

The 1960 Snowstorm

At 11.00 am on Monday, 18th January, the four-coach diesel train incorporating units from Peterhead and Fraserburgh ran into an 8 ft deep snowdrift in the cutting 300 yards north of Newmachar Station. 57 passengers were stranded. Neither road vehicles nor a relief train from Aberdeen could get through. By nightfall some food had got through by Landrover, but not enough for everyone; volunteers walked into the village for more. The 57 passengers then walked along the line to where the relief train was stuck. This eventually got back to Aberdeen at 6.00 am on Wednesday, 20th January. (Alan H Sangster, *The Story and Tales of the Buchan Line*, Poole, 1983, 26-29.)

The cutting which caused all this trouble runs for about a mile between Westside and Rainnieshill. The surface is about 140m (460 ft) high while the cutting becomes almost 18m (50 ft) deep.

Chapter XIII
The Church in the Life of the Community since 1804

When Mr William Stronach demitted office as Newmachar's minister in 1804 to be succeeded by Alexander Simpson, there was only one church and, more importantly, everyone in the parish could be regarded as a member of the national, established Church of Scotland. Even if, as we have seen (Chapter VII), significant changes were in train by the 1790s, the Church was still a vital part of Scottish life. It was at the centre of the intellectual renaissance which was the Scottish Enlightenment. Even more obviously, it was at the centre of everyday life where it remained paramount in the control of moral behaviour and education. Within the next half-century or so the position would change radically. One immediate and obvious sign in Newmachar was the addition of two more churches to the parish, the Free Church in 1843 and the Episcopal Church in 1858. The signs of economic change — the turnpike road, the newly enclosed fields and eventually the railway — were accompanied by and perhaps linked to less obvious manifestations of an even more profound change. This was the increased secularisation of society. Secularisation began to erode the authority of the Church and hence its ability to claim the right to regulate education and moral behaviour. (There is a useful general discussion on the extent to which Scottish society did become secularised in the early nineteenth century in T.M. Devine, *The Scottish Nation 1700-2000*, London, 1999, p. 363ff.)

Whatever the extent of secularisation, it would be entirely wrong to assume that the Church became irrelevant. The great majority of people were believers in the sense that they instinctively assumed (without necessarily being able to formulate the idea in words) that there was something beyond the material world. It was conventionally and normally taken to be one of the functions of the Church and its ministers to provide congregations with means of giving expression to this feeling. A second assumption which most people would have made in 1804 was that believing in God implied that Christ's injunction that one should love one's neighbour as oneself meant that the Church had a duty not only to try to guide personal behaviour and even social relations, but also collective behaviour in political and economic matters. In other words, the Church does have to engage with the world. Just how it should do so was perhaps the fundamental problem underlying the Disruption of 1843. The Disruption was the most important development not only in the history of the Church but in the history of Scotland in the nineteenth century. Could church, state, and society be one and indistinguishable as in John Knox's vision? This was an important question in Newmachar as elsewhere and it was to be a descendant of John Knox, Alexander Thomson, who had a key role in the outcome in the parish. By 1929, however, perhaps it had to be admitted that Knox's vision was not appropriate for the modern more secular world and reunion came; one of Newmachars's new churches soon disappeared.

The other church established in the nineteenth century has lasted into the 21st century. This is All Saints' Church at Whiterashes., The persistence of episcopalianism in the north east of Scotland and its re-invigoration in the earlier nineteenth century was to have its impact on Newmachar.

Newmachar Parish Church 1804-1843

The *Rev. Alexander Simpson* served as minister from 1804 until he died in 1840. He had been born in 1757 and gained an M.A. from King's College in 1777. He became schoolmaster in King Edward - where he taught 27 pupils and it was he, rather than the minister, who was asked to write the *Statistical Account* for King Edward. (*OSA*, Vol XV, pp. 254-264.) Writing at the time of the most extreme revolutionary sentiments and activities in France in 1792-3, Simpson pronounced that

> It is highly reasonable, that an order of men, by the fruit of whose labours all are fed, should enjoy such a competence as to make their condition easy and comfortable.

Simpson moved from King Edward to become schoolmaster at Turriff and wrote the *Statistical Account* there also. Although stated in less potentially revolutionary terms, the Turriff account (*OSA*, Vol IX, pp. 519-537) again makes clear Simpson's strong belief that tenant farmers should be given the opportunity to better themselves. Is this mildly revolutionary streak what lies behind Simpson's willingness to become chaplain to a Freemasons' Lodge in Newmachar; did he even initiate it? (See Chap. XXII.) Perhaps, too, his interest in agricultural improvement had at least something to do with the great changes in agriculture in the parish in the 1830s. (See Chap. IX.) Here, indeed, if this is so, was the church engaging with the secular world. One would like to know much more about Alexander Simpson and his ministry at Newmachar; there seems to be regrettably little information about him. The Kirk Session records may repay further study but they seem to suggest that the conventional pattern of the minister and session trying to maintain moral discipline remained. One Thomas Rae was regularly accused of fathering illegitimate children between 1812 and 1826. As far as the services are concerned, music must have been part of the worship as in 1825 there was a Precentor called John Berry. (Pigot's *New Commercial Directory*, London, 1825. The Kirk Session records for this period (CH 2/281/6) are almost entirely concerned with discipline.)

George Moir (1807-1857) and the Disruption in Newmachar

The *Rev. George Moir* was parish minister from 1840-1843 when he went 'out'. He had been born in 1807 and had taught at Madras College in St Andrews before coming to Newmachar. However, there is little information on his early life. This is disappointing given his great importance in the history of the parish. Nevertheless, it is clear from the *New Statistical Account* he wrote in 1842

(Vol XI pp. 1025-35) and other evidence that the Earl of Fife had done well in choosing such an active and intelligent man to be minister. His short ministry in the established church meant a refurbishment of the church and the manse.

More important was the well-regulated system of sabbath schools which he set up, his encouragement of the continuing work of a general library and of the religious library which he established. His parishioners had already presented him with a clock in appreciation of his work. (Information from Major Irvine who was asked to keep the clock by Mr Moir's daughters.) Moir's enthusiastic activity was a practical expression of the beliefs he clearly held as an adherent of the evangelical party during the Ten-Year Conflict which preceded the Disruption.

REV. GEORGE MOIR : 1840-1857.

The Ten-Year Conflict

Since there is so little information about Alexander Simpson's ministry, it is difficult to say how the Ten-Year Conflict may have affected Newmachar. Clearly, when Moir became minister he was influenced by the vision of Thomas Chalmers that Scotland should continue to be divided up into relatively small communities as parishes. Chalmers saw such communities as the best means by which the new social formations created by the Industrial Revolution could be brought once more into a godly commonwealth. The Chapels Act of the Assembly was designed to make the vision possible; it was not enough in the eyes of the evangelicals simply to build more churches, which was something the Church Extension Act provided for. However, the greatest arguments came over the Veto Act which gave adult male members of a congregation the right to veto the candidate presented to a parish by the owner of the patronage (which had been re-established in 1712). The Auchterarder and other cases saw challenges to the Veto Act on the grounds that it infringed property rights which were recognised by the civil law of the United Kingdom. Arguments over such matters seemed to bring into question the Church of Scotland's position as an established church. Yet the evangelicals did not want disestablishment so much as 'sphere sovereignty.' (*Dictionary of Scottish Church History and Theology*, p. 247.) The argument on this matter not only raised the question of whether the Church was above the civil law but also the political issue of whether Scotland had the right to be and to remain different from the rest of the United Kingdom.

It seems unlikely that many ordinary churchgoers in Newmachar were concerned about Scotland's constitutional position or even the possibility of the Earl of Fife losing his right to nominate the parish minister. However, there is another more general social level on which one can discuss the Disruption. The Free Church initiative, especially in urban situations, can be seen as a desire on the part of newly emerging middle class figures to 'break the dominance of the older, professional and commercial elites.' (S.J. Brown.) In a rural parish like Newmachar, by the same token, some of the tenant farmers and shopkeepers might be expected to support the Free Church. More research needs to be done on Newmachar to establish just what social dividing lines there actually were, if they existed at all in the parish. All that can be said with confidence is that the more skilled tradesmen — which meant, for example, the Cothal Mill weavers (whether or not most of them lived in Newmachar) — like those in other areas, sought their own independence and importance through identification with the Free Church. (On the general question of the Disruption, see the essays in *Scotland in the Age of the Disruption*, ed. S.J. Brown & M. Fry, Edinburgh, 1993 and further references there.)

The Free Church 1843-1929

By November 1842, it was reasonably clear that some ministers and laymen were likely to leave the Church. George Moir obviously expected to do so and he and his supporters were able to start building their new church well before the formal break of May 1843.

When he spoke at the Aberdeen Synod in April 1843, Moir seemed most concerned about the way the Veto Act affected the status of ministers (*Aberdeen Journal*, 19 April 1843) but as mentioned earlier (Chapter VII), he was clearly much affected by Bisset's views on patronage from well over a century earlier. Moir attended the great meetings in Edinburgh in May 1843. He returned to Newmachar and on Thursday, 1st June, Alexander Thomson laid the foundation stone of the 'Free Protesting Church.' Three days later, on the Sunday, as the Kirk Session records simply state, Mr Moir preached and intimated his secession from the established church. (CH 2/281/6.) For a short time the new congregation met in a barn at Mameulah but by 6th August it was possible to assemble in the new church. This was probably the first Free Church in Scotland to become operational after the Disruption. (W. Ewing, *Annals of the Free Church of Scotland*, 2 Vols, Edinburgh, 1914, 2, 188.)

Judging by the fact that in five years' time the number of communicants would be 515, the initial group that 'went out' must have been substantial. Although this sort of number was common in towns, it was less common in rural parishes. Ewing says the membership in 1848 was 450. What perhaps was even more significant for Newmachar was the fact that Moir had the backing of two very substantial and influential laymen. *Captain Thomas Shepherd* of the Indian Army (see Chap. XVI) had been involved in the Ten-Year Conflict and the final assembly of the old church in 1843. In that year he was the tenant at Straloch House and immediately offered shelter to Mr Moir. Shepherd is a figure who deserves more research; presumably even while in India he was affected by the Evangelical Revival of the early nineteenth century.

Even more important was the support of *Alexander Thomson* of Banchory-Devenick (1798-1869) who was also the proprietor of the Rainnieshill estate. Thomson could trace his ancestry back to John Knox. He was in a position to provide the land on which the new church was built. This was at the crossroads in the middle of the village on the site of what is now *Carousel* and its car park area. A little later he provided the land for a manse, on rising ground just to the west of the village (879197). (*Guesses at Truth*, 1913, pp. 3-5.) Alexander Thomson was putting into practice what he preached to the leading figures of the new church. If it really was to be an alternative Church of Scotland, not just a sect, its ministers needed to be properly housed; he persuaded the new Free Church Assembly to set up a building fund. He had been a key figure in the final stages of the Ten-Year Conflict trying to avert crisis by negotiations with the Earl of Aberdeen and Sir Robert Peel. Altogether, Alexander Thomson was a remarkable man. A polymath scholar, traveller and collector, he was also a

major landowner, a Tory, a social reformer with some claim to be seen as the Scottish Lord Shaftesbury. His nineteenth century biographer is so intent on making him an Evangelical saint that he misses many key issues — including the fact that Newmachar and Mr Moir were important to him during the Disruption because Moir 'went out' whereas the minister in his main parish, Banchory-Devenick, did not. (George Smeaton, *Memoir of Alexander Thomson of Banchory*, Edinburgh, 1869, pp. 284, 289, 301 and *passim*.)

The Free Church Manse (later the West Manse, now Westgrove House)

The site of the Free Church manse was said to be one that Mr Thomson had envisaged as the location for a substantial house for himself. A croft tenanted by a Mrs Watson must have been displaced to make way for the new house. (Rainnieshill Estate Map, 1841.) The incoming wife of a twentieth-century minister found the house difficult to run with the water supply in the house having to be pumped up from a well, and a cooking range which used up lots of coal and was very difficult to manage. (Information from Mrs M. Nicol, daughter of Mrs C.M. Kerr.)   Mr Moir had gone south to England to raise money (presumably from English evangelical and nonconformist churches).   He returned to move into the manse late in 1844 - together with his new wife, Ellen, whom he had met on the English expedition.   Did she find the house as difficult to manage as her successor 80 years later?

George Moir, Free Church minister in Newmachar 1843-1857

The support both practical and moral which Moir received from Thomas Shepherd and Alexander Thomson puts his sacrifice in going out in some sort of perspective.   Nevertheless it was a sacrifice of position as an active and successful minister, earning a regular stipend, and as the tenant of the commodious manse which had been repaired and refurbished for his use.   He gave this up for what in 1843 would have seemed a very uncertain future.

All the indications are that George Moir successfully began to build up the Free Church as an active entity and moreover one which maintained friendly relations with the Established Church.   However, he died at the comparatively early age of 47 in 1857.   Mrs Moir lived until 1896.   Their daughters remained unmarried and lived at Connel Ha', Cothal, well into the twentieth century.

Rev. Alexander Thain, 1858-1864 and Rev. James Duguid, 1864-1909

Alexander Thain's short ministry was affected by the strong evangelistic attitudes he learned from his friend Robert Murray McCheyne of Dundee, and also, less fortunately, by the loss of large part of his congregation when the Crombie Mill at Cothal was finally closed; the business relocated to Grandholm and the workers moved to lodgings in Woodside to be closer to their work. (*Guesses at Truth*, p. 7; *Dictionary ... Church History*, pp. 504-5.)

Duguid's ministry by contrast was long.   The congregation steadily recovered in numbers but was never to be as large as it had been in the 1840s.   On the other hand, the support of the largest landowner in the parish, Mr John Gordon Cuming Skene of Parkhill (c.1826-1882) must have been of great service to the Church.   Mr Duguid took a full part in village affairs, being involved with the work of the Parochial Council and the School Board.   It was he who had to make the decision to close the Free Church School and transfer the pupils to the new Board School system in 1873.   During his ministry, the Free Church was to become part of the United Free Church in 1900.   There is what looks like a human tragedy in connection with music at the Church round about this time. The Duguid family were musical (testimony of Mrs Nicol) and he would have wanted good music in church.   In St Machar's Cathedral there is a memorial plaque to the Cathedral's last precentor, John Gordon Robertson.   The plaque adds that his eldest son, William, was 'first organist and choirmaster of New

Machar Free Church.' He died in December 1899 when he was only 19 years old. (The existence of the plaque was pointed out by Mr Alec Hay of Wood Cottages.)

Rev. D.R. Kerr, 1909-1929/32

The Rev. David Kerr was the last United Free Church minister of Newmachar and for three years minister of what became, after the Reunion of 1929, the West Parish of Newmachar. David Kerr, born in 1871, was a distinguished and scholarly man. He had published a work entitled *St Andrews in 1645-6*, Edinburgh, 1895. As noted already, he had clearly begun to make some investigations on the history of Newmachar but never had the opportunity to write up his results for publication. The little book *Guesses at Truth*, produced by Mr Kerr, includes his invaluable account of the Disruption in Newmachar, photographs of all four of the Free Church ministers and, the main purpose, a selection of verses or hymns chosen by various of his acquaintances. The selections are interesting in themselves. Mr McGregor, master at Whiterashes School, chose to quote David Livingstone: "Fear God and Work Hard." Mr G.A.M. Burnett of Elrick House chose a humorous quotation in French to the effect that life is like a slice of bread on which 'il y a beaucoup plus de margarine que de beurre.'

When appointed, Mr Kerr was unmarried. He was to serve with the YMCA in France during the Great War when he also met and married his wife who then joined him in Newmachar. An extremely talented lady, Mrs Cecilia Kerr was the daughter of a Free Church medical missionary in India, Dr James Sommerville, and had been born in Udaipur. As this book's cover shows, Mrs Kerr was a very capable amateur artist. She was also a violinist and revitalised the church choir and musical life in Newmachar more generally, not least through her activities with the WRI of which she was an enthusiastic member and Secretary, working with Miss Annie Knight to establish a WRI choir. For a time she even managed to assemble an orchestra for the Free Church. (From a press cutting in the possession of Mrs Nicol.) Mrs Kerr died in 1983 and is buried with her husband in the Newmachar cemetery.

Mr Kerr himself made a considerable impact on the village by setting up and running a scout troop; the photograph (see Chap. XXII) shows the troop going off to camp on Tyrebagger Hill. Perhaps there was an element of rivalry here for the scout troop was obviously in competition with the Boys' Brigade Unit run by the Established Church organist, Mr Murphy, and Henry Catto who had actually started the unit. (See Chap. XXI.)

Mr Kerr was well known outside the parish because he was chosen as Moderator of the Free Church Presbytery of Aberdeen. As Moderator in the middle 1920s, it became his task to negotiate the reunion in 1929. He died comparatively young in 1932. Mr Jaffray's very warm tribute at the memorial

service referred to Mr Kerr's 'high moral character', and 'intellectual gifts'.
(Quoted by kind permission of Mrs Nicol.)

As a result of the end of Mr Kerr's ministry, the West Parish was soon merged with the East — the original church. For a short time the kirk building continued to be used for worship but was then sold to a private business. Plans to turn it into a village hall were abortive and it was finally demolished in 1975. The sketch from memory was made by Mrs Elizabeth Walker. The demolition marked the end of an episode which had begun with the Disruption and had had a considerable impact upon Newmachar and its people for some 75 years. Its long-term significance is difficult to assess because the period when the Free Church was in existence coincides with material and social changes which affected the standing of all churches.

The Established Church 1843-1929

The Disruption was not the disaster for the Established Church that might have been predicted. Its authority in matters of education and morals was perhaps on the wane in any case. In the 1850s it became freer and more egalitarian socially, more liberal in its doctrine. (Brown, p. 24.)

The *Rev. Alexander Allan (1816-1866)* had been schoolmaster and then minister in Newhills before taking over from George Moir in 1843. Mr Allan has the credit of avoiding the kind of bitter rivalry between the two churches which was apparent in some places. He died in 1866 and was succeeded by one of Newmachar's most outstanding churchmen, the *Rev. William Robertson Bruce (1835-1901)*. Born in 1835, he was educated at King's College before

becoming a schoolmaster at Urquhart. He married Elizabeth Cruickshank in the year before he was called to be minister in Newmachar. Mr and Mrs Bruce had a large family of ten children. Hence the addition of a new east wing to the manse, which was later demolished in the 1960s. Three of their sons were to make their careers in South Africa. One of them later gifted £500 to the church. (*Third Statistical Account*, p. 158.) Their daughters, when grown up, helped out with teaching at the school during staff absences. Mr Bruce was chairman of the School Board for over twenty years and perhaps his greatest public achievement was to guide the board through the first crucial years of its existence. He had to balance the traditional expectations of the heritors to control important matters in the parish against the expectations of elected members and the parents of the children. He seems to have been firm but tactful, an ideal person to get a new public service off on a sound footing. (See Chap. XVII.) A natural chairman, Bruce was equally sensible and firm on the Parochial Board which was responsible for looking after the poor and many other problems. (See Chap. XIV.) He was naturally a very respected and influential figure in the councils of the church and it was a well-merited reward when the University of Aberdeen made him an honorary D.D. in 1895. Mr Bruce's long ministry came to an end when he died in 1901. The memorial plaque in the church refers to his 'sympathetic kindness' and this is by no means the only evidence that behind the skilful chairman and church statesman was a warm human being.

The **Rev. Robert Nelson** held the incumbency for only two years from 1902-4 and was succeeded by the **Rev. Alexander Hood Smith (1866-1927)** who served at Kemnay before coming to Newmachar in 1904. Alexander Smith in many respects sought to carry on Mr Bruce's tradition of churchmanship plus public service. It was also during his ministry that the church was renovated and refurbished in 1913. In 1840 George Moir had relocated the entrance to the east end of the church and added a vestry area. Now the church was re-orientated with the communion table at the west end. As a consequence, the galleries on the west and south sides had to be removed. New seating, a new communion table plus a rather splendid pipe organ were installed. A little later, a stained glass window by Douglas Strachan, which is widely admired, was commissioned. This was in 1916 at the instigation of Miss Margaret Crombie in memory of her parents James and Katherine Crombie. (See Chap. XVI.) Its historical reference encompasses St Machar, David I and William the Lion, all of whom made grants which affected Newmachar, plus the Bishop's Loch. (See Chap. III.) Mr Smith's relations with the Free Church seem to have been smooth. He died in 1927 leaving £1000 to the Church. (*Third Statistical Account*, p. 158.)

The Reunion

The **Rev. Andrew M M Giles**, became minister in 1927 and was to remain at Newmachar until he transferred to Broughty Ferry in 1941. It was during his ministry that the Reunion took place. The arrangements were negotiated with Mr Kerr who, of course, was also responsible for wider questions relating to the Reunion for the Aberdeen Presbytery of the United Free Church. The arrangements for Newmachar were comparatively simple: the two churches would remain in being as the East (former Established) and West (former UFC) Kirks, it being understood that they would unite when next one or other of the ministers died or moved to another charge. In the event that happened very soon with the death of Mr Kerr in 1932. The terms of the subsequent reunion in Newmachar were that the older church would become the church for the united congregations and sessions although the former UFC church would be used once a month. (In fact, this proved inconvenient and the building was sold in 1936.) All the elders were retained and Mr Giles remained minister with his residence as the manse. The West Manse was to be sold. (Act of Union: a handwritten agreement dated July 5th, 1932, in the possession of Mrs Nicol.)

As far as one can judge, the congregations of the two churches settled together reasonably smoothly; indeed, there had been a fair amount of co-operation before the reunion. *Mrs Elizabeth Walker* remembers the organists at both churches and singing practice in the manse in Mr Giles' ministry. She regrets that the 1913 organ was removed from the church in 1969 and an electronic one put in. *Mr Bert Sangster* by contrast was officially attached to the Free Church but confesses to having played outside when his parents believed him to be at Sunday School; he was careful to return home when he saw the other children coming out of church. Not all church teaching was treated solemnly. Whether from either church or school is unsure but Sundays in Newmachar taught him and his friends that

> If you don't wear a dickie and a tie, ay ay,
> You won't get to heaven when you die, ay ay.

The Episcopal Church from 1858-2001

Disabilities on Jacobite 'non-qualified' Episcopalians were removed in 1792. This, plus the continuing success of St Paul's Church in Aberdeen, one of the formerly 'qualified' episcopal churches (i.e., for those prepared to pray for the Hanoverian Kings) meant that Anglicanism flourished in the region. (Patrick Jones, 'The Qualified Episcopal Chapels of the North East of Scotland, 1689-1898', *Northern Scotland* 20 (2001) 47-69.) It was ironic, incidentally, that Alexander Thomson found sermons by evangelical Anglicans at St Paul's preferable to those preached by the 'moderates' of his own Church of Scotland in the 1820s and '30s. (Smeaton, pp. 117-8.) Generally, though, there was more emphasis on an elaborate liturgy than might be found in the Church of Scotland — or the Evangelical wing of the Church of England. In Scotland, the revival of spiritualism and liturgy had been connected with the name of John Skinner (1744-1816). Not only had he been instrumental in getting penal laws removed in 1792 but he also began the process of creating or re-creating what became seven territorially-based bishoprics. Thus by the earlier part of the nineteenth century, the Episcopal Church was growing stronger and was in a position to

respond to a very influential manifestation of the need to engage with the sublime rather than the material world. This was the tractarian or Oxford movement in the Anglican Church. It was Bishop Forbes of Brechin (1817-1875) who introduced tractarianism into Scotland and gave Scottish Episcopalianism a distinctively 'High' or Anglo-Catholic character - often combined, however, as in Forbes' case, with an acute concern for social problems. (R. Strong, *Alexander Forbes of Brechin*, Oxford, 1995; R. Strong, *Episcopalians in Nineteenth-Century Scotland*, Oxford, 2001.)

It was in 1858 that Major Ramsay established an Episcopal church at Whiterashes. It was both a school and a mission church from Old Meldrum. In 1880 the church, shown above, was formally conveyed to the Episcopal Church and consecrated. But only between 1896 and 1920 did it have the services of a resident clergyman. Hence from 1858 to 1896 it was looked after by the Old Meldrum priests, J. Davidson, 1859-62, and W.Y. Moir, 1862-1896. The All Saints' priests were R. Mitchell, 1896-8, Alfred Wild, 1899-1907, James Fowler, 1907-08, and John Threlfall, 1908-1920. Thereafter it was again under the wing of Old Meldrum with Alexander Macpherson to 1936 and later from 1962, after a period of little use, Canon A.B. MacGillivray. (D.M. Bertie, *Scottish Episcopal Clergy 1689-2000*, Edinburgh, 2000 p. 535; information from Major Irvine.) Through the energy and dedication of lay reader Kenneth Chilles, All Saints' Church resumed regular services during the 1990s.

All Saints' Church is a well-proportioned small building. It has striking stained glass windows designed by Sir J.W. Comper, including one in memory of Miss Christian Ramsay (1833-1905), daughter of John Ramsay II.   George Davidson recalls the priests in charge, Mr Wild and Mr Threlfall, and fêtes at Straloch in aid of church funds. (*Memories of Whiterashes*, pp. 9-11.)

Ernest Gregory, 1874-1967

If you enter the little Episcopal Church of All Saints', Whiterashes, erected in 1858, you will notice among the other interesting features, a charming pulpit carved by Ernest Gregory.

Ernest was born in Tarporley, Cheshire on 5th October 1874 and became at the required age a choirboy at St Helen's, the parish church there. Most days on his way home from school, Ernest would stop at the carpenter's workshop in the village and watch intently how the work was done, and especially the carving, which was a regular part of the carpenter's work in the late 19th century. This was all the training that Ernest ever had in woodwork, for at a very young age he was entered in the service of the Bishop of Manchester, who, he recalled, was bald except for a fringe round the back of his head. On one occasion Ernest related that his barber asked, 'Much off, My Lord?' to which the Bishop replied, 'Yes, if you can get it.' Ernest Gregory went from the Bishop's service to that of a Canon Cooper of Cuckfield, Sussex, being promoted to

footman. Incidentally, Canon Cooper is commemorated on one of the stained glass windows, gifted in his memory at All Saints', Whiterashes. He was a regular visitor to Straloch, being a friend of the Irvines and Ramsays. By the time Ernest had been thoroughly trained in the duties expected of one in service in those days, a butler

was required by the Irvines at Drum Castle and Canon Cooper duly recommended him for the post in about 1890. After some years at Drum, where his photograph may be seen, he was asked to move to Straloch with Mrs Irvine of Barra and Straloch, widow of the 21st Laird of Drum. At Straloch, Ernest met Jane, the girl who was to be his life's companion, and a very successful marriage it turned out to be. Four children were born in five years, the last surviving until 1990.

While at Straloch, Ernest found time to exercise his artistic talent and this is how the pulpit, which was dedicated on Easter Day 1904, came to be carved. [It is shown on the accompanying photograph.]   Ernest Gregory lived into his nineties but the rest of his life is another story.

Kenneth E. Chilles (Mr Gregory's grandson)

The pulpit was installed in All Saints' in time for the Easter Services in 1904 when it was reported that the numbers attending were greater than ever before. Each of the six panels has a different design of which the main elements are: Keys, IHS, a Lily and Crown, a Cross, the Passion Flower and the emblems of the Trinity. (*The Buchan Churchman*, 10 (1904) 55, 68-69.) This remarkable piece of craftsmanship is one of the few outstanding public works of art in Newmachar yet it is little known. There is also at All Saints' a handsome brass lectern which commemorates Major Henry Nares.

The Church of Scotland and Newmachar 1929-2001

Mr Giles was succeeded as minister by the *Rev. Henry Thornton (1911-1978)*. Educated in Edinburgh, he graduated from the University with a 'first' in Mental Philosophy having undertaken additional studies at the Universities of Bonn and Heidelberg. After assistantships at Ormiston and Kelty he came to Newmachar in 1942. Despite far from robust health, it became his practice to make his visits around the parish and to Kingseat Hospital (then a naval hospital) by bicycle.

As a result of his German contacts, Harry Thornton had met and married Agathe, a teacher of Classics. Life in the manse in the midst of the war was not easy. Harry Thornton's father, who had been caretaker at 121 George Street, Edinburgh, the Church of Scotland headquarters, came to help out. Chickens and ducks were kept to provide additional protein in the form of eggs. Mrs Thornton tried to keep goats as well. The billy goat regularly stood on the roof of the steading and once slipped his chain to stand on the roof of the house itself. The large garden was kept in order by Mr Third, the grave digger/sexton until he was conscripted. Mrs Thornton, with a young child and then a new baby born in the manse, could not easily manage such a large area. (Information from Mr Bernard Thornton, son of Harry and Agathe, now a writer and teacher in New Zealand who has vivid childhood memories of the manse. The sister born here in 1946 is now a Jungian analyst.)

Arriving with a very young child in the middle of the war with all its difficulties and shortages and having to manage an old-fashioned manse cannot have been easy for Mrs Thornton. Her German background must have meant additional problems. In what follows, there is an account of her memories of the manse but echoes, too, of some of these problems of adjustment. It is clear that the District Nurse, Nurse Macrae, who assisted at the birth of Alison, became a good friend and counsellor.

The drawing room had a red carpet and a black upright piano, with a large fireplace on the west wall. It was an amazing room, with its colours of black and red and white, coupled with its views to the garden, big trees and landscapes beyond - it was a most beautiful place! You looked out through a bay window to mighty trees - ashes. You looked out of the window onto a broad drive with enough room to take a horse and carriage, bounded on the far side by a honeysuckle hedge which went the breadth of the garden. There were lovely scents in the evening after a warm day.

The dining room had red linoleum on the floor. The furniture was lovely…it all had to be left behind…I hankered after it for the rest of my life…an octagon-shaped, light oak table, and four chairs with red leather seats. This room had a bay window too, facing south.

The congregation were very proud of the new coal-burning stove they had put in the kitchen, the latest thing in technology. I had never had to manage one like it in my life. (They had no clue of the amount of hurdles I had to overcome in all directions.) I had to be there most of the time, minding it. It used to go out on me.

Beyond the kitchen, on the east side, was the maid's room. The Boy Scouts, in the village, kept their drums there. Bernard was wanting to play with them; I didn't know if they would like that. I should have got him a drum of his own.

A door from the kitchen led through into the 'dairy', where they used to make butter and cheese. There were stone shelves along the east wall.

Beyond was the washroom with windows looking to the east. A door led out into the yard. Bread was put on the bench in the washroom to keep it fresh. I had to watch that I didn't leave the door open, or the goats would eat it. There were two stone tubs under the window. And to the right of the door, as you came in, was a copper. I used it not for boiling clothes, but for bottling fruit. There was a hand-driven mangle between the two tubs. I got terribly tired in that place.   There was no technology to help me. But there was electricity; some people didn't have that. The organist was Miss Crombie.   In her house in 1954 when we revisited Newmachar, there was still no electricity.

Behind the glebe house, was a byre in which the ducks and goats lived. Beyond the byre was a barn/coach house, which was used in the past for sheltering a coach and horses. In our time, Grandpa (Harry's father) kept his saw horse there, and regularly cut wood on it for the fires.

The villagers had plots on the glebe, which was ploughed up to provide food in wartime.

The staircase between the ground and first floors went up and virtually doubled back on itself. It was steep, with no carpet and painted brown. There was a landing halfway up. In the left back corner of the landing stood the grandfather clock. On the same level was a bathroom and a toilet off it.

The floor above the ground floor we referred to as 'upstairs'. Straight ahead was Alison's bedroom (a dressing room in the 1926 floor plan). On its left was the main bedroom, the same size as the nursery. A toilet table, with a big beautiful round mirror, stood across one corner. From the window you could see Lochnagar. And beyond the main bedroom, at the end of the passage was the guest room. To the right of the staircase was a room that wasn't used much. To begin with, the maid Edith who came with us from Fife and Keltie, slept there. It had a huge brass-knobbed double bed in it.

Beyond this room was Bernard's nursery. In the back right hand corner there was a table. You could lay a baby on it to change its nappy. It had six-inch sides, so the child didn't roll off. Next to the table was a wood stove against the west wall. We had to remove ash each day. It was damped down at night and went through the night. 'Eggs' of coal burnt down to a fine ash. It had cellophane windows and you could see the flames licking up inside it. The window faced south, to the right of it stood Bernard's cot. Bernard could roll it to the window to look out at the cows and the moon.

The stairs went on up to the attics. We didn't go up there often. Only two spacious rooms. To the left was the one where the apples were laid to ripen and store. They did well up there. Cox's Orange Pippins. Gorgeous. We planted an espalier-form apple tree against the western wall of the garden.

I had forgotten how much I enjoyed the garden. But it was far too big. Surrounded by stone walls. Across from the front door, a wrought iron gate - with a fence along either side along the drive - led into the garden. Honeysuckle wound itself around the fence. I loved its scent in the warm summer evenings.

I remember once when Harry (Mr Thornton) was away at a meeting, it was winter, with the snow lying all deep around the manse, there was a blackout. Bernard and I went around this great dark stone house, about our chores and tasks, by the light of a single candle. It was very hard, but it was like a fairy tale, with a full moon outside reflecting off the snow, and shining into the house through all the windows.

If I was worried, or didn't know anything, I was on the phone to the nurse, Margaret Macrae. She was the most wonderful friend.

Agathe Thornton, 2001

Mr Thornton met a convalescent at Kingseat who was brother to a minister in New Zealand and fired Harry Thornton's interest in that country. In 1947 he decided to go there to a lectureship in philosophical psychology at the University of Otago. Mrs Thornton resumed her classical studies and became professor at the University.

Mr Thornton was succeeded in 1948 by the **Rev. Harold Ross 1948-1958.** Harold Ross was born in 1891 at Fraserburgh. His varied early career included service in the Great War in Salonika and working as a student missionary in Ferryhill before he was ordained into the Free Church ministry in 1921. He was the author of the highly valuable description of New Machar provided in the *Third Statistical Account of Scotland* which is drawn on elsewhere in this book. Here his son provides a brief memoir of the ministry of Harold Ross in the parish.

Educated at Robert Gordon's College, Aberdeen University and Christ's College, my father had held Ministries at Gorebridge, Troon and Dundee before being inducted Minister of New Machar in June 1948. This large country parish was in sharp contrast to Dundee where he had had a congregation of a thousand members drawn from many parts of the city.

Church services in New Machar were thinly attended and it took some time before numbers increased. The Sunday School, Bible Class, Women's Guild and Choir attracted more members as new ideas were introduced. There was already a well-established Boys' Brigade Company. Congregational visiting had always been one of his priorities and he was very aware of his responsibility to all people in the Parish, whether or not they had any church connection. He enjoyed cycling the length and breadth of the parish, visiting every cottage, house and farm in order to get to know people. Often the visits were to fields or steadings as people went about their daily work. These visits were in addition to the pastoral care of the sick, the housebound and those with particular needs.

Close links were established with both the New Machar and Whiterashes Schools. Kingseat Hospital was the largest employer in the Parish and although unfortunately he was not chaplain, many of the staff were members of his congregation. Outwith the Parish, he played a full part in the Presbytery of Aberdeen and in Ministry and Church Extension.

My parents had always been accustomed to callers at the Manse and were pleased when the community learned that they were welcome either for pastoral or social visits. The large house and substantial gardens provided both hard work and relaxation, especially when the Church Fête was held there. The garden was highly productive and the profusion of daffodils each Spring meant City congregations could be supplied.

It was in Newmachar that I met my wife and we were married by my father in 1959. Ill-health had brought about his retirement in November 1958. He died at the age of 69 in 1960 and my mother at the age of 87 in 1982.

Angus B Ross
March 2000

In 1959, the **Rev. John Gibson**, shown here with the elders, became minister and served until 1962 when he left to become lecturer in Hebrew at the University of Edinburgh. The **Rev. John M. Paterson** was minister from 1963 until 1968 when he transferred to Ferryden. In 1968 the **Rev. William Claydon** arrived as

minister. Born in 1920, he had an interesting and varied background as a Salvationist and attended the William Booth Memorial Training College before serving in south-west Scotland. Later he met members of the Original Secession Church and then the Nazarene Church which he served in London, Blantyre and Belfast before becoming a Church of Scotland lay reader; he was ordained after further study. During Mr Claydon's ministry, the church pews were repaired and cleaned, the pipe organ removed and an electric one installed and the area under the gallery was refurbished for use as a meeting area for the Women's Guild and other organisations. Many changes were made to the church surroundings but the most striking innovation

was the installation of the back-highlighted cross behind the communion table. The Church also decided to build a new, modern manse beside the original 1781 structure. This was done in 1986.

(The foregoing is based principally on a small cyclostyled pamphlet 'A Brief Sketch' by Mr Claydon, issued in 1983. This is a remarkably frank autobiographical work.)

The **Rev. Ian Dryden** was inducted as minister in June 1988 and served until his retirement in February 2001, when he was succeeded by the **Rev. Manson Merchant**. During Ian Dryden's ministry impressive celebrations were held in 1991 to mark the bicentenary of the Church building itself. The Moderator of the General Assembly attended some of the events. At the beginning of the New Millennium celebrations, sixteen ladies of the Guild decided to mark the occasion with a co-operatively-produced banner, 'the product of many hours of painstaking needlework.' It now hangs in the church and shows a group of people around the cross with the words 'Gather together. Be glad and rejoice.' In the fellowship area of the church there is a communion table and chairs made out of old pews by elder John Gordon who also designed the banner.

In the following account, Ian Dryden describes the church and reflects on some of these developments. Under his stewardship, the membership had advanced to 593 in 1999. There were 37 elders, a Women's Guild of 29 and a Sunday School of 66. Contributions for all purposes totalled well over £36,000 annually.

(i) The Bicentenary Celebrations, 1991

In preparation, a programme of interior decoration and refurbishment of the church was carried out, including the replacement of the organ. The most spectacular aspect of the refurbishment, which as well as re-painting included new carpets and curtains, was undoubtedly to return the sweeping, arched, pine roof beams and carved supports to their glowing wood. Money to finance the whole project was raised in record time. One of the most successful efforts proved to be a cookery book made up from recipes donated by members of the congregation. Funds were also boosted by a well-supported roup at which everything from a bicycle to a bathtub had come under the hammer, and an outstanding craft fayre. The church celebrations to mark the Bicentenary were well and truly launched with a Burns Supper and Ceilidh and continued with a birthday party for the senior citizens, a Gospel Concert for the young folk, a flower festival, fashion show and a St Andrew's Night Ceilidh in Kingseat Hall.

The Rt. Rev. William Macmillan, Moderator of the General Assembly of the Church of Scotland, visited Newmachar for the occasion and voiced his appreciation of the tremendous effort that had been expended in planning, fundraising for and supporting what proved to be a truly memorable event.

(ii) The Parish Church

The 1639 structure was described as a plain rectangular building with round windows at either side. The present building was erected some 200 years ago in 1791 to replace the original 17th century building. In the Reformed tradition, the preaching of the Word of God was central and so the interior of the building would have been dominated by the pulpit placed in the middle of the long south wall, well lit by windows and around which the people might gather. The fact that the finer stained glass windows are to be found on that wall confirms that the congregation was facing that way. Following tradition established in medieval times, the door for the people to enter the church was what is now called the back door, in the west wall where the belfry was placed. When completed, the church had galleries round three sides of the interior and pews in an open square round the pulpit. Some forty years later as times grew more prosperous, the new present entrance to the church was created and included the stairs, the vestry and the double doors.

The church in its present form is the result of a complete renovation and reconstruction carried out in 1913 with new pews, organ and communion table installed. The beauty of the building was further enhanced by the gift of a colourful stained glass window showing St Machar and aspects of parochial history. It was designed by the notable artist, Dr Douglas Strachan, and presented in 1915 to the Church by Miss Margaret Crombie as a family memorial.

Throughout its history, the Church in its provision of places of worship has sought to respond to the needs of people, alterations in its building reflecting changes in society itself. At the time of the bicentenary in 1991, a programme of refurbishment was carried out making the building in the words of most visitors, warm and welcoming. As a millennium project The Kirk Session is currently undertaking an ambitious project seeking both to bring the facilities of the 200 year old building up to a standard acceptable for the 21st century and to meet the requirements of an expanding village. What is planned is a two-storey extension which take the front door to the street, providing disabled access and toilet, a spacious vestibule, better toilet accommodation, a refurbished kitchen and meeting room facilities.

(iii) The Place of the Church

Whatever changes take place the Church will continue to be a landmark, a testimony in stone to centuries of religious devotion. For well over 200 years the Church, proclaiming the Gospel and providing a Christian presence, has figured largely in the life of this parish and community. It was and remains for many a focus for all the key events in the lives of individuals - their celebration of birth, death and marriage. Nor did the community ever fail to return and give thanks at harvest time or to remember its deliverance in time of war. Largely, too, it marked the major festivals of the Church such as Easter and Christmas. From the Church's teaching, from its fellowship, folk have drawn strength over the centuries to face the challenges and tragedies of life. God willing this will always be the case.

No longer, however, can the Church claim to be the dominant presence in the community that it once was. Its role in parish relief, in schooling, in caring for the sick has been largely taken over by agencies of the state. Nonetheless its influence is still exerted through the membership of the Church and the leading roles they often play in village organisations. By the same token the parish minister no longer holds the once powerful and privileged position of former days, commanding respect as of right. In today's world such respect is earned only through service to the people of the parish.

Ian Dryden

****

The church building from the exterior is seen in the photograph with Chapter VII.

Chapter XIV
Civil Government c. 1800 to 2001: Politics, Law and Order,
the Poor Law and Local Government

Until the Local Government (Scotland) Act of 1889 became operative in 1891, the parish of Newmachar remained split into two halves. The northern part was a part of the county of Banff - a consequence of the fact that most of it was part of the Straloch estate originally owned by a Banff family. This northern half of the parish was separated from the south by a strip of land 300 yards wide which was technically part of the parish of Udny - in this case because it was part of Torryleith estate property. Both the strip and the southern part of New Machar parish were part of the County of Aberdeen.

This peculiar and anomalous situation was only one sign of what, to modern eyes, seems a chaotic system of local government with all sorts of different authorities overlapping in their functions and jurisdictions. For the most part the system before 1889 had grown up in a haphazard way in the seventeenth and eighteenth centuries. The surprise is that it should last as late as 1889 in essentials. That it did is probably in the main a consequence of the continuing power and influence of the major landholders - the heritors. This is not to say that no attempts were made to change the situation earlier in the nineteenth century. Indeed, the earlier part of the century is often called the 'Era of Reform.' The reforms, however, tended to be piecemeal and because this was the case, the confusions of function overlap tended to get worse.

The problems in the nineteenth century that a modernising economy threw up were social problems which the old machinery was hardly fitted to solve. As pointed out in Chapter XIII, the Church found it very difficult to continue to enforce social discipline. In the field of education (Chap. XVII), social needs and parental expectations put strains on the system of parochial schools and various expedients were tried until in 1872 it was decided to set up a national system of public schools. Law and order problems grew beyond the capacities of parish constables. As far as can be ascertained, even the major upheaval of the enclosure movement in the 1830s did not produce disorders in Newmachar. What would have been obvious, however, was the problem of poverty. Old style crises of rural society such as those of the 1690s and the early 1780s tended to be the result of adverse weather conditions with resulting bad harvests. In the early nineteenth century this sort of crisis (at least in eastern Scotland if not in parts of the Highlands and, of course, Ireland) was less of a problem because food could be brought in easily. On the other hand, the increasing orientation of Newmachar agricultural activity to market demands and the sharpening of economic distinctions between farmer employers and labour led to new causes of poverty. The operation of the trade cycle of alternating booms and slumps affected even predominantly rural areas. Satisfactory solutions to the problems of alleviating, much less of curing poverty, began to seem beyond the capabilities of the heritors and kirk session. The state would step in to try to improve and regularise the system of poor relief.

Political Change

It seems unlikely that the official politics centred on government and parliament in London caused much stir among people in Newmachar in the early nineteenth century. In the 1806 election, for example, only one of the County of Aberdeen's 126 electors lived in Newmachar. This was Peter Burnet of Elrick House. He voted for the losing candidate Alexander Hay. (John Patrick, 'The 1806 Election in Aberdeenshire,' *Northern Scotland* 1 (1973) 151-176.) Presumably Mr Ramsay at Straloch had a vote in Banff. The Great Reform Act did not make much difference; the County Parliamentary representatives were chosen by a still very small number of electors. Generally, the Tories held the county through the influence of the Earls of Aberdeen although the Liberals were to capture the county in 1857. (*Papers on Scottish Electoral Politics*, ed. J.I. Brash, Edinburgh, 1974 p. 220ff.)

General Administration

An act of 1667 had established Commissioners of Supply who, working through the heritors in any local area were supposed to arrange valuations and resulting taxation and to manage the maintenance of roads, bridges and so on. The commissioners were forced to adopt an improved system of valuation in 1854 and, though they lingered on, they lost most of their functions in 1889.

There was a system of Lord Lieutenants and Depute Lieutenants representing the Crown in the counties. Strictly speaking, their original function was to raise and train the militia - a military force recruited by ballot and highly unpopular. In practice, the Lieutenants had more popular success with genuinely volunteer forces set up later. They took on other functions such as becoming magistrates and were generally leaders of local society. Naturally, the Earl of Aberdeen was normally Lord Lieutenant but John Ramsay III became Depute Lieutenant as later did his great grandson, Major Irvine.

Law and Order

From 1661 there were supposed to be two constables in each of Scotland's parishes. This rarely became the case because it was difficult to find suitable men and even more difficult to raise money to pay them. Technically, it was the job of those appointed as justices of the peace to appoint the constables for any parish. J.P.s dealt with minor criminal matters and were supposed to enforce legislation. The administration of justice at a higher level became more efficient when hereditary sheriffdoms were abolished in 1748. By and large sheriffs were drawn from, allied to, and appointed by the landed classes and this was the case for Aberdeenshire. (Ann E. Whetstone, *Scottish County Government in the*

Eighteenth and Nineteenth Centuries, Edinburgh, 1981; James E. Shaw, *Local Government in Scotland*, Edinburgh, 1942; Christopher Whatley, *Scottish Society 1707-1830*, Manchester, 2000, pp. 147, 286-90; David Moody, *Scottish Local History*, London, 1986, has a useful appendix on Local Government functions, pp. 146-153.)

For a parish like Newmachar, the crucial figure in the nineteenth century was the village constable. There is no evidence of any police function in the parish earlier than the 1830s. In fact there were various police acts in the 1830s and '40s but the crucial one for Newmachar was 1839 when the Commissioners of Supply were empowered to establish rural constables. From about that time there seems to have been a police presence in Newmachar with a police constable based in the village up to the later twentieth century. John Forbes was in office in 1841; he was only 20 years old. William Booth was also 20 in 1851 but Alex Matthew in 1861 was 24. By 1891 a police station and house had been established and William Scott was the constable. (Census Returns and Valuation Rolls.)

The police house was on a site between the parochial school and the church (now replaced by a pair of bungalows on School Road). There was a cell attached to the house. (Testimony of Mr Bert Sangster.) Later, the police house was moved to a larger building on the Old Meldrum Road. It is now privately owned, but has kept its name of The Police House. For the most part, the Newmachar constable no doubt dealt with minor crimes of drunkenness and poaching etc. although there was a case of sheepstealing in Whiterashes in 1912. (*Aberdeen Journal*, 19 March 1912.) Police were supposed to deal not only with crime and related matters but also public needs such as water supply, sewage and scavenging. In practice they were ill-equipped to do so and more and more of such functions were taken on by the Parochial Boards originally set up in 1845 to deal with Poor Law administration.

The Parochial Board, 1845-1895
At the parish level, the relief and management of the poor was the major problem, the Act of 1579 having established the key principle that authorities could 'Taxe and stent haill the inhabitants within the parochin acording to the estimation of their substance.' (Jean Lindsay, *The Scottish Poor Law...1745-1845*, Ilfracombe, 1975, provides background and examples from the Northeast.)

The authorities were the minister and kirk session meeting jointly with the heritors. Half the financial burden would fall on the heritors and half on their tenants. Powers were further defined in 1698 following the disastrous famine years of the 1690s when perhaps a fifth of Aberdeenshire's population died.

By 1842, the general level of prosperity in New Machar had increased at the cost of a higher proportion of poor; there were now 32 poor out of a population of 1262 compared with 12 out of 1031 in 1790. The annual cost of relieving the 32 paupers was £52.16s. Then in 1845 the Scottish Poor Law Act established parochial boards made up of heritors, kirk session representatives, magistrates and two elected representatives. While the basic composition of the Board represented the traditional power structure in the parish, the addition of elected representatives was a sign of changed times. Moreover, there was to be a salaried official to administer the system and the local surgeon, John Christie, was to advise the board on medical matters. Much hinged on whether a claimant was considered fit to work. 'Outdoor relief' in the form of grants of money or sometimes supplies, eg of coal, might be provided to the relatively able-bodied. Those who needed 'indoor relief' - that is accommodation in a poor house had to be sent in to Aberdeen or perhaps Old Meldrum until Newmachar got its own poor house. Of course, the Aberdeen House of Refuge had to be paid for looking after any of Newmachar's poor.

The first election to the board proved interesting. The Rev George Moir (Free Church) was proposed by John Law, the Innkeeper, and Mr Dawson; Mr James Leslie (Merchant and Postmaster) was proposed by Mr William Singer, the tailor, and Mr George Smith, the shoemaker of Reisque. Both were appointed to the Board. In the early days the major heritors thought it appropriate to send lawyers along to the Board meetings to represent them. John Gordon of Parkhill at least, assumed his representative should be Chairman. But by the 1860s it was becoming apparent that it was more convenient all round if one or other of the two clergymen in the parish took the chair.

The first meeting of New Machar's Board was on 25th September 1845 when 29 poor were identified and Mr A. Harvey was appointed Inspector of Poor. A little later, the Parochial Schoolmaster, Mr McHardy became Assistant Inspector. The first case dealt with was Susan Buchan, a 74-year old widow from Burnside, Kinmundy. She was a partially-disabled domestic servant. She was awarded 12s 6d quarterly. For the next 50 years nearly all the cases involved agricultural labourers or domestic servants.

Extracts from the Minutes:

9 Feb 1846: Janet Laing claimed for her child alleging that Robert Duncan, a farm servant at Swailend (Mr Low) was the father; he denied it. Awarded 1s. 6d for six weeks pending a court case.

9 March 1846: Voluntary subventions of £50 from the Heritors and £50 divided between the Kirks were suggested but Free Church unhappiness meant a rate had to be fixed (see below).

7 Jan 1847: Alexander Walker of Old Town of Brownhills has a wife lodged in Aberdeen Lunatic Asylum but is father of a family by a second marriage. Required to pay £5 a year towards the cost of lodging his first wife at the Asylum.

22 Feb 1847: Alexander Gibbon complains of his assessment for the poor rate; it is reduced by 1s 10½d.

27 Aug 1847: Is Alex Niven the father of Barbara's Findlay's child?

24 Oct 1848: Measures are to be taken to compel residents to remove nuisances which might cause cholera.

(Minutes of the Parochial Board , 1845-56, AC 6/59/1)

There was some initial difficulty in Newmachar over raising money. At first, they tried to proceed by donations: the proposal was that the heritors should raise £50 and the Kirk and Free Kirk £50 between them. But John Thomson of Mameulah, representing the Free Kirk, was doubtful whether they could raise enough. In fact £100 was not enough anyway. In the end, the provisions of the Act allowing a rate to be set had to be applied. Heritors were to pay half what was needed and tenants the other half, individual payment being in proportion to their rents. The table shows how money was raised.

How the costs of Poor Relief were met in New Machar

In 1847, the gross value of owners' rentals was	£4786. 3s. 4½d.
the rental of tenancies was	£5386. 17s. 5d.
A rate of 5d on owners yields	£99. 14s. 2¾d.
4½d on tenants yields	£102. 16s. 4½d.
providing a total of	£202. 10s. 7¼d.

Property	Owners £ s d	Tenants £ s d
Parkhill	24 5 5	25 4 3½
Straloch	24 7 4	24 7 7½
Elrick	21 15 0	21 9 7½
Rennieshill	14 6 0	14 11 0¾
South Kinmundy	6 10 8¾	6 9 7½
North Kinmundy	5 16 10	5 17 8
Kingseat	1 12 8½	2 0 1¾
Mr Allan (Church of S)	12 11	12 0
Mr Moir (Free Church)	7 3¾	6 9

(Parochial Board Minutes 7 Jan 1847 & 8 Jan 1848, AC 6/59/1)

The Case of Emelia, Martha and Helen

On 30 October 1848, three very small girls aged seven and under turned up at the tailor's shop of Mr Alexander Burgess at the Kinmundy crossroads, having walked from Old Meldrum. Their mother, Matilda Smith, had died of scarlet fever. The stepfather of Emelia and father of Martha and Helen had deserted them. He was Angus Robertson, a one-legged man who travelled the country renovating hats. The village constable and Mr Harvey eventually hired a horse and cart to take the three girls to the House of Refuge in Aberdeen.

There the girls stayed until July 1849 when the New Machar Board decided that the charges of 2s 6d per week per child were too much for the ratepayers and sent them to live with the widow Garden who was prepared to accept only 5s per week for all three. The School would give free education to them. Soon Mrs Garden was asking for clothes for 'they came from the House of Refuge almost in a state of nudity.' Clothes were supplied but then the widow asked for shoes but these Inspector Harvey 'did not consider necessary during the Summer months.'

By August 1849, Emelia was about nine years old and was therefore expected to be able to earn some money by herding sheep or the like. Even so, the cost to the Parish went up to 6s per week. Clearly the hat renovator had to be found to take responsibility for his children. It cost £6 to find Angus Robertson but apparently he was persuaded to take the children back. New Machar Parochial Board was relieved of the costs of £15 per annum and Emelia, Martha and Helen disappeared from history. (AC 6/59/1.)

From 1863 there was a separate register of children. In 1868, for example, Catherine Pipe aged two years had to be provided for because her mother had died and her 'father' (who denied paternity) would not support her. Against such distressing cases can be set the fact that there were only thirteen child paupers up to 1913.

Gradually, the parochial boards were given responsibilities beyond looking after the poor, notably the registration of births, marriages and deaths in 1854 (which put an extra halfpenny on the rates), the appointment of a vaccinator and other medical and sanitary officers and the care of lunatics. There was especially a concern about the cleanliness of byres on farms which produced milk; regular limewashing was required. There were ten such farms in 1887 with Mameulah, Westside, Old Goval and Ord of Elrick the most important.

Mr Harvey resigned in 1852 and a new Inspector, *Mr James Glashan*, was appointed. He served until 1876 when his son and successor proved less than satisfactory (see below). Through the 1860s and '70s there were usually about 20-25 poor on the roll. It became customary for either the *Rev James Duguid* of the Free Church or *Rev William R Bruce* of the Established Church to chair the Board and the two churches appeared to co-operate sensibly.

Minutes:

16 April 1870: two extra beds to be taken at Old Machar Poorhouse.

4 Feb 1873: Poor on roll up to 40; a Law Agent appointed.

26 Mar 1884: Mr Peter McAllan, assistant to Mr Cooper (merchant of Summerhill) to become Registrar of births, marriages and deaths at £8 p.a. [He remained in office until he died in 1929.]

16 Nov 1886: The byre at Woodend Farm had not been cleaned and limewashed. Therefore James Henderson is no longer allowed to sell milk.

9 Mar 1887: All future meetings would be in the Public Hall (ie the former school).

20 May 1895: All the books of the Parochial Board were handed over to the new Parish Council.

A Scandal

On the retiral of Mr Glashan as Inspector of Poor in 1876, *Mr Allan Glashan*, presumably his son, was appointed to replace him. But on 14 Jan 1884, it was reported that the younger Mr Glashan had collected £180 10s 6d from ratepayers but recorded only £163 10s 2d. It was further reported that 'The disappearance of money from the safe is still shrouded in mystery and that the Police authorities have been unable to throw any light on the matter.' The Board referred to Mr Glashan's 'gross and culpable negligence in leaving the safe unlocked which he confesses he frequently did…His services as Inspector ought not to be retained.'

The Poor's House at Newmachar

21 Oct 1854 Mr Stephen, on behalf of the Heritors, intimated that they had built a range of dwelling houses for the use of the poor which they offered to hand over on the following conditions, viz.,

That the houses with all their appurtenances should be used by the Parochial Board during the pleasure of the Heritors, free of rent; that the Board agree to pay any Fire Duty liable on them by the Proprietor. (AC 6/59/1.)

The Poor's House was a constant source of discussion and decision for the Parochial Board and for its successor from 1895, the Parish Council.

3 Nov 1890: The well at the Poorhouse had run dry.

2 & 30 Aug: 1892: The cost of deepening the well is 2s. per foot. It is complained that the rooms in the Poorhouse are smoky. (AC 6/59/3)

11 Feb 1896: Jessie Abel refused to go into the Poorhouse. Ann Lumsden, the matron, resigned and, with some dissent of the Council, Mrs Agnes McGregor was appointed in her place.

27 July 1897: A mangle is bought for the house for 32s. Each of the ten adult residents would receive 2s 6d as a Diamond Jubilee gratuity.
(Parish Council Minutes, AC 6/59/4.)

The position of matron continued to cause problems. Another new one was needed in 1899 and no fewer than fourteen ladies applied for the position. *Maggie Collie* was appointed but she fell and injured her arm and so in March 1900 Mrs I. McLean became matron.

Mrs Nicol (testimony of Nov 1999) remembers Mrs Craig as being Matron in the 1920s. Mrs Walker (testimony of October 1999) once lived at Cunnighar Cottage near the Poorhouse on Disblair Road during the post Great War period and sometimes her mother, Mrs Cooper, used to help out the Matron, Mrs Tait. There were two parts to the Poorhouse. In one, Mrs Tait cared for two orphaned boys named Duncan and 'Auld Mary', a blind lady, while in the other Mrs Bruce, a married couple and a mentally-handicapped person looked after themselves but under Mrs Tait's superintendence.

The poorhouse was knocked down in the 1960s and replaced with two modern bungalows.

The Poor House, Disblair Road, Newmachar c.1910

The Parish Council 1895-1929

On 20 May 1895 the Parochial Council, which had been in existence for precisely fifty years, handed over all its books and records to the new Parish Council. (AC 6/59/3) Following the 1889 Local Government Act, the Parochial Boards were in an anomalous position in relation to the new County Councils.

So the 1894 Act set up Parish Councils which were to be largely elected. These councils in turn were to elect one of their members to sit on the district committee of the new County Council (in Newmachar's case, this would be the Aberdeen District of Aberdeen County Council). The responsibilities and powers of the Parish Councils over burial grounds, libraries, rate assessment and still, as yet, the Poor Law, were carefully defined.

The Rev. William Bruce resumed his place as Chairman of the new council in Newmachar and Mr T. Fraser became the Newmachar representative on the District Committee, but soon resigned on becoming a County Councillor. His place on the District Committee was taken by Mr Stoddart. Much of the old type of business came before the Council. Could a new clothes pole be obtained for the Poor's House, could something be done about smokiness in the Matron's room and could the Council afford to buy linders for a poor lady? The local rate was set at 7½d which on a rateable value in the parish of £9387 yielded £293-6s-10½d. But now government grants made the total income up to £368. In addition a school rate of 7d was set.

Under the 1894 Act, heritors in a parish could seek to be relieved of their responsibilities for burial grounds. Accordingly in 1901, the Newmachar heritors asked the Parish Council to take over responsibility for the kirkyard and all its graves. The Parish Council refused; they feared inheriting debts and expenses. However, the heritors insisted as they said the legislation entitled them to do. They also insisted that the Council must become responsible for the new burial ground which was planned for School Road. There was a public meeting on the issue on 27th June 1901 - 99 years and ten months before another public meeting on kirkyard problems which have been exercising the current generation of Newmachar's residents. It seems that the Parish Council was persuaded that it must take on the responsibility for both the old and the new burial grounds and, of course, their successors, Aberdeenshire Council, remain responsible. (AC 6/59/4: Minute Book 1895-1909.)

By 1906 the elected representative on the District from Newmachar was Alex Reid, a farmer of Eastertoun. It is interesting to note that the Aberdeen District Committee was still dominated by the major lairds, Mr Crombie of Parkhill, Mr Burnet of Elrick plus some of the larger tenant farmers. (*Aberdeen Almanac for 1906.*)

By this period, too, the Parish Council itself was becoming a more sophisticated body, setting up its own sub-committees for Finance, the Lodging House, and Burial Grounds. Four rates were set - for Poor, Registration, Burials and Education (although the Education Board remained separate). Just after the Great War broke out it was judged unwise to go ahead with the creation of a 'Central Pleasure Ground' in the village. Instead, the Council was soon involved raising money to help the French of the invaded district, or Prisoners of War and children of soldiers killed in action.

On 11th December 1917 it was suggested that a few lectures on vegetable growing might be helpful for Newmachar residents (since this was a period of food shortages in Britain as a result of German U-boat activity). Mr Hood Smith, the minister, had allowed the East Glebe land to be taken over for allotments. However, it was reported of the allotments:

> They were well cultivated and produced an abundant supply of potatoes
> and other vegetables. This district is wholly agricultural and those
> holding plots are acquainted with agricultural work and the Council
> are of the opinion that lectures are unnecessary.

In July 1918 Mr Harvey of Monykebbock died having been Chairman of the Council for 16½ years. He was said to have been characterised by his 'urbanity and fair-mindedness.' The *Rev A. Hood Smith* took his place.

Less than a month after the Armistice in 1918, Mr Murray moved that a memorial should be erected 'to those who had fallen in the recent war.' The result is recorded in Chapter XX. The Parish Council became formally responsible for the memorial in 1924.

During and after the war, the poor continued to be a subject of major concern and the Council were pleased in 1921 to receive a donation of £5 from the Newmachar Horticultural Society to help alleviate their problems.

1922 was a landmark date in social provision when the first public housing in Newmachar was built on Disblair Road. The new council houses were named Ash, Beech, Elm, Larch, Oak and Rowan Cottages. A landmark of a different kind was the winding up of the Rainnieshill Estate in 1922-3. This was the estate once owned by the Thomson family who had such an impact on the parish. (See Chap. XIII.) The Parish Council bought two small houses for public purposes - although not without some haggling over the price with lawyers.

By November 1923 the Council found themselves protesting at the Government's intention to abolish Parish Councils. Despite this the Council continued to be very active, trying for example, to buy the Village Hall arguing that the trustees committee set up when the building was acquired was now 40 years old and self-perpetuating. They failed to dislodge the trustees as a lawyer was found by the trustees to defend their position.

There was a little more success eventually in getting Aberdeen County Council to renovate the Monykebbock Churchyard - something their successors on the Community Council in the late 1990s failed to achieve. By September 1928 the Council thought a speed limit was necessary for the village. Aberdeen County Council did not agree. (AC 6/59/5.)

In 1929 Mr Peter McAllan, who had been Inspector of Poor for 44 years and latterly clerk to the Council, died. He was said to have displayed 'tact and devotion'. By this period there were ten poor and five lunatics. In 1929 argument raged again about Monykebbock and the condition of the War

Memorial.   The arguments became intense enough for Mr Souter, the headmaster, to be voted out of his position as Chairman of the Council. Almost as its last act as it faced abolition under the 1929 Local Government Act, the Parish Council finally obtained control of the Village Hall. On 7th May the affairs of the Council were wound up.   There was a balance of £13-0s-5d to hand over to Aberdeen County Council. (AC 6/59/12.)

From the 1929 Act to the 1973 Act
A full set of records of Aberdeen County Council's proceedings exist and from this can be constructed an account of decisions that impinged on Newmachar. It must be said, however, that it was unfortunate that Newmachar now had no local elected council of any kind, the School Board also having been superseded by the County some ten years before. There were, of course, economies of scale as a result of the County Council taking over all local functions and access, also, to much more expertise in the shape of salaried officials.

There was a realisation that there had been local losses as well as county-wide gains in the operation of the 1929 Act. Accordingly, the 1973 Act set up Grampian Region but also, for certain functions, Districts - which were supposed to be more responsive to local needs. Newmachar became part of Gordon District. Even more significant was the fact that there was provision for the setting up of Community Councils.

Newmachar Community Council's constitution dates from 1978. Although it has nothing like the power of the old Parochial Board or Parish Council, it is at least closer to ordinary residents than the old Aberdeen County Council or Grampian Region and now Aberdeenshire authorities.

Once again, the records exist for the history of the Community Council to be written. There are its own minutes and the Newsletters which it has published since 1978. The major issues tend to involve planning matters. The Grain Store at Whiterashes in 1984 led to the Community Council being at odds with their elected councillor, Mr Paul Miller. Despite the Council's protests, the store was opened in 1985 and the Ombudsman did not uphold the Community's complaint against Gordon District Council.   1988 saw the first (then unsuccessful) attempt to put up Christmas lights. 1991 saw great arguments about the proposed sand and gravel quarrying at Greendams Farm. Again the Council's protests were unavailing. Following the closure of Kingseat Hospital, the Council began to concern itself about what sort of housing development would come to the site. Ironically, on this occasion, it approved the developer's plans only to see them turned down by Aberdeenshire on the advice of Historic Scotland. There is now a speed limit in the village but a pedestrian crossing is needed. As noted in the case of the burial ground, some local problems seem not to change even if a new millennium has arrived. There is now fruitful co-operation with the elected councillors, Jock McGregor (up till 1998) and latterly

Dr Martin Ford, and through them to the Area Committee of Aberdeenshire Council. A Forum of Community Councils also exists. It is to be hoped that at last the right balance has been struck between central provision and local interests. The heritors could manage things easily enough in 1800; unfortunately the Community Council does not have the powers that they were able to deploy.

The Opening of the New Village Hall on February 14th 1955
(See Chapter XXII)

Chapter XV
Great and Small Houses in the Nineteenth and Twentieth Centuries

Chapters V to IX have shown the importance of the emergence of the larger estates as economic units. They were also important social units well into the twentieth century. Unless the laird was living elsewhere, each estate's life was centred on the great house where the proprietor and the family lived. The great house also provided the points of contact with the wider world of the county, Scotland and Great Britain. In the homes of the most important figures, business was transacted, political negotiations took place and administrative matters were arranged. Less formally, country house parties and sporting occasions provided the means by which the leading families forged links with one another at the county and national levels. Straloch House provides the best examples of these aspects of life in Newmachar simply because some of the evidence is available, but it is clear that the other estates and houses functioned in a similar way.

Only two of the great houses remain as notable examples of architecture. Ian Shepherd judges Straloch House to be 'serene' but is more critical of the near contemporary Elrick House as 'crisp, if a little bland.' Parkhill House, whatever grandeur it might once have had, is now demolished. (Ian Shepherd, *Gordon, An Illustrated Architectural Guide*, Edinburgh, 1994, pp. 218-18.)

Rather smaller estates like North and South Kinmundy were hardly in the same league as Straloch, Elrick and Parkhill. Nevertheless they, too, had importance for their tenants. Some of the tenants themselves became important enough men to rival smaller landowners in property. Enclosure meant that many farmhouses now became substantial dwellings. The Harveys at Monykebbock are an example of an important tenant family. In a different way, the manufacturing Crombie family also grew important enough to rank with the major lairds well before the end of the nineteenth century. Changing economic conditions meant more well-built stone houses were erected in Summerhill village in the nineteenth century; indeed for the first time what can really be termed a village emerged after about 1840. (See Chaps. XI and XXIV.) Perhaps, but more slowly, the standard of living for the rural labouring families also began to improve.

One important fact to remember about households in the nineteenth century is that even the proprietor of a small house would employ one or two servants. Both of the manses in Newmachar in 1881 had two servants living-in. Swailend Cottage in the 1840s and '50s had five servants and a boy. At Straloch House in 1851 there were nine living-in servants plus a butler installed in a separate house. This little community existed within the much larger community of the estate and farm workers. A related fact is that domestic service represented almost the only possible means of employment for women; to become a lady's maid in one of the great houses was to have one of the plum jobs.

Each house, whether large mansion or relatively modest 'two up-two down' village house with one maid of all work, represented a family centre which was both an economic and social investment. The great houses and estates affected the lives of many people. But there is also information on one or two less important houses.

Straloch House

As Chapter VII has shown, the Ramsay family began its association with Straloch in 1770. John Innes, who took the name Ramsay after marrying Mary Ramsay, died in 1814. Their son, also John, married Susan Innes (1802-1887). This John died in 1832 when their son, another John Ramsay, was only one year old. As Chapter XVI shows, Susan Innes had a sister, Christina, who had married William Shand, attorney and West Indies planter who had retreated from his creditors to Straloch in 1835. Then in 1844 the widow, Susan, married Captain William Henry Nares of the Royal Navy and they lived at Straloch.

Captain Nares himself was a widower with children, four surviving including a young son who was to become Admiral Sir George Nares (1831-1915) and a daughter Maria who married John Gordon Cuming Skene of Parkhill.

The last John Ramsay had actually been born in 1831 at The Burn, Fettercairn, then owned by William Shand. Presumably, John Ramsay's mother was visiting her sister. The young John Ramsay in 1832 became the owner of Straloch but was also at the centre of a network of family relationships which embraced the Ramsays, the Innes, the Shands, the Nares and, slightly more distantly, the Gordon Cuming Skenes of Parkhill. Through his great grandmother, another connection, as Chapter VII shows, was the Shepherd family. Captain Shepherd lived at Straloch for a time up to 1844.

John Ramsay grew up and became a scholar of Trinity College, Cambridge, and could have become a don, but thought he must return to relieve his mother, Mrs Nares, of the management of Straloch. Perhaps mother and son did not see eye to eye about everything. When some stables were burnt down in the 1870s the replacements, built at her son's direction, were so little to her taste that she had a new path built beside the burn in Middleton Wood so that she did not have to walk past the new buildings. But she loved the garden shown here. Mrs Nares died in 1887. (Information from Major Francis Irvine; Temple, pp. 321-9; Henderson, pp. 450-2.)

The importance of John Ramsay as a public figure in Aberdeenshire has been described in connection with the development of transport. (Chap. XI.) He had a wide circle of friends and acquaintances. Probably his closest associate was his cousin, Alexander Shand.

Alexander Innes Shand (1832-1907)

Shand was the son of William Shand and his wife Christina Innes and like his friend and cousin, John Ramsay, had been born at The Burn. He graduated from King's College, Aberdeen, in 1852, and eventually became a lawyer but practised little and eventually moved to the south of England and began to write for *The Times, Blackwood's Magazine, The Saturday Review* and other periodicals, especially about his travels to Europe and America. As a correspondent he reported on the Franco-Prussian War in 1870. Shand also tried his hand at novels without great success. Even so, the great Anthony Trollope nominated him to the Athenaeum Club. Trollope's rather barbed joke was to make Shand the model for Alfred Booker, a minor and slightly dubious character in *The Way We Live Now* (1873) 'who was not above writing favourable reviews of inferior books in exchange for similar favours for his own.' One of the novels Booker reviewed was *The Wheel of Fortune* which echoes Shand's own novel, *Fortune's Wheel.* An alternative theory is that Shand was represented in Trollope's novel by 'Ferdinand Alf' a hard-bitten editor. Whichever version is right, Shand got his revenge with a rather patronising review of Trollope's work in 1877. All this serves to indicate that Shand was a well known figure in the Victorian literary world. He seems frequently to have visited Straloch and some of his writings, especially his 'Memories of Gardens' originally published in *The Saturday Review*, and in 1908 as a book, describe Straloch. Similarly, his *Shooting* (1899) draws on his sporting experiences on the Straloch lands. (Information from Major Irvine; *DNB*; R.C. Terry, *Oxford Companion to Trollope*, 1999, pp. 487-8; W. & J. Gerould, *Guide to Trollope*, 1983, p. 29; N.J. Hall, *Trollope*, 1993, p. 412.) Shand described Straloch's walled garden as 'lying fair square like a New Jerusalem.' There were clove carnations with 'a bouquet suggestive of the Spice Islands or a bottle of old Burgundy.'

W. S. Gilbert

W. S. Gilbert had become a friend of Ramsay's although it is not clear how, and it seems that he was a frequent visitor to Straloch in the 1870s. Early in his

career, Gilbert had intended to enter the Army but the Crimean War ended too soon. He therefore became a captain in the militia - in this case the third battalion of the Gordon Highlanders. He retired in 1883 with the rank of major. One oddity about Gilbert's association with Straloch is that he did not like shooting. What did he do whilst all the house party members went out killing pheasants? (*DNB*, which however, does not mention Straloch; information from Major Irvine.) The photograph was taken in Aberdeen at the time of one his visits. Perhaps Straloch was above all an agreeable retreat from arguments with Sir Arthur Sullivan.

Shooting Parties

A game book of 1869 indicates what kind of sport men like Shand, if not Gilbert, would have enjoyed at Straloch. On October 26th and 27th for example, a largish party was assembled. It included Major John Ramsay himself, H. Nares, Sir G. Abercrombie, William Forbes, Sir A. Grant, Major King and others. 77 pheasant were shot on the first day and 69 on the next, 40 and 33 hares, 39 and 29 rabbits but only seven partridge on each day. All this was achieved despite drifting snow. The book indicates how the shot game was disposed of. Some went to tenants and friends such as Mr Cruickshank at Sittyton or helpful people like the Stationmaster at Dyce, but the greater part went to market; shooting was not an entirely uneconomic operation.

Mary Ramsay, Mrs Irvine (1859-1938)

Although John Ramsay clearly lived life to the full as a public figure and country gentleman, his personal circumstances had elements of tragedy. In 1858 he had married Leonora Bond who bore him a daughter, Mary, in 1859. But in 1862 there was an accident: Mrs Ramsay's crinoline caught fire, she was badly burnt and subsequently died of pneumonia. John Ramsay did not remarry and when he died in 1895, it was once again - as in 1787 - a Mary Ramsay who inherited the estate. Mary had in 1882 married Francis Irvine of Drum. She ran Drum for a time after her husband's death but when her eldest son, Alexander, came of age returned to Straloch and, aided by her aunt Christina Ramsay (1833-1915), looked after it until her second son, Quentin Irvine, came of age in 1909. In 1908 she initiated the building of St Mary's Chapel at Straloch for family services and burials. 'Mary and her father had owned Straloch for 107 years between them when she died in 1938'. (Major Irvine's testimony.) George Davidson remembered Mrs Irvine as a good and improving landlord and also

Straloch Tenants at Major Irvine's Coming of Age

recalled the celebrations when Quentin Irvine came of age; there was a great bonfire on Torryleith Hill. (Davidson, p. 15.)

Mrs Quentin Irvine was active in many local concerns during and after her husband's lifetime. She became President of the County of Aberdeen Branch of the British Red Cross Society. She had been closely associated with the formation of the Women's Rural Institute in Newmachar in May 1926 and became its first president.

Mr Quentin Irvine died in 1941 and was succeeded by Major Francis Irvine who has up to 2001 kept the estate going as an entity and a sporting estate.

The Grampian Field Sports Fair

The most notable example of Straloch's continuing importance for field sports was the Grampian Field Sports Fair which was held every year from 1985 to 1998 in the Front Park. Gun dogs, archery, falconry, rifle and air-gun shooting, fly casting, clay pigeon shooting were among the attractions, whilst there was usually a pipe band to enliven proceedings. Also associated with Straloch is the British Bavarian Warmblood Society; there is an important collection of stallions, mares and foals owned by Mr and Mrs Fichtner who now live at Sittyton. In 1996 the Fair, renamed the County Fair' attracted 15000 spectators. (Information from Major Irvine and Grampian County Fair programmes.)

Elrick House

As Chapter VII has shown, the Elrick estate was owned by the Burnett family from 1663 and the present splendid Elrick House built in the 1780s. John Burnett (1745-1822) was succeeded by his son, Peter (1792-1870). It seems that this Peter Burnett spent much of his life in Italy, possibly for health reasons. He it was who is supposed to have brought back the 'Fassfern Rose' a Jacobite rose from the villa in Rome once occupied by Bonnie Prince Charlie, a specimen of which grows in the Elrick gardens. Because Peter Burnett spent much time out of the country, Elrick House itself was often occupied by short term tenants. Much the same situation seems to have continued under the fourteenth laird, also Peter, after he inherited in 1870.

J. W. Cruickshank (1842-1918)

Perhaps the most distinguished and interesting figure among the nineteenth-century Elrick tenants was John W. Cruickshank. He occupied the house from about 1882 until 1892. It may well be because Cruickshank, too, frequented Italy that he had had contact with the Burnetts. However, Cruickshank had other important links with the area since he was part of the Quaker family associated with Sittyton and its cattle. (See Chap. IX.) John Cruickshank was the nephew of Amos and son of Anthony who had developed the famous breed of shorthorns. John apparently spent some time helping his uncle Amos with

Tenants at Elrick House in the Early Twentieth Century

A Shooting Party at Elrick in 1911

(Both photographs by kind permission of Mr and Mrs Alexander Ingram)

the cattle business. But this was after he had served an apprenticeship as an engineer in Leeds and then engaged in cotton spinning in Blackburn. Back in the Northeast, he took over the Oatmeal Milling Company at Lethenty, which seems to have been started by his grandparents, became a director of the Aberdeen Jute Mill and also the North of Scotland Bank. Lethenty is shown in some of his photographs and the mill can be seen alongside the branch railway line which formerly linked Inverurie to Oldmeldrum. Presumably he became prosperous enough not only to live at Elrick but also to develop his real interests which were in photographing mediaeval, mainly early Christian, art and architecture in Italy. With his wife, Alice (1861-1920), he wrote studies of art and compiled a number of guide books to Italy and particularly to its Christian Art, eg. *Christian Rome* (1906) and *The Smaller Tuscan Towns* (1912). It is not clear how far these interests had developed whilst Cruickshank was a tenant of Elrick. Whilst living there he clearly intended to identify himself with Elrick and Newmachar, and got himself elected to the School Board for the period 1882-85. Later on, however, he seems to have decided to move south and built himself a large house at Haslemere in Surrey. At that time, about 1892, he liquidated his milling business and sold the premises. So his real life began when he was fifty years old. He died in 1918, leaving 1000 volumes of art works, religious and historical studies, plus thousands of photographs and negatives, to the British School in Rome. There were some platinum as well as nitrate prints which were very effective in portraying the interiors of buildings and the texture of stone used. It seems that even in the 1890s Cruickshank was using a telephoto lens to catch the detail high up in roofs. His photographs are important in their own right and also as a record of much important mediaeval architecture. Cruickshank himself said that his aim was to understand the monuments he photographed 'as material embodiments of the spirit of the age.' Romanesque and Gothic architecture attracted him most and he disliked St Peter's in Rome. Cruickshank's work and particularly his photographic legacy is now being re-evaluated for the British School as a result of the initiatives taken by Professor Alistair Crawford. He believes Cruickshank to be one of the finest of architectural photographers who, despite his Quaker background, displayed a real passion for his subject and a great willingness to experiment.

(This account is based on information supplied by Professor Alistair Crawford, originally of Fraserburgh, now of the School of Art at the University of Aberystwyth and on his preliminary article, 'John William Cruickshank (1842-1918), Mediaeval Photographer' in *Studies in Photography* (2000-2001) ed. Julie Lawson, Edinburgh, 2002.)

Elrick in the Twentieth Century: Mr and Mrs Burnett-Whyte

It would appear that Mr Burnett himself became resident at Elrick in the early 1900s. Photographic evidence shown here suggests that Elrick became again the centre of an active agricultural estate and also a great house where country pursuits took place. Nevertheless, the Burnett family appear to have been unable to maintain the estate after the Great War and in 1926 it passed into the hands of an Aberdeen advocate, Mr Burnett Whyte. He and his wife became active in the parish and its various organisations. Mrs Burnett Whyte was the president of the WRI for many years, and used her gardens for summer picnics, when the members' children were invited to enjoy the grounds. After 1939, she also organised work parties to knit garments for the troops, and entertained convalescent patients from Kingseat Hospital at Elrick during the war when it had become a military hospital. After the death of Mrs Burnett Whyte, the estate and the house was sold to Mr Charles Ingram in 1956. (See Chap. XXIII.)

Parkhill

By 1850 the Parkhill estate embraced most of the southern part of Newmachar and land in the parishes of Old Machar and Dyce. At its centre was a house, refurbished in 1861, described in 1901 as a 'handsome and commodious' mansion, (F.H. Groome, *Ordnance Gazeteer of Scotland*, Edinburgh, 1901, p. 1285.) which is no longer in existence. John Gordon Cuming Skene, (1761-1828) (see Chap. VII) took over the estate in 1815 after a distinguished military career. His son of the same name (1826-1882) was a powerful and influential man who unusually, though by no means uniquely among landowners, supported the Free Church. He was chairman of the School Board from 1879 until his death in 1882 and also a member of Dyce and Old Machar Boards. A director of the Infirmary in Aberdeen, he was also a Depute Lieutenant for the County. He married a daughter of Captain Nares and thus had strong links with Straloch. Eleven carriages followed the coffin on his death and obituaries described him as 'the poor man's friend' because of his concern for social and religious matters. (*Aberdeen Journal*, 10 March 1882.) His son and heir, Alexander, (1857-94) followed the family tradition of army service, fighting in the war against the Zulus in 1879 before returning to take over Parkhill. His son, John Gordon Cuming Skene born c.1886 had to sell the estate in 1927. The mansion house itself had been leased for some time to James Edward Crombie of the famous cloth firm and he eventually bought it; his widow remained in the house until the 1960s.

Gavin Greig (1856-1914)

Gavin Greig was born in the North Lodge on the Parkhill Estate. Although his later career as a schoolmaster, playwright and, above all, collector of folk songs developed when he was at Whitehill, three miles from Maud, his early life at Parkhill was important. Encouraged by Mr Cuming Skene, the young man became closely involved with the Free Church and its music. In fact, he spent so much time on church music, it is said that his academic work at Dyce Parish School, and the Old Aberdeen Grammar School rather suffered: he was fourth bursar rather than first when he went up to King's College in 1872. After graduating, this brilliant young man entered the Free Church College intending a career as a minister. However, what today would not be seen as a scandal at all in his relationship with Mary Moir, who was to become his wife, meant he had to withdraw from the College. The loss to the College and the Free Church was a gain for the music and the culture of the Northeast. His early life in Newmachar was at least an important formative influence in preparing Gavin Greig for his enormous achievements in the years that were to follow. It is of interest, but not necessarily gratifying, to note that the funeral oration for Greig referred to his Newmachar origins debarring him from being a real Buchan man. (This short account is based on information provided by Dr Ian Olson, long associated with editing the *Greig-Duncan Folk Song Collection* in the eighth volume of which his definitive biography of Greig will appear in 2002. Dr Olson has also prepared the entry on Greig for the forthcoming *New DNB*.)

Rainnieshill

The Thomson family had taken possession of the Rainnieshill estate from the middle of the eighteenth century. The owners were largely absentee, their main holdings and mansion house being at Banchory-Devenick. Nevertheless Rainnieshill functioned as a very efficient agricultural unit in the nineteenth century. The estate was of great importance to the history of Newmachar for two particular reasons. The laird, Alexander Thomson (1792-1868) was (see Chap. XIII) a key figure in the events surrounding the Disruption of 1843. Because Newmachar had a minister who went out and his own parish minister did not, he took a close interest in the Free Church in the village. The second reason is that the Rainnieshill estate included most of the area of Sumerhill village which was built up as a settlement and site for several small businesses with the encouragement of Thomson.

A good example of this is provided by the origins of 'Naringa' at 5 Disblair Road whose history is described by its present owner, **Dr John Beattie**.

The triangular area of land on the western boundary of the United Free Church, owned by Alexander Thomson of Banchory, was leased at a rent of one pound a year, to Mr John Reid, who was living at the Mill of Cavil. The 99 year lease was signed in December 1849 and obliged Mr Reid to build within one year, 'a substantial dwelling house of stone and lime and covered with slates to the value of at least twenty pounds Sterling', and to maintain the house at that value. Mr Reid and his wife Elspet (Prott) named the house 'Cavil Cottage' and it retained this name until 1946 when it was changed to 'Naringa'. The property was bounded on the south and west by Cunninghar farm, occupied at that time by Mr Andrew Gibbon, and Mr Reid was obliged to enclose the land with stone walls or dykes. A 20-foot deep stone built well still exists close to the southern boundary. At some time, in the first half of the 20th century, the lean-to extension on the east side of the house is thought to have been used as a dairy. The property has been owner-occupied for many years and has been modified on several occasions, notably in

1979, when the western end was partitioned and sold for the construction of a house at 5A Disblair Road. A further substantial extension to 'Naringa' was built in 1993.

Name	Occupation	Dates	Price
Mr John & Mrs Elspet Reid	Retired Miller	1849-1859	£20
Mr Anthony Beveridge	House Carpenter	1859-1907	
Mr William Beveridge		1907	
Mr William Gauld	Dairyman	1907-1917	
Mr & Mrs George Christie	Merchant	1917-1928	£145
Mr Harry Duncan	Postman	1928-1932	
Mr & Mrs Hugh Kennedy	Retired Gamekeeper	1932-1943	
Mr & Mrs Alexander Fraser	Commercial Traveller	1943-1946	
Miss Annie Ingram		1946-1949	£900?
Mr John Law	Retired Farmer	1949-1971	£2,250
Mr & Mrs Iain Mackinnon	Technician	1971-1973	£4,200
Mr & Mrs Steven Cameron	Chef	1973-1981	£12,750
Mr & Mrs Nigel Mortimer	Helicopter Pilot	1981-1988	£26,000
Dr & Mrs John Beattie	Research Scientist	1988-	£46,500

After Thomson's death, George Thomson of Pitmedden bought the Rainnieshill estate. He was succeeded by his son, Cornelius. From 1900 William Watson, a whisky manufacturer, owned the estate but, like Parkhill, it was soon to be broken up.

North Kinmundy and South Kinmundy

All Kinmundy properties had been held by the Earl of Aberdeen but in 1846 North Kinmundy was sold to Alexander and William Stephen. (Temple, p. 301.) and remained in this family's ownership until the early 1900s. Alexander Wilson, a Civil Engineer, married Elizabeth Stephen and became a J.P. and long-time member of the School Board. They lived at Kinmundy House. However, in 1907 North Kinmundy was acquired by the Trustees of the Cruickshank Botanic Garden in Aberdeen who maintained the estate as an entity. For many years the Trustees would not sell individual properties to the tenants but policy changed and from 1956 the estate was sold off mostly to their tenants. (Testimony of Mr A. Low; AUL Ms 2769.)

Kinmundy South was for many years owned by the Rev. William Mearns and then by his son, Rev. D.G. Mearns of Oyne. William Mearns lived at Woodlands for a time in the 1860s and the younger Mearns in the 1890s but it seems they must have been absentee landlords for most of the time. (Valuation Rolls.)

Other Properties

Kingseat passed into the hands of the City of Aberdeen by the end of the nineteenth century. (See below, Chap. XXI.)

Among lesser houses one of the most interesting is the now demolished **Swailend Cottage** on the site of Newmachar Golf Club House. Despite its name, this was a very substantial house occupied for many years by James and Katherine Crombie and their large family (see Chap. XVI) and later by a succession of tenants including Captain Shepherd (Chap. XIII) and Captain Mars Mourier Pohle - who sounds interestingly exotic. **Monykebbock** was a substantial farmhouse and home to the leading tenant farmer of nineteenth century Newmachar, William Harvey, (1802-1879). He became an M.A. and married the daughter of a naval surgeon late in life and had a large family. His brother was an advocate in Aberdeen. The 1781 **Manse** and the **Free Church Manse** are described in Chapter XIII. In a different but no less important way than the great mansion houses they were also centres of social networks in the nineteenth century.

Each of the houses in Newmachar can be shown to have a fascinating history of its own because each is so intimately bound up with the people who lived in it.

Chapter XVI
Some Connections with the Wider World

As Scotland's connections with the wider world extended from the sixteenth century onwards, there were implications for a parish like Newmachar. There are at least echoes of what were once strong ties between Northeast Scotland and the Baltic and Northern European areas. It was after the Union of 1707 that opportunities for contact with the non-European world greatly increased. As Britain built up an Empire and, much more important, wider spheres of trade and influence all over the world, many individuals were drawn into activities or contacts overseas. The North Sea contacts became relatively less important while the Atlantic system of trade with its focus on the Caribbean and its slave plantations became a vital interest. Then in turn, came the decline of that system and the 'swing to the East', especially of course, India, but also increasing trade to China. These are all developments which have some reflection in Newmachar and, indeed, some impact upon it. So, too, do later nineteenth-century developments when Britain's global supremacy was marked, among other things, by its sending out a series of distinguished scientific explorers one of whom was born in Newmachar.

The Seventeenth Century
Robert Gordon was clearly in touch with the world of geographical enquiry centred on the Netherlands in the early seventeenth century although there is no evidence that he ventured across the North Sea. (See Chap. VI.) Many others from the Northeast did but Newmachar seems not to have produced any of the soldiers of fortune who fought in the European wars of the seventeenth and eighteenth centuries. However, there is the interesting case of Vice-Admiral Sir David Mitchell (c.1650-1710). He is now chiefly remembered for his service in England's navy and for bringing Peter the Great of Russia to London in 1698. He assumed the arms of 'Mitchell of Tillygreig'. (Paul Dukes, 'Some Aberdeen Influences on Early Russian Enlightenment', *Canadian American Slavic Studies*, 13, (1979) p. 445.)

The West Indies and the Atlantic Trade: William Shand at Straloch
John Shand (1759-1825) was an attorney at law who worked in Jamaica. There he acquired several estates, became involved in politics and also extremely rich - rich enough to return home and buy two large estates and, when he died, to leave £5000 each to his ten illegitimate children by his Negro or mulatto 'housekeeper', Frances Brown. (*Lady Nugent's Journal...* 1801-1805, ed. Philip Wright, Kingston, 1966, p. 316.) John Shand's younger brother, William (1776-1845), began to help manage the Jamaica properties in 1818. Under his direction, meticulous lists were kept of the names, ages, and condition of all

slaves and of all the correspondence with the merchants who handled the sales of the slave plantation products - principally sugar and rum. William Shand also preserved much of his private correspondence.

William inherited everything on his brother's death. His first wife having died, he returned to Scotland in 1827 and courted 'the lady who is to be my Rib,' Christina Innes, daughter of Alexander Innes of Pitmedden (with whom he already had business connections). The Innes family was intimately linked with the Ramsay family of Barra and Straloch. (See Chap. VII and Chap. XV.) Mary Ramsay had married John Innes (1755-1814) who adopted the name Ramsay. Their eldest child, John Ramsay, married another daughter of Alexander Innes, Susan (1802-1887). Hence this John Ramsay and William Shand had married sisters and it was not surprising when Shand ran into acute financial difficulties that he should retreat to Straloch where he spent the last ten years of his life from 1835 to 1845. These were clearly not happy years. Shand was declared bankrupt and also said by some of his creditors to be insane.

William Shand was in part a victim of changing circumstances. The slave trade had been abolished in 1807 for British subjects and in 1833 the status of slavery itself was to become unlawful in the British Empire. The West Indies trade was no longer the most important part of Britain's overseas activities and the 'West India interest' was no longer able to bend Parliament to its will. Even so, a prominent group of Aberdeen and Northeast 'proprietors and landholders' had petitioned Parliament in 1831 not to abolish slavery. Despite his association with Shand, Ramsay of Barra seems not to have signed the petition - possibly because there was a noted abolitionist tradition in another branch of the Ramsay family, encouraged by the influence of the greatest of Newmachar's ministers, Thomas Reid. The Shand connection with Straloch is simply one illustration of the way Newmachar, like practically every other part of the United Kingdom, became involved in transatlantic relationships and questions involving slavery and its abolition. (The story of William Shand is based on the evidence contained in his papers in the possession of Major Frances Irvine of Straloch, who kindly allowed the author access. Major Irvine has now generously made this important collection of papers available for study by placing them on deposit in the Aberdeen University archive collection as Ms 3652.)

The Indian Connection and Katherine Crombie née Forbes of Swailend and Goval

It was suggested in Chapter VII that India-derived money made it possible for John Burnett (1745-1822) to build Elrick House. Another possible son of John Burnett, Alexander, described as 'late of Bengal' was buried in the kirkyard in January 1811. (Temple, p. 298 but Henderson, p. 459, questions whether this Alexander Burnett was the son of John.) Newmachar Baptisms, Marriages and Deaths Records (General Register House) name a Captain William Burnett of the East India Company (in fact, the army) and residing at Elrick as being present as witness at the baptism of his nephew in May 1831. Clearly at least two generations of the Burnett family of Elrick were heavily involved with India.

Yet another connection with the East India Company comes in the person of Captain Thomas Shepherd (died 1875) who was to play an important part in Newmachar affairs. He was a cousin or second cousin of Mary Ramsay (died 1811), mentioned above, through her grandfather the Rev. Thomas Shepherd, minister of Bourtie. Thomas Shepherd, having presumably retired from India, became tenant at Straloch sometime before 1841. He married into the Innes family and his daughters were baptised in the Free Church. In fact Shepherd supported George Moir at the time of the Disruption, having him to stay at Straloch until the Free Church manse was ready, and becoming an elder. (See Chap. XIII.) Later, when Captain and Mrs Nares resumed residence at Straloch in 1845, Captain Shepherd moved to Skene.

Somewhat later, two sons of William Smith, a tenant farmer on the North Kinmundy estate, were engaged in trade in the East. Their deaths are recorded in the kirkyard: one at Shanghai in 1863 and the other at sea near Rangoon in 1876. (Headstone in New Machar Kirkyard, no. 139 on the list made by Ms Sheila Spiers.)

Katherine Scott Crombie (1812-1893)

By far the most interesting Indian connection with Newmachar is that of Mrs Katherine Crombie who is buried in Fintray churchyard with her husband, James Crombie (1810-1878) of Swailend Cottage and then Goval Bank. Katherine was the daughter of Theodore Forbes (1788-1820) of Boyndlie near Fraserburgh, who, like several others from the many branches of the Forbes family, had sought employment and fortune in India after completing his education at Marischal College, Aberdeen. Three of his brothers did the same. As was not uncommon at this period, he had a liaison with a woman in Aberdeenshire and also an unofficial wife in India. The Aberdeenshire partner was Ann Macdonell who bore Theodore a son, Frederick, in 1808. In India, there was Eliza Kewack who was a member of the Armenian community living in Bombay. She was with Theodore when he acted as East India Company agent in Mocha (on the Red Sea coast) and also as a representative of Forbes & Co, one of the great Indian 'country traders' and banking houses in Bombay. This had been set up by a different branch of the Forbes family, based in Upper Donside and then headed by Sir Charles Forbes. Eliza bore Theodore Forbes two children, Katherine and Alexander, born in Mocha in 1815. When Eliza complained that Theodore seemed to be losing his affection for her, it seems they agreed to part and to send the children back to Scotland to be brought up at Boyndlie and educated, as far as the boy was concerned, at Marischal College.

The son by Ann Macdonnel, Frederick (1808-1841), was also educated at Marischal College, qualifying as a surgeon and, like his father, proceeding to

India - in his case to join the Indian Navy. Also like Theodore, Frederick had intellectual inclinations and explored the Somali coast of North East Africa. Then he decided to travel home as an explorer via Afghanistan and Persia. He was murdered in a remote part of what is now Iran at Lake Seistan. Frederick seems to have been especially fond of his half-sister, Katherine, and they frequently corresponded. Frederick also liked her husband James Crombie whom he made one of his executors.

Both Ann Macdonnel and Eliza Kewack for long received pensions on the basis of funds deposited in Forbes & Co. by Theodore and by Frederick. Katherine herself had inherited 50,000 rupees from her father. This would have represented about £5000 and was no doubt a very useful dowry for the business man and woollen manufacturer, James Crombie, of the Cothal Mills. The two were married in 1838; they appear to have had a long and happy union. They lived first with their eight children and six servants at Swailend Cottage - a large house on the site of what is now the Newmachar Golf Club clubhouse. The family then moved to Goval Bank, where Katherine developed a talent for growing geraniums, winning prizes for them at the annual shows. One of their daughters, Margaret, gifted the stained glass window in New Machar Church to commemorate her parents. One of Katherine's other daughters, Jane, married into the Littlejohn family and so became the great-great-grandmother of the late Diana, Princess of Wales.

James Crombie no doubt benefited from his wife's Indian money at a crucial stage in his career. It is worth noting that his father, John Crombie (1782-1858), who had developed the woollen manufacturing business at Cothall, had married into the important Monykebbock family, the Harveys. (See Chaps. VII and XV.) Hence the Crombie business and the Crombie family supplemented local wealth by an infusion of Indian wealth and this was to their advantage. (The preceding account is based on the correspondence of Frederick Forbes with Katherine Forbes and other papers preserved as Forbes Papers in the Centre of South Asian Studies, University of Cambridge; the papers of Theodore Forbes among the Ogilvie-Forbes collection preserved as Ms 2740 in the Aberdeen University Archives; Roy Bridges, 'The visit of Frederick Forbes to the Somali Coast in 1833', *Int. Journal of African Historical Studies*, 19 (1986) 679-691 and other references there.)

Mrs Kerr, Newmachar

A rather later link with India may be mentioned. Mrs Kerr, the wife of Mr D.R. Kerr, the last U.F.C. minister in Newmachar, had been born in India and spent her early life there. She came from a medical missionary family. (See Chap. XIII.)

Scientific Exploration: the Deep Ocean and the North Pole. The work of Admiral Sir George Nares F.R.S.

Captain William Henry Nares (1788-1867) of the Royal Navy owned a property at Danestone on which he lived after a distinguished naval career. It seems that

he and the Ramsay family became friends and he was staying at Straloch in 1831 when his wife, Elizabeth, née Dodd, gave birth on 24th April to their son, George Strong Nares. Mrs Nares died, as well as five of her other children, after successive outbreaks of scarlet fever in 1835-38. The owner of Straloch, John Ramsay, had also died a year after his son, also John Ramsay, was born leaving his widow, Susan, née Innes. In 1844 the widower, Captain Nares, and the widow Susan Ramsay were married, with Captain Shepherd as one of the witnesses. Thereafter, Captain and Mrs Nares lived at

Straloch with the Captain drawing half-pay from the Admiralty. His son, George, was naturally a frequent visitor when on holiday from school, the Royal Naval School, New Cross. He formally entered the Royal Navy in 1845 at the age of fourteen. He was a midshipman on various ships including HMS *Havannah* on the Australian station, was commended for trying to save the life of a man who fell overboard as the ship was returning round Cape Horn and obtained his lieutenant's certificate in 1852 after further studies at the Naval College in Portsmouth.

Finding a means of distinguishing oneself was not easy in the navy in an era of peace. This explains why Nares was willing to go on an Arctic expedition. He wrote home to his father saying 'I hope you will not be very angry at what I have done!' He had had the temerity as a 20-year old to go along to the Admiralty to try to persuade an Admiral to post him on an expedition. The Admiral refused to see him but a Commander spoke for him and he was appointed to one of the many expeditions sent in search of Sir John Franklin. This 1852-4 expedition gave Nares the experience of sailing north and west into the Canadian Arctic as far as Melville Island and then proceeding on foot with sledges much further north. The ships were trapped in the ice and tedium was relieved by educational lectures - by Nares among others - and amateur theatricals. Nares played 'Lady Clarse' in 'the amusing historical drama Charles the Second.'

As a full lieutenant Nares subsequently became a gunnery officer for a time, saw service in the last months of the Crimean War and was then asked to take on the training of naval cadets. Nares appears to have been competent in everything he did and this experience led to his writing *Seamanship* which became the standard Naval training manual for many years. Nares' favourite sister seems to have been Maria; she maintained the Newmachar connection by marrying J. Gordon Cuming Skene of Parkhill in 1856 but died two years later leaving a son, Alexander, who inherited Parkhill. Thus the Nares were intimately connected with two of Newmachar's leading families. George Nares himself married in 1858 a Maria Grant who died in 1905. Hydrographical Survey work in a paddle-steamer, the *Salamander*, off Queensland and elsewhere followed from 1865. Nares began to gain experience of techniques for surveying the sea bottom and this led to his next appointment and in many ways his most important contribution to scientific knowledge.

HMS Challenger

In the middle of the nineteenth century, there was a growing interest in ocean currents and the way they were generated. Moreover, one or two marine biologists were beginning to think there might be life in the ocean depths although the orthodox view was that life was impossible there. In 1873 the Admiralty was persuaded to convert the warship HMS *Challenger* into a floating laboratory for a group of scientists to investigate these problems and Nares, already promoted to Captain, was given the command. As can be seen from the illustration, the *Challenger* was actually a steamship with sails and with it Nares became the first to take a steam vessel south of the Antarctic Circle reaching 66° 40' S. But most of the work was tedious dredging work. Nares made some useful innovations in trawling techniques and also, perhaps most important of all, pointed to the existence of the mid-Atlantic ridge.

Nares was seen as a firm and fair commander who managed the difficult task of reconciling the interests of the scientists and of the sailors with great tact. He therefore seemed to be the ideal man to be appointed to command Britain's next major Arctic expedition in 1875-6. The principal object was simply to reach the North Pole and explore the northern coasts of Greenland. Thinking continued to be affected by the erroneous idea that open, unfrozen water would be found near the North Pole. Nares took the *Alert* and the *Discovery*, a steam sloop and an ex-whaler, and they were to go through what is now called the Nares Strait between Greenland and Ellesmere Island. Of course they could not get through but Nares did reach 82° N. and then sent out sledge parties which did useful exploration with one reaching over 83° N.; this was a record for some years. Scurvy broke out and Nares had the courage to disobey his instructions and save

life by bringing the expedition home.

Some controversy followed over whether Nares could have prevented scurvy with more lime juice (which is now known to be of little use as a preventative). Perhaps Nares was unfortunate, also, to be the man who showed that big ships and heroism were not in themselves enough to get one to the North Pole. Nevertheless, Nares was given a knighthood, became a Fellow of the Royal Society and a gold medallist of the Royal Geographical Society. His account of the expedition, Narrative of a *Voyage to the Polar Sea* was modestly successful. The copy now at Straloch House is inscribed 'Susan Nares with much love; from her affectionately attached stepson.'

Nares subsequently sailed the *Alert* to the Straits of Magellan and retired from active service in 1886 as a Rear-Admiral. He held several other sea-related posts and died in January 1915. 'Quiet and reserved' yet also a man of action, Nares tends to be forgotten, his fame eclipsed by that of Shackleton and Scott. His name does survive, not only in the 'Nares Strait' but also 'Nares Land' in Greenland, two Capes in the Canadian Arctic, 'Nares Harbour' in the Admiralty Islands and the 'Nares Deep' in the Atlantic. In addition the naming of the deep sea crinoid, *Promachocrinus naresi* commemorates him. He certainly deserves to be remembered as one of the most distinguished people to have been born in and connected with Newmachar. (Nares, Correspondence with his father, National Maritime Museum XNAS1; Margaret Deacon and Ann Savours, 'Sir George Strong Nares,' *Polar Record* 18 (1976) 127-41; G.S. Nares, *Narrative of a Voyage to the Polar Sea during 1875-6*, 2 vols, London, 1878; L.P. Kirwan, *The White Road*, London, 1959. Eric Linklater, *The Voyage of the Challenger*, London, 1972 is an excellent popular account of the expedition. Dr Deacon has kindly allowed me to see the results of her research on Nares and the text of her article on him which will appear in the *New D.N.B.* I am grateful also to Ann Savours (formerly of Aberdeen University Library) for help and advice, and to Major Irvine of Straloch. Oliver Nares has set up a website on the Nares family which has been of aid to me.)

No doubt other Newmachar families could point to overseas connections. The evidence of the Kirkyard has already been noted in some cases but there are others where the headstone evidence is all that seems to be available. For example, there is the memorial to John Black, a merchant and member of the Council in Halifax, Nova Scotia, who died in September 1823 aged 61. Then there is the intriguing headstone commemorating Edward Wilhelm van Laer of Bielfeld, Westphalia, Prussia, who died in October 1876. It is not clear precisely what his connection with Newmachar was although possibly there was a link to the Clark family at Kinghorn. (Spiers List.)

From a much earlier period there is the evidence of the graveyard at Monykebbock; here is commemorated George Davidson, sometime shipowner in Aberdeen, who died in December 1784. He came originally from the Pinkie Mill.

Not commemorated in Newmachar itself, finally, are some casualties of the *Titanic* disaster of 1912: Andrew Johnston, his wife Elizabeth and their two children were third class passengers who died when emigrating to the New World.

Chapter XVII
Education 1621-1918

The 'readers' given the responsibility of looking after the church at Monykebbock in the 1570s (see Chap. VII) were probably expected to provide some education. Whether in fact they or the first minister, James Hervey, did do any teaching is open to question. This is only one of the many obscurities about the early history of schooling in Newmachar. In fact, it is difficult to say precisely when the parochial school was set up. For later periods, however, there is a very full and interesting collection of primary source material which would repay much more detailed examination than has been possible for this and the following chapter.

The Legislative background
Whatever educational facilities Scotland may have been able to offer in the mediaeval period, it is not likely that any of them were of any benefit to Newmachar. At the Reformation, John Knox (one of whose descendants was to have a profound effect on church and educational life in Newmachar (see Chap. XIII) set out the ideal of the Kirk being the community. To achieve this there would need to be a school in every parish. Subsequent Acts of the General Assembly or Parliament in 1616, 1633 and 1693 tried to achieve that aim. The fixing of a minimum salary for a schoolmaster of 100 merks (£5-11s-1d) in 1696 and attempts to force heritors to ensure schools were set up and premises built for them were not always successful. The 1803 Act tripled the minimum salary. In the Northeast, the Dick bequest made it possible to augment salaries from about 1830. Even if there was a parochial school, as happened in Newmachar, some parents might prefer to send their children to schools run as a private adventure. Enforcement of adequate religious and academic standards depended on the Minister, the Kirk Session and the Presbytery. At the very least the 3 Rs, the Catechism and perhaps a little Latin and Geography would be taught.

In the early part of the nineteenth century, there was increasing state intervention in the form of inspections designed to ensure certain standards as a condition for the awarding of grants. Grants began in 1834. The Privy Council Committee which organised grants and inspections from 1839 was too inclined to assume Scottish education was like that in England. Nevertheless real progress was apparent even if the multiplicity of schools, the varied sources of finance and the equally varied approaches to actual teaching, again as in Newmachar, made for confusion. The Argyll Commission of 1864-7 produced a massive report on the situation and recommended the setting up of a Scotch Education Department to preside over a series of local boards elected by all those paying at least a £4 rental, whether men or women. The 1872 Act followed and Newmachar elected its first school board in 1873.

Rosemary O'Day, *Education and Society 1500-1800*, London, 1982, pp 223-5; James Scotland, *History of Scottish Education*, 2 vols, London, 1969, 1, 106-204, 189-204, 228-253; D.J. Withrington, *Going to School*, Edinburgh, 1997 pp. 6-67; R.D. Anderson, *Education and Opportunity in Victorian Scotland*, Oxford, 1983.

Newmachar's Schoolmasters, 1621-1874
William Tullidaff
The honour of being the first person named as a schoolmaster in Newmachar parish belongs to William Tallidaff or, probably, Tullidaff. He is recorded in a Privy Council action of 25th July 1621 as 'skuilmaister in Straloche.' Another action of 12th October makes it clear that he was the son of Thomas Tullidaff, minister of the kirk at Foveran who lived to be 98 years old. (*The Register of the Privy Council of Scotland*, Vol XII, Edinburgh, 1895, pp. 551, 581; *Fasti Ecclesiae Scoticanae*, new ed., 1926, Vol VI, p. 193.) There is no further information about Tullidaff nor his activities at Straloch. It seems possible that he was employed by Robert Gordon to educate his numerous children and that perhaps other children, as was not uncommon, were allowed to join the classes.

William Mitchell and his successors
Whatever Tullidaff's position, it does not seem he was regarded as the parochial schoolmaster. The first name to appear in the Kirk Session records is that of *William Mitchell* in June 1673. Presumably, therefore, the school was established in that year or earlier but there is no direct evidence. Mitchell died in 1681 and another *William Mitchell* was appointed in the following January. Conceivably this is the same William Mitchell who became Minister of the parish in 1706; schoolmasters were often potential ministers waiting for a call. If this is so, it was this Mitchell who was slandered and physically assaulted by the schoolmaster in 1711, *William Gordon*, who was soon dismissed. *Robert Smith*, 1696-8, *John Gordon* 1701? and *John Harvey* ?1710 are the other masters of this period of whom we know nothing. *William Johnston* who served 1717-1720 was session clerk and precentor as well as teacher. No doubt he needed the money as did his successor, a *Mr Mair*, who had great difficulty in getting the heritor living at Swailend to pay his proper share of the master's salary.

Mr William Henderson, 1725-1769, is the first of the schoolmasters to have served for any length of time. We know that he was qualified in Latin, Arithmetic and Music. He died in 1772 at the age of 86 and his grave is in the kirkyard. His wife lived on until 1798. She had had to sew the communion linen to raise a little money on her husband's retirement. Henderson's successors, *James Shirras*, 1769-70, and *William Dauney*, 1770, were not long in post but *Alexander Watt* probably served from 1783 for almost twenty years. Without naming him, Mr Stronach, the minister, tells us that his salary and perquisites were about £15 per annum (compared with his own stipend of about £40). The *OSA* also tells us that the school itself was 'hard-by the church' - the building which is still there but now in use as a builder's store.

From 1802 to 1835, the schoolmaster was *William Buchan* who was a graduate of King's College. By 1829 the Dick Bequest had made it possible to raise his salary to £27. Buchan had various other functions in the parish, not least taking the censuses in 1821 and 1831. *Colin Falconer* was schoolmaster from 1835 probably to 1844 when he was succeeded briefly by *William McCulloch* and then from 1845, right up to beyond the formation of the board in 1874, by *Donald M'Hardy*. M'Hardy was also Inspector of the Poor; he was to cause the new Board a certain amount of difficulty.

(The list of schoolmasters and their doings is derived principally from Ian J. Simpson, 'Education in Aberdeenshire before 1872' Aberdeen University thesis, 2 vols, 1942. A shorter version was published, London, 1947.)

The Mid Nineteenth Century: The Parochial School and some new schools
In 1838 a Parliamentary Enquiry revealed details of schooling in Scotland. The Parochial School in Newmachar had 56 pupils, boys and girls, who attended on average, for four or five years and only one teacher, Colin Falconer. The pupils paid 2s.6d, 3s or 4s, according to their position in the school but they were all taught in one class with some separate attention for beginners. There was also a Sunday class. No playground was available. Colin Falconer was a King's College graduate and received £30.00 p.a. He taught English, Arithmetic, Geography, History and Religion but did not have Latin classes. Rewards for pupils were to be promoted to a higher position in the class.

There was also at Rosehall an 'adventure' school run by *Alexander Elrick*. He had begun classes in 1812 and now had 76 pupils pursuing much the same sort of curriculum as in the parish school where Elrick had himself been educated. He seems to have had no higher qualification. Elrick added singing as a subject and fees at Rosehall were slightly higher than those charged in Summerhill. Rosehall was inspected by the minister and also offered three Sunday-school classes. Pupils were offered no rewards but bad conduct might mean admonition or 'slight corporal punishment.' (Answers Made by Schoolmasters in Scotland . . , Parl. Papers C64, 1841.)

By 1842 according to Mr Moir, there was another adventure school and he characterised their teachers, including presumably Mr Elrick, as being 'in humble circumstances and of limited education' yet 'assiduous in their endeavours to promote the spiritual as well as intellectual improvement of the children.' There were also now three 'Sabbath Schools.' Their 120 children had to come to the church in Summerhill every month to be examined. (*New Statistical Account* Vol XII pp. 1033-4.) Clearly the active and efficient George Moir had revitalised the Sunday-school movement. He also tells us that a library had been established in the parish in 1816 consisting of 470 volumes and that he himself had just set up a religious library.

The main library was one casualty of the momentous changes which were to come in 1843 but which also produced yet another school. The Disruption (see Chap. XIII) not only produced a new church but, almost immediately, a new school. (*Guesses at Truth*, Aberdeen 1913, p. 6.) The classes seem to have been held in the new Free Church itself. By 1872, the school was restricting its intake to girls of whom there were then 36.

Yet another all-girls school had been set up as an adventure school at Parkhill and this had 80 pupils in 1872. There were 115 pupils at the Parochial School but the largest roll was actually at Whiterashes where there were 147 pupils at the Episcopalian School. This was not so much because there were large numbers of Episcopalians as because the northern part of the parish together with adjacent areas of the Fintray and Udny parishes needed provision. (AC 5/70/1: New Machar School Board Minutes, 28 April 1873.)

The Episcopal School had been set up by Major Ramsay in 1858 together with a mission church. Classes were held in the Church vestry. (Information from Major Francis Irvine.)

By 1872, therefore, Newmachar had four schools providing an education for almost every child under 13; only three children were recorded as not at school in 1872. By the standards of the time a very reasonable elementary education was being provided. It is also apparent that parents' expectations were rising and that both the parochial school and private school managers were finding it hard to finance the buildings and teachers who could meet those expectations. Government grants did not solve the problems and so the 1872 Act came.

The School Board in Newmachar

Initially, the elections for the seven members of the board attracted great interest. This early experiment in democratic control of a major sector of everyday life did have important implications. It is notable that in the very first election Mr George Pittendrigh, general merchant in Whiterashes, received the highest number of votes although only three more than Major Ramsay. How difficult did Mr Pittendrigh find it to sit on the same board as his landlord, Major Ramsay? Elections were held every three years but in later years were often uncontested. Over the period 1873-1897 in all 24 men served on the Board; only one lady stood as a candidate but withdrew before the 1879 election; her husband, Will Murray, carpenter and wright, was re-elected instead as the representative for Summerhill. Of the 24, four may be classified as landowners or gentry, with Major Ramsay of Straloch the most prominent. Mr Peter Clark, an advocate, in effect represented an absent landowner's interests; clearly it was still thought appropriate to try to ensure that each of the estates had its place on the Board. There were two ministers, Mr William Bruce of the established

Church who was chairman of the Board from 1873-1901, except for 1879-1885, and Mr James Duguid of the Free Church. For most of the time the two men appeared to co-operate sensibly but there clearly were tensions not made explicit in the minutes; the Free Church sometimes seemed to be in alliance with the Episcopalians against the 'establishment'. There were two shopkeepers, Pittendrigh for Whiterashes and Cooper for Summerhill, and three tradesmen but the largest group, understandably in a parish like Newmachar, were tenant farmers. The tendency over the whole period up to 1918 was for the landowners to lose interest and for the proportion of tenant farmers to increase. Throughout, the churches continued to have an important influence. (The figures are based on an analysis of the information in AC 5/70/1, the Board Minutes, by Mrs Jill Bridges.)

While there is some evidence of, for example, a reluctance on the part of Major Ramsay to relinquish his traditional responsibilities as a landowner and heritor, or on the part of Mr Bruce to lose the minister's accustomed power to determine the way education should be organised, the Board in general seems to have approached its tasks with a great sense of the importance of its work. In fact, religion caused no difficulty: it was agreed that non-denominational religious instruction should be offered in all schools.

The first rate was fixed at 3d in the pound. One of the earliest problems was how the Episcopal School at Whiterashes was to be brought into the Board system. Major Ramsay wanted to set up a separate board combining the northern part of the parish with part of Udny and to retain some personal control of the school and its building. He lost this argument: the Episcopal Church School as such was closed in 1876 and a board school was built at Whiterashes. For the main parochial school in Summerhill, the major problem initially seems to have been how to replace the ageing and presumably inefficient John M'Hardy. When he did agree to go, after withdrawing his resignation more than once, there were numerous problems over a pension, the schoolmaster's house and his furniture.

William Scott, a 'brilliant mathematician' took over as head teacher and seems to have been a great success: he raised the school from 'the low level at which he found it' in 1876 according to Mr Bruce. (AU Ms 2546.) Unfortunately his successor was described by an inspector as 'unintelligent and unhappy' and thereupon resigned.

A Model of New Machar School

Mr Bruce thought the Returning Officer had misconducted the School Board election in 1879 and felt strongly enough to resign from the chairmanship and the board for three years. More important was the achievement of the Board in bringing about the building of three new purpose-designed schools. The new one in Summerhill, on the site of the present (2001) school, accommodated the infant and female departments, with boys attending up to the age of eight and girls up to thirteen. The contract for £832 to build the school went to Mr Will Murray, the local joiner and wright - who was also a member of the Board. The other schools were at Parkhill, which cost £217-9s-0d, and Whiterashes. Piped water was to be provided for all these schools. When the new school at Summerhill was later enlarged to enable the amalgamation of the boy's school with the other departments into one school in 1885-6, what had been the old parochial school building was bought for £50 for the

Whiterashes School

community as a village hall, which it remained until 1955. The members of the Board were assiduous in visiting the schools, trying to assure themselves that standards were being maintained, that there were supplies of books or that the drains were not blocked; there was much to be said for the system of local responsibility which was characteristic of the Board system. (AC 5/70/1.)

The Life of the Schools

Much can be discovered from the Admissions register of the schools. It is clear that often, because of the feein' system, the children of farm labourers tended to move in and out of a particular school. Some support is given to the idea that schools were levellers in that children of rich and poor sat together there. Certainly the Summerhill School showed the ministers' children, and those of other professional people and prosperous tenant farmers sitting for at least part of their school lives with labourers' children. (AC 6S/G491/4, Registers of Admissions.) However, it is the Log Books which provide the most detailed insights into the everyday lives of the teachers and their pupils.

The Free Church Girls' School had ceased to exist although the premises continued to be used for a short time. Its pupils were transferred to the new Board School whose new teacher, *Miss Euphemia Young*, was not impressed by these pupils: they were 'quite [meaning entirely] ignorant as regards notation.' (AC 6S G49/1/1.) At the main school, ie what now became New Machar Public School, the new regime meant academic change as Latin and Algebra were introduced. Yet some things did not change: boys were cautioned not to climb on the wall behind the School. Some Scotch songs were being taught in 1877. Inspectors' visits meant the anxiety of wondering if the grants for subjects would be withdrawn. In 1875 lack of discipline was noted and in 1880 a considerable deficiency in penmanship, but a year later - more seriously - the inspector threatened to withdraw grants for Arithmetic and also advised that 'Drill should be brought into greater prominence for the better regulation of routine movements and of School conduct generally.' In December 1887 Standard II were having to attend for special practice in Arithmetic every night. By 1890 some senior boys were able to take Map Drawing and extra Arithmetic while the girls did Sewing.

The greatest problem was attendance even after it became compulsory from 1878; at harvest, turnip singling and potato lifting times the senior pupils in particular did not turn up. But illness could be the cause; only 23 pupils out of 106 were present in January 1882 because of measles. At other times, as in January 1875, snow made roads impassable; in 1895 the heating pipes inside the school were frozen solid! If teachers were absent, Miss Bruce, the minister's daughter helped out.

In October 1900 wash hand basins were installed in the lobbies - 'which is a great assistance to cleanliness in sewing and drawing.' Later that year Annie Wildgoose was absent on account of her weak eyesight; another pupil, from a well-known Newmachar family, was debarred from school because of ringworm. On 9th December 1901 the school closed as a mark of respect on the day of Dr Bruce's funeral. In February 1904, the teachers were complaining like those a century later of excessive administrative chores. (AC 6S/G49/1/1.)

At Whiterashes, a piano was acquired in 1896. The head teacher was *John McGregor*, remembered as a tall man with a pointed beard. The school was more than just a school: it became the social centre where, for example, a lending library functioned. Miss Annie Knight of Sittyton gave music lessons there; she later moved with her two sisters to a cottage at Elrick House, continued to give music lessons, and set up and trained the WRI choir. Miss Sim, who was to have such a long career at Newmachar School, became an assistant in about 1910. (Davidson, *Whiterashes*, pp.17-18.)

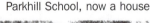

Parkhill School, now a house

The End of the School Board
The 1918 Education Act abolished School Boards and control of the public education system passed to County Boards. These lasted for barely ten years; in 1929 the County Boards were subsumed within the County Councils. There was certainly a loss of local control and responsibility but this has to be balanced against the larger resources in materials and expertise which the County could provide.

Chapter XVIII
Education since 1918

During most of the twentieth century Newmachar maintained three schools. One was in the village and later became what was known as a Junior Secondary School. In other words, pupils could stay there until they reached school leaving age, which had become 14 in 1901. Those able to pass the appropriate examinations and aiming at higher or further education needed to take the Higher Leaving Certificate and so would go on to Senior Secondary School at Inverurie, or Ellon (by train - this was á popular and convenient option while the railway operated) or Aberdeen. Under the 1945 Act, all secondary education became free. Parkhill and Whiterashes remained as one or two-teacher schools, effectively working as primary schools though sometimes with classes beyond the primary stage. In 1965, the introduction of 'comprehensive education' meant a few large 'academies' and the relegation of schools like New Machar to be simply primary schools whilst Whiterashes and Parkhill were closed. For many years Whiterashes School remained with its two schoolrooms still just as the last pupils and teacher had left it: books open on the desks, chalk writing on the blackboard, all rather like an educational *Marie Celeste*. The two rooms have latterly been integrated into the former schoolhouse which is now a private home.

The Life of New Machar School
For the twentieth century, the evidence of the Admission Register (AC 6S/G49/1/4) and the County Council Education Committee Minutes is available but, once again, it is the School Log Book which provides the most full and illuminating picture of the work of the teachers and their pupils. This can be supplemented by the direct testimony of living members of the community.

Mr James Souter, Head Teacher 1915-1943
James Souter's long career in charge of New Machar School meant that he had a very significant impact on the lives of large numbers of Newmachar children. Sometimes the impact was too literal: many informants (eg Mr George Rennie) remember him as excessively physically violent - although not to girls. (Testimony of Mrs Elizabeth Walker.) Some of the boys had a theory that he became especially irritable after he had had his hair cut! (Testimony of Mr Norman Duncan.) Miss Sim, who lodged with the Souters in the schoolmaster's house, was often a calming influence and 'knew how to handle him.' Adults outside the school, too, such as the U.F.C. minister, Mr Kerr, and members of the Parochial Council often found Mr Souter difficult to deal with. (Testimony of Mrs M. Nicol.) He sometimes acted in an unreasonable and erratic way over announcing the results of the vital public examinations. (Testimony of Mrs Ada Ross.) Many informants

believed that it was a medical condition - diabetes - which made James Souter erratic or unreasonable in his behaviour. It is also notable that there are many who remember his excellence as a teacher, especially for mathematical subjects; Mr A. Low testifies for example to the way in which Mr Souter's tuition had helped him towards a qualification in electrical engineering. Inspectors in 1930 referred to his 'able and sympathetic management.'

James Souter was born in 1880 near Monymusk and graduated M.A. from King's College in 1903. After spells of teaching in Banchory, Dunottar and Cushnie, where he was first a head, then Cultercullen, he took up the head-ship at New Machar on 5th October 1915. (T. Watt, *Roll of Graduates of the University of Aberdeen 1901-1925*, Aberdeen, 1935, p. 564.) Some surprise was caused when he volunteered for military service in July 1918 and then resumed his teaching duties in January 1919. He retired in 1943 when the School presented him and his wife - also a teacher, a stalwart of the WRI and well liked (testimony of Mrs Agnes Cran) - with an electric standard lamp.

A School Group from 1934

Miss Sim had died with tragic suddenness earlier in 1943 having been at New Machar School for 32 years. She had taught both the infant and the (senior) qualifying classes. She was very well liked and respected. *Miss Norrie* had taught for even longer - 40 years. She was very strict but fair (Mrs E. Walker). She died in 1926. *Miss Ruby Jack* arrived in 1930 from New Deer. She taught the younger children, working in the former school building - by then officially the Village Public Hall. She founded and ran the Newmachar Girl Guides Troop. She was 'lovely, respected and will always be remembered by 'her' children.'

(Testimonies of Mrs Dorothy Smith and Mr George Rennie.) *Miss Ann Whyte* who taught Primary II was a 'nice enough lady' but she 'tended to screech'! (Testimony of Mr Rennie.) She settled happily in the village at Cunninghar Cottage and then the former Police Station by the Church, after her retirement in 1964. *Miss Isabella Finnie* appears to have been a somewhat eccentric lady given to falling asleep at her desk. Allegedly better qualified than Mr Souter, she did not see eye to eye with him on many matters. He reported adversely on her in the log book. To pupils she was known as 'kipper.' Was this because she was red-haired or by transference from 'finnan haddock'? (Testimony of Mr George Rennie.) An actual kipper was once fixed under her desk and left to smell by some of the boys who also - in self defence? - buried her tawse in concrete. (Testimony of Mrs Penny.)

There are memories, too, of Whiterashes teachers. *Miss Duguid*, a strict but good teacher, took the infants. She played the organ at Whiterashes Church and also produced concerts. The older children were taught in the 1940s by *Miss Johnston* who was always calm except, it seems, when there was thunder which frightened her very much. She was an excellent teacher. (Testimony of Mrs Marie Cameron.)

Jottings from the Log Book at New Machar School (AC 6S/G49/1/3)
In 1918, Newmachar, like most of the rest of the world, was affected by the influenza pandemic. Many pupils were absent and the school was closed completely in October. The coal strike in 1920 meant shorter school hours because of the fuel shortage. Despite this, the roll went up to 138, apparently because several pupils transferred from Disblair. Measles became a problem in May and June of that year.

The Rev. Mr Hood Smith for several years gave addresses, as in 1923, on 'Rights of Citizenship and Patriotism.' Psalm 100 as well as 'Rule Britannia' were sung.

By 1930 there were 168 on the roll and Mr Souter was supported by five female assistants. The major visible development during the 1930s was the modernisation of the 1880s building including the heating system and the addition of several new classrooms. In the years up to 1934 the Village Hall - the former school building - had needed to be pressed into service again for the infants department. (Testimony of Mrs Dorothy Smith.) The result of the new work, reported an inspector in 1935, was a 'pleasing, airy and well-equipped school'. One new entrant in 1938 (Leslie Keith) could not believe how big the windows were! There were now good facilities for the post primary education of those senior pupils who did not go on to senior secondaries. (Whether the curriculum they were offered was a sensible one is another matter although at least there were classes in English, French and Latin to the Higher level for the academically inclined.)

The school treat to celebrate George V's Silver Jubilee in 1935 was to be taken to the Astoria Cinema in Aberdeen.

In 1936 electric light was installed in the school. It seems odd that this had not been done in the previous year's modernisation. It is odd, too, that not a single bulb fused until December 1938; perhaps the lights were seldom used.

Like schools all over the rest of the country, New Machar School was closed for the national emergency on September 1st 1939. Then 84 evacuees arrived from Broomloan Road School, Govan, with three teachers. (See Chap. XX.) The 'phoney war' encouraged most to go home but by the middle of 1940 things were more serious; the fitting of gas marks and air-raid drills became standard and some pupils applied for evacuation overseas. Soon, however, the Rev. Mr Thornton was able to tell the school about 'The Empire's Greatness' and in 1945 the school closed to celebrate V.E. and V.J. Days.

The Post-War School

Cases of scabies were being spotted in October 1946. At this same period, there was a greater demand for child labour for potato lifting (tattie picking) than could be easily met and two-thirds of the senior classes were absent.

Mr McKee, the head teacher, was worried about coping with the effects of the school leaving age finally being raised to 15. Fierce blizzards raged in January and February 1947; fewer than half of the pupils were able to get to school. In January 1948, the County Director of Education thought it worth confirming that the name of the school was 'New Machar' and not 'Newmachar'. The flag was raised on Empire Day. New food ration books were issued in June and eleven pupils passed the junior Leaving Certificate. In 1949 the school picnic was held at Fraserburgh with a special train being hired; funds to help meet costs had been raised by a

school concert and gifts of food promised for goodie bags. During the 1949-50 winter months, the soup kitchen had served 9145 meals. But from 1952 meals were brought in from Dyce.

A service was held in February 1952 to mark the death of the king. Measles remained a frequent cause of absence in 1952-3 with the infant class reduced by half in January. In February 'the worst storm in memory' broke out over the district; three window panes were blown in and electricity supplies failed. But in May pupils received gifts to mark the Queen's Coronation. Two groups from 1953 are shown on the preceding page.

In 1956 Mr *George McKee* retired as head teacher after thirteen years in Newmachar and 48 years as a teacher. He was succeeded by *W. Allan Lamont*, 1956-1962, who introduced a prize-giving ceremony for the first time in 1957. Major and Mrs Irvine presented the prizes. Mr Lamont also introduced the house system, the two houses being named 'Elrick' and 'Straloch'. Miss Lesley Moir left to take up a teacher's post in Tanganyika.

The great snowstorm of January in 1960 (see Chap. XII) severely affected the school. Local children were taken home under escort 'as they could not have survived alone.' Others had to wait in school as did the eight staff but everyone was in good spirits even after the electricity supply failed. A student teacher, Miss Smith, who walked from Whiterashes to the school suffered from frostbite. The Quatercentenary of the Reformation was celebrated later in the year. Mr Lamont refused to ask his staff to help collect National Savings; they already had too many 'extraneous duties.' New classrooms began to be built. Foot and mouth disease was confirmed at Kingseat Farm and every animal on the farm was slaughtered. As a result of quarantine controls, attendance at school dropped severely.

In the following year the first threats to the existence of the Secondary classes emerged.

In 1961-2 there was a considerable turnover of staff with seven new appointments including the head teacher, Mr *A.F. Robertson*, 1961-69. Under his direction the school seemed to proceed smoothly for the most part. However, a sign of unwelcome social changes was that police visited the school in connection with an assault case involving pupils in 1967. Two pupils from Sierra Leone were admitted; were these Newmachar's first overseas students? The first child with English as a second language did not arrive until 1991.

By 1969 the school roll had gone down to 137 as more senior pupils went to classes elsewhere. Mr *J.C. Rollo*, 1970-1986, took over as head teacher in January 1970. Large Christmas services conducted by Mr Claydon with much musical input from the pupils became the norm. Snow conditions closed the school in March 1979 but in the same month most of the teachers were out on strike - an increasingly frequent occurrence during the 1980s. On the other hand, the school roll began to go up again as more houses were built in the village; it reached over 200. Yet another building extension began to be planned by 1980. Mr *Walter Baxter* took up duty as janitor and amid all his other duties managed to keep a photographic record of the new building work. In 1981 *Mrs Sheila Reid* began to teach at the school - temporarily at first. She became Senior

Teacher in 1989 and Assistant Head Teacher in 1992. In 1984 power failures were still being experienced; on one occasion the school was closed for almost a week. By this time the roll was up to 250. In 1985 the school earned a prize under the 'Keep Grampian Beautiful' scheme for being the best kept school in the Gordon District.

Tragically, Mr Rollo died in January 1986 and was replaced by *Mrs E.J. Jarman*, 1986-1999. In 1987 the school became responsible for four flower tubs in the main street under the guidance of the Garden Club. Expeditions to Disblair Woods to study lichens, and to Drum Castle and Crathes Castle were organised. The number of houses in the school increased to four for 1988's Sports Day - Alpha, Bravo, Charlie and Delta and, another sign of a new world, a milk bar started up in the school in 1989.

Miss Pauline Dow became acting head teacher in 1992-93 and again in 1994-6 whilst Mrs Jarman was on secondment. There were now 287 pupils and 12 permanent teachers. By this time, the Parent Teacher Association had become a key part of the school scene. In May 1999, *Mrs Jean Yacamini* became head teacher, to be greeted a few days later by the problem of intruders; a security system had to be installed. But the normal life of the school went on. An After-School Club was set up in 1999 and new software was introduced for the school's computers. (New Machar School, Log Book, 1946-1999.) In 2001, yet another extension was in the course of construction.

As New Machar School entered the new century and new Millennium in January 2001, it could look back on at least 328 years of continuous existence. Perhaps William Middleton and Mrs Yacamini would find their problems not too dissimilar: attendance, curriculum, obtaining adequate accommodation and resources from the controlling authority, whether the heritors or Aberdeenshire.

New Machar School Group in 1932

Chapter XIX
Contributions to the History of Newmachar by pupils at New Machar School and Dyce Academy

During 2000 certain pupils at both schools produced the following contributions for *People and Places in Newmachar, Past and Present*.

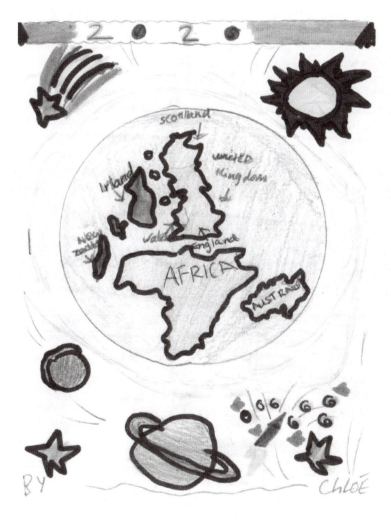

Chloé Hunter's drawing in her folder about the future

I am most grateful to the pupils, whose names appear below, and to their teachers, at New Machar School, Mrs Wendy Kelman and Mrs Alison Thomson, at Dyce Academy - Miss Seonag Robertson. The Dyce survey is reproduced in full although unfortunately without colour for the pie-diagram. It was also not possible to reproduce all the brightly coloured pictures drawn by the New Machar pupils nor to reprint all their mini essays. But everyone who took part is recorded.

New Machar School:
A survey among Primary 4/5 pupils on life in Newmachar in 2000

My name	When my family came to Newmachar	What I want to be
Nicolas Bell	1999	Actor in Hollywood
Siobhan Brown	1985	Vet & work in Africa
Laura Bruce	1983	Hairdresser
Amanda Cator	Before 1964	Actor
Mark Esson	1993	(Not stated)
Alexander Faulkner	1997	(To live in Florida)
Sarah Gordon	1993	Singer
Kelly Green	1963	(Not stated)
Chloé Hunter	1992	Netball Teacher
Sara Keene	1999	Model
Ryan Knight	1995	(Not stated)
Kyle Lawrie	1995	(Not stated)
Andrew Logan	1986	Footballer
Hannah McPherson	1993	A Model
Angus MacSween	1989	Footballer for Scotland
Ryan Melvin	1965	Footballer
Kelly Mitchell	1982	Pop Star
Stacie Morgan	1998	Vet
Christopher Ryan	1997	Fireman
Douglas Smart	1999	Footballer
Peter Stephen	1996	Aberdeen Footballer
Kevin Taylor	1999	(Not stated)
Matthew Todd	1989	Snooker Player
Lisa Youngson	1992	Vet

General results of the family survey conducted by the children.
Out of 24 families surveyed, 3 had been in Newmachar for thirty years or more, 6 over ten and 15 for less than ten. The children also asked their families what

Newmachar Past and Present

new or improved facilities they thought should be introduced in the village. The results are shown in the next table. All recently arrived families said they found Newmachar and its people welcoming. The only adverse comment was Mark Esson's: "We thought the community was friendly but were surprised by the ferocity of the wind."

Siobhan Brown wants to be a Vet

Hopes for the village in the future:

Principal Hopes:		Mentioned once:
Doctors' surgery	14	Bigger school
Community Centre/Hall	9	More car parking
Chemist	8	Pedestrian crossing
Bank	8	Disco
More shops	5	A focal point
Facilities for young people	2	Fewer shops
Sports Centre	2	Police house
Better roads	2	More houses
		Swimming Pool

Lisa wants her home to look like this

****

Dyce Academy: Newmachar Millennium Project 1999-2000

Researched and written by

Hannah Abel	Neil Bruce
Stacey Clews	Samantha Grant
Caroline de Hart	Suzanne McMurtry
Mhari Mackay	Dawn Riley
Amy Ward	Kay Morris
Louise Stratton	

Introduction

We are S1 pupils at Dyce Academy who carried out a study on Newmachar today. We looked at Education, Fuel, Industry, Character of the people and how long families have lived there. We compared the information from the questionnaire we gave out to 27 S1 pupils from Newmachar, to the *Statistical Account of Newmachar* in 1842. This is what we found out.

Education

The Statistical Account tells us that there were three schools: a parish school and two run by the teachers. The teachers of the parish school lived in the school. They taught reading, writing, arithmetic, geography and English.

Today there is only one primary school in Newmachar which no teachers live in. The subjects taught are Maths, Physical Education, English, Drama, Music,

Home Economics, Art, Topics and Religious and Moral Education. French is also taught to P6 and P7.

Sunday School was another aspect we looked at. Sunday School in the 1800s was very popular. It was attended by 120 people under the age of 14. There were three Sunday Schools. Nowadays, only one Newmachar S1 pupil goes to Sunday School. Instead, the pupils prefer to watch TV, play sports, playing the computer and playing with their friends.

Fuel

Most people living in Newmachar in 1843 used to have peat fires. From our survey of S1 pupils from Newmachar we found out what kind of fuel they use nowadays.

What type of fuel do you use?

This shows that electricity is most popular but no-one uses peat now. We also found out that people who had oil had their tank refilled every 3-9 months. Coal fires was another item we investigated. Only one pupil had a coal fire but five pupils used to have one. We think this is probably because coal fires are hard work and need cleaning often.

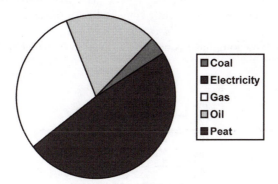

- Coal
- Electricity
- Gas
- Oil
- Peat

(Figures: Coal 1; Electricity 13; Gas 8 [LPG: survey taken before town gas laid on]; Oil 5; Peat 0.)

Industry

We asked S1 pupils from Newmachar what their parents work as today, how long they have lived here and what services there are in Newmachar. We wanted to compare it to 1843.

In 1843 most people used to work as farmers, though some must have been mill workers as the Statistical Account mentions 'several corn mills'.

Jobs of Parents

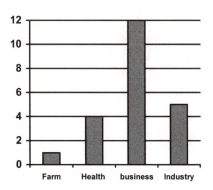

With our results we found out that most parents work in industry and business nowadays, not farming.

We asked S1 pupils how long their parents have lived in Newmachar to find out how many families have recently come to live in the area.

How long have your parents lived in Newmachar?

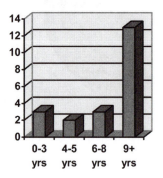

With our results we found out that most parents have lived in Newmachar for nine years and over, but there are some people who have more recently moved in.

We also asked if pupils' grandparents came from Newmachar. Only one out of 26 came from Newmachar so families have not been here long.

We asked S1 pupils what new services they would like to see in Newmachar.

What services should be built in Newmachar?

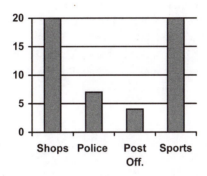

Almost everyone said there should be more services.

Twenty out of 27 people thought that there should be more shops and sport facilities in Newmachar and a majority of people thought that there should be a police station. Not so many people would like to see a separate Post Office from Forbuoys (now Mace). This means that if the people get what they want then a couple of new shops might be built and we might see more sports facilities in Newmachar. So, in the future there might be more buildings and Newmachar will keep getting bigger.

Character of the People

When we looked at the *Statistical Account* we didn't really understand most of it but what we did understand was that the people were described as sober, industrious and intelligent. We wanted to find out if that was still the case today.

In the year 2000 most of the people questioned, twenty out of twenty seven, thought that the people are still friendly and intelligent. But only nine pupils said that people are hardworking and respectful in Newmachar!

We also asked a question about new problems in Newmachar. Seventeen of the pupils think there is a problem with alcohol but not so many think there is a problem with drugs. Seven pupils said there was a problem with drugs and vandalism.

We think that the character of the people in Newmachar in the year 2000 has changed since 1842 as there are new problems with alcohol and drugs. However, there are a lot of good things about Newmachar as people are friendly and cheerful. 23 out of 27 pupils said that they were friendly. Newmachar is still a nice little village to live in.

Conclusions

After doing this questionnaire we have found that Newmachar has changed drastically thoughout the years from 1843 to the year 2000. Examples of this are that Newmachar has become a larger village. Also there is only one primary school where there used to be three in 1842. We also found that the main job is not farming anymore. Most people work in industry and business.

Chapter XX
Wars and Rumours of Wars

Newmachar has been fortunate in having no castles and, except as a secondary route to the north from Aberdeen, little intrinsic strategic importance. The inhabitants have avoided military engagement when possible but served with gallantry and dedication in national wars.

The **Battle of Barra** was fought close by at North Mains Farm (797263) in May 1308 and must surely have affected Newmachar. John Comyn and his allies precipitately fled 'Quhen thai saw the nobill king cum stoutly on foroutyn fenyeing.' (John Barbour, *The Bruce*, ed. A. Duncan, 1997 p. 330.) So Robert the Bruce and his Anglo-Norman followers destroyed the power of the Celts and Picts in the Northeast; the Gordon, Fraser, Forbes, Burnett and Irvine families now took control.

Groome's *Gazeteer*, which gives no source, says the **Battle of Monykebbock** was fought in 1647. This was more likely a minor skirmish between the Covenanters' Army trying to get rid of remaining Scottish royalists, and the Marquis of Huntly, a 'ditherer, much dependent on the advice of astrologers' who quickly fled to the Highlands. (Testimony of Prof. David Stevenson.) No tradition about this battle seems to have survived locally. Newmachar's relative insulation from the troubles of the Civil Wars must owe much to the fact that Robert Gordon of Straloch was something of a mediator between the factions who accepted the decree which said he should be left alone to continue his cartography. (See Chapter VI.) Later in the century, there was certainly no enthusiasm for serving in the Militia — or paying for it. Robert Burnett of Elrick complained that a greater burden was placed on Aberdeenshire than Angus or Fife in 1687-8. (*Register of Privy Council of Scotland* 3rd series XIII, 357, 367.) Robert's son Andrew, with William Gosden of Goval, was equally reluctant to pay a tax to the Earl of Mar and the Jacobite rebels of 1715. (J. Allardyce, *Historical Papers … Jacobite Period*, New Spalding Club, 2 Vols. 1895, I: 47-8.)

The altogether more serious affair of the **Jacobite Rising of 1745** saw the inadequate government forces of Sir John Cope camped at Parkhill on 'Cope's Butts.' They could not prevent the rebel army from marching the length of the parish in February 1746. John Bisset, a former minister of Newmachar, naturally took a close interest and reported with approval that the Duke of Cumberland had arrived by April; the Duke took the road via Newmachar to Old Meldrum in his pursuit of the Young Pretender. (Diary of John Bisset, *Spalding Club Miscellany*, 1841, I: 379, 388-9.)

There were no more battles on Scottish soil but Newmachar residents became much involved in international wars. For example, William Gordon Cuming Skene of Parkhill, despite his 'constitution being naturally delicate', served in the Peninsular War of 1813 and then against Napoleon again in France itself in

Stewart Cooper
1918
A soldier in the
Gordons killed in
France

Tom Rearie
Also in the Gordons
(See Chap. XXIV)

Dedication of the memorial in the Cemetery 1950

1815. (Temple, p. 316.) Closer to home, the Militia riots of 1797 were survived and Newmachar men more willingly served in the Dyce, Newmachar and Fintray Company of the Volunteers. They wore smart red and yellow uniforms and knew that they would not be sent overseas to confront Napoleon. (D. Sinclair, *History of the Aberdeen Volunteers..*, Aberdeen, 1907, pp. 131-2.) Some one hundred years later, the **South African War** had echoes in Newmachar with fund-raising events and a great celebration of the fall of Pretoria in June 1900 with children marching round the village to the music of a brass band. (*Aberdeen Journal*, 11 Jun, 13 Aug 1900.)

The Great War was a more serious concern as the names of 31 dead on the War Memorial testify. By December 1914, wounded soldiers from the front were being brought back to Aberdeen and several Newmachar farmers with others got together to ensure a daily supply of fresh milk for the hospital. (Testimony of Mrs Agnes Cran, née Burgess, whose father farmed Highlands at the time and contributed, as did Messrs Anderson of Mameulah, Murray of Rainnieshill, Cowie of Chapel of Elrick, Dawson of Brownhills, Gray and others of Kinmundy, Cow of Ord, Rennie of Westside, Harvey of Monykebbock, Wilson of Argo. See also *Aberdeen Journal*, 3 Dec 1914.)

Meanwhile, the Parish Council had already organised collections for the children of fallen soldiers and the relief of French provinces overrun by the Germans. Other flag days or war savings and war bond days followed. By December 1917, German U-boats had sunk enough transatlantic shipping to make food very short in Britain. Local authorities were urged to provide allotments for people to grow their own vegetables; as noted in Chapter XIV, this was happening in Newmachar, as the 'abundant supply of potatoes' proved. (AC 6/59/5, 25 Aug 1914, 31 Aug 1915, 4 Jul 1916, 11 Dec 1917.)

On 10th Dec 1918, Mr Murray proposed that a war memorial be erected and a public meeting was organised. Oral tradition suggests that there was argument about whether the memorial should be in the cemetery or on the rough knoll to the south west of the village 'known as Shand's Wood' (ie the 'Shannie'). Another village oral tradition holds that Miss Shand, who used to work the croft on the east side of the knoll and whose name is perpetuated in the popular name for the site, wanted the land to become a play area for children after her death. Perhaps Mr Peter Burnett of Elrick, the actual owner of the land, was aware of this when he offered to gift the knoll to the Parish Council for the memorial. The gift was accepted and building began in 1922 with Kingseat patients helping at the site. The memorial was in place by 1924. During this period, and to its credit, the Parish Council declined to put on an exhibition of 'trophies' captured from German soldiers. (*Ibid.*, 10 Dec 1918, 20 Jan, 23 Mar, 27 Jul 1920, 6 May 1924; Testimony of Mr Bert Sangster.)

The names on the memorial include holders of the M.M., the D.C.M. and the M.S.M. Sixteen of the 31 were in the Gordons. One of these was Stewart Cooper, shown in the photograph. His loss meant hardship for his widow but, fortunately, his parents were able to look after his daughter at the Corseduick Croft. (Testimony of Mrs Elizabeth Walker, daughter of Stewart Cooper, who also kindly provided the photograph.)

As a result of the **Second World War**, sixteen new names had to be added to the memorial. They included those of two ladies, Elizabeth Burnett of the Civil Nursing Reserve and Helen Farquhar who had been attached to R.E.M.E. In many ways the impact of the new war was more immediate than had been the case in 1914. On the morning of Sunday, September 3rd 1939, even before Mr Chamberlain had spoken at 11 am, patients began to be moved out of Kingseat Hospital which now became *HMS Bacchante*, a naval hospital. (Testimony of Mr J. Imlah.) Casualties from the sinking of the *Royal Oak* soon arrived. In the cemetery there are simple but dignified headstones marking the graves of 61 naval or merchant marine sailors who died at Kingseat. Queen Elizabeth visited the hospital in 1940.

Soon after the outbreak of War, an L.D.V. unit , soon to be known as the **Home Guard**, was set up for Newmachar. Henry Catto was in charge as Platoon Sergeant. The platoon trained in the grounds of Elrick House. Each night, two men were detailed to stand duty at a post on Beauty Hill where watch could be kept for any signs of German invaders from the North Sea. In case they *did* come, a secret cache of arms, ammunition and explosives was established in the woods south of Straloch not far from Woodend Farm; guerrilla fighters would have the means to attack the enemy and his installations. (Testimonies of Mr J. Imlah, whose father worked at Kingseat farm and was in the Home Guard; of Mr H.G. Catto, Sgt. Catto's son and Mr H. Barclay, formerly of Woodend.)

Various air encounters and accidents are recalled including a German plane which crashed near the gates of Straloch, an RAF plane which went down one evening near Brownhills and another near Chapel of Elrick. (Testimonies of Mr C. McLaughlin who lived at Straloch whilst his father, a leading eye surgeon, served at Kingseat; Mrs M. Bogdan; Mr J. Imlah.)

Meanwhile, Mrs Rennie of Kinghorn caught a 'German spy' one late summer evening while raspberry picking. On being challenged, the 'spy' said 'Na, Na, Nae me! A'm fae Turra!' In fact, he was working for the Ordnance Survey. (Testimony of Mrs C. Penny, Mrs Rennie's daughter.) There were light-hearted moments at other times, not least when concert parties were organised for war causes. (See Chap XXII.) The Women's Rural Institute organised a War Work

Party and by April 1940, sugar rationing was limiting the entries for cake-making competitions. Yet something like a normal programme of activities and meetings was organised as well as concert parties for convalescents from Kingseat and fund-raising activities for prisoners of war and their families. V.E. week in May 1945 was marked by the singing of Psalm 124. (Minute Book of Newmachar SWRI, 16 Sep 1939, Apr, Jul 27 1940, 25 Jul 1942; Committee Book 1940-1946.)

Evacuees

Extracts from New Machar School Log Book:

1 Sep 1939	School closed for national emergency.
2-8 Sep 1939	School used as a billeting office for evacuees from Glasgow. Three rooms scrubbed out and disinfected. 290 evacuees passed through the School.
11 Sep 1939	School reopens; double shift working is arranged so that 84 Glasgow children might be taught by the three teachers who came with them.
28 May 1940	47 evacuees remain on the School roll.

(AC 6S/G49/1/3; AC 6S/G49/2/4.)

Mrs Mitchell (formerly Miss Cowie) was on the committee set up under the chairmanship of Mr Charles Ingram to receive the evacuees and arrange their accommodation. They arrived at the station by rail on a very dark night. Many were crying. Using her car, Miss Cowie began to take evacuees to their allotted hosts. One took one look at the Glasgow child and refused to accept him. Later that night, Miss Crombie of Swailend reported that her evacuee had 'escaped'; Miss Cowie had to scour the country for him. One family from Glasgow lived in the house formerly the Free Church stables (behind the present Butcher's shop). The mother always wore a fur coat, whatever the weather. She complained of the lack of a fish and chip shop in the village. Tragically, the family decided to return home only to be killed in an air raid. Most of the evacuees did drift home. (Testimony of Mrs Margaret Mitchell.)

For the men and women who were called up, the reality might be, for example, to march all the way to Nairn, to endure much boredom and then to be carried right round Africa via Capetown to reach Egypt and the Western desert in time for the Battle of El-Alamein. John Mearns was wounded and taken back to Cairo where he encountered the assistant from the Butcher's shop in Newmachar who, sadly, was shortly to lose his life. (Testimony of John Mearns.)

In 1950, a second memorial was dedicated to all the war dead, local and from elsewhere, by the Rev. Harold Ross who had himself served overseas in the Great War. The simple cross stands just inside the Cemetery. The original memorial remains in its place on the 'Shanny'. In her admirable history of Newmachar, Mrs Imlah described the site as having an 'air of peace and sanctuary'. This was in 1965. (C. Imlah, 'History of Newmachar', p. 9.) Unfortunately, in 2001 the site was overgrown and full of rubbish, while the steps and even the memorial had been vandalised. Repairs have been made and it is to be hoped that the memorial can be preserved at least until the centenary of peace in 2018.

The War Generation
Children at New Machar School in 1939
The teacher is Miss White

Chapter XXI
Kingseat Hospital 1901 - 1995

The Kingseat estate in Newmachar comprised three farms, Kingseat itself, Nether Kingseat and Cockcairn. After 1746, it was owned by a variety of groups or individuals the most notable of whom was Sir Thomas Blaikie (1802-61), a very wealthy Aberdeen 'developer' who was also Lord Provost in 1839-46 and 1853-56. Famous at the time for having an Aberdeen house with inside lavatories — indeed, two or three on each floor — he bought Kingseat in 1859. The Rev. William Gordon acquired the estate in 1874 but just over twenty years later was induced to sell it to the Aberdeen District Lunacy Board. The Board was looking for an alternative to the Cornhill building which, despite its elegant Archibald Simpson architecture, was more a place of confinement than a hospital. Investigations were conducted and Alt Scherbitz near Leipzig was the model which inspired the Aberdeen planners to produce something which was revolutionary for Britain. What was proposed was a country setting with plenty of space and fresh air plus the opportunity for patients to work on the land.

The key innovation at Kingseat, therefore, architecturally and medically, was the erection of villas in a spacious setting (as seen in the 1906 plan and the cricket photograph). Building began in 1901 but it was not until 1926 that the last of the ten villas was completed. Mr Birnie, of Reisque, a master builder, had an important hand in the large-scale works which the hospital necessitated. (Testimony of Mrs Ada Ross, the daughter of Mr Birnie.) Nether Kingseat continued to function as a farm but Kingseat and Cockcairn became part of the hospital policies and their buildings were altered or demolished. The new hospital needed its own water and Rainnieshill estate was temporarily purchased to ensure an adequate supply. A new short stretch of road had to be built from the crossroads below the station to the bridge so that coal could be carried to the villas. This, incidentally, created the now dangerous corner at the southern end of the railway bridge. More positively, there were telephones, and electricity was laid on from the beginning. Some local people began to acquire jobs as plumbers, builders, gardeners, cleaners etc. New inhabitants, including doctors, nurses and ancillary staff arrived. A nurses' home was built on the site and houses for other staff nearby. The population of the parish of New Machar rose from 1,393 in 1901 to 1,882 in 1911.

On 16th May 1904, the first 261 patients were admitted. One year later, there were 478. A remarkable medical experiment had begun and what was to prove a thriving new community had been created within the parish.

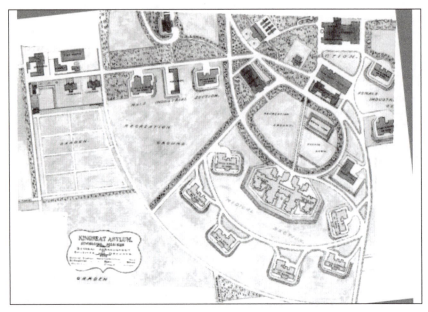

Kingseat Plan as in 1906 (By courtesy of Mrs Ellen Robertson)

A cricket match in progress at Kingseat, probably during the 1920s.
The character of the architecture is apparent.
(From an undated postcard)

Kingseat c. 1920-1979

Dr Charles Angus was the first Medical Superintendent but died young and it was Dr Hugh de Maine Alexander who really shaped Kingseat during his reign from 1906 to 1933. He was the only doctor present during the Great War. Dr J.S. Annandale was in charge from 1933 to 1939. Everything was highly organised and the somewhat sparsely-furnished wards were kept spotlessly clean and polished. Basically, 'kindness…adequate food, exercise, freedom where possible and work' was the treatment. Able-bodied patients did do farm work although occupational therapy was perhaps not much developed otherwise. The total atmosphere is described as 'good humoured, friendly and warm-hearted.' (1979 Booklet.)

Where is King Malcolm's Seat?
The story of Malcolm III sitting on the stone at Kingseat is not, like most 'ancient' traditions, one invented in the nineteenth century. The name appears on Robert Gordon's map of c. 1637 (see Chap VI) and there is no reason to doubt that Malcolm rested at what is a superb vantage point just to the north of the *original* Kingseat Farm (901193). Maybe the tale of the water from Betteral Well is invented. Maybe the stone which used to be shown to people before 1901 was no more than a stone but it seems a pity that it has disappeared — presumably as a result of all the building works after 1901. Could it be found and made a feature of the new Kingseat which is arising in 2001?

Mrs Dorothy Smith, whose father was a nurse until his unfortunate early death in 1934, testifies that Kingseat was indeed a happy place for staff of all grades and for the patients. Physical standards of living were in advance of their time; when Mrs Smith and her mother had to move from Wood Cottages into the village, they very much missed having electricity and an inside bathroom. **Mr H.G. Catto** also lived at Kingseat from 1922 and remembers it as a lively, largely self-supporting community. Younger members like him attended Craigie School and then went on to New Machar School. Later, Mr Catto was to cycle regularly into Aberdeen for classes at school and university on the bicycle bought for him at £6-10-0.

After the interval of the Second World War when the Hospital was taken over by the Navy (see Chap. XX), the Mental Hospital was re-established in 1946 under Dr Adam Milne. In 1956, Dr Ronald Stewart took over. Co-operation with other parts of the health and social services and with the University Department of Mental Health developed. Links with the wider community of Newmachar became even closer as chiropody and baby care clinics were set up in the 1970s together with a domiciliary nursing service. **Mr A. Low** points out that the existence of Kingseat meant that, in all sorts of ways during the post-war period, Newmachar had much better facilities than most other villages in the County of Aberdeen. As well as the medical services, there were football and cricket fields, a bowling green, and badminton courts, while a drama group, choirs and many other social activities flourished. **Mrs Ellen Robertson**, herself a nurse, whose father-in-law Mr Alistair Robertson (shown here) was head gardener, also mentions the wealth of activities and the community spirit. A vivid particular memory is the devastating effect on the trees around Kingseat of the great storm of 1953.

Mr Dave Lee began to work as a student nurse in the early 1970s. His very first day was memorable. Nervous and dressed in what was then a fashionable pink and white shirt plus 'kipper' tie, he encountered suspicion from one of the older members of staff who thought his clothes would frighten the patients! Fortunately, another responded: 'Leave the loon alone; I didnae fight in a war just so folk could be judged on the colour o' their sark.' Dave became good friends with both. Later, he was to have the interesting experience of visiting a direct copy of Kingseat Hospital in New Zealand — even down to the name. This has suffered worse indignities than Kingseat, Newmachar, at one time becoming a prison. (Testimony of Dave Lee.)

Mr Henry Catto

Mr Henry Catto joined the Kingseat community in 1922. Mr Catto was a plumber to trade and no doubt helped to keep the hospital infrastructure functional. Yet it is his other activities for the hospital and the wider Newmachar community which are so notable. He sang in the Church choir and was in charge of the Newmachar

unit of the Boys' Brigade. The photograph here shows some of the boys at their summer camp in 1932; Mr Catto can just be seen on the right of the picture. Both Henry Catto and his son (who is on the left in the picture) were notable cricketers who played for Kingseat in the inter war period against various Aberdeen Grades sides. Both staff and some of the patients were encouraged to play. During the War (see Chap. XX) Mr Catto became the sergeant of the Home Guard platoon.

After 1979

The advent of new kinds of drugs meant that many people with mental health problems could be treated as day patients; Kingseat's airy villas began to seem inefficient and out of date. In practice, the hospital became increasingly a refuge for geriatric or alcoholic patients. By the early 1990s, it seemed sensible to forsake the villas for modern buildings and facilities on the original Cornhill site in Aberdeen. Kingseat was finally closed on 31st March 1995 after a phased withdrawal from the site. Some of the staff transferred, too, leaving Newmachar. Others continued to live in the parish and commuted to Cornhill. Not a few chose to take early retirement and remain in Newmachar. After an interval as a Fire Brigade and Police anti-terrorist unit training ground, the Hospital site is scheduled to be developed as a housing complex. There are plans eventually to add facilities for light industry and services so that a source of local employment is created. It is to be hoped that in its new form Kingseat will serve the community as well as did the hospital.

(*Kingseat Hospital 1904 - 1979. A 75 Years Commemorative Booklet* is the source for some of the basic information in this chapter. This has interesting illustrations which provide a vivid impression of the social life connected with the Hospital. Dave Lee runs a web site devoted to reminiscences and records of Kingseat such as the experiences of a group of student nurses who arrived from Mauritius. They found Kingseat and Newmachar somewhat bewildering.)

Chapter XXII
Newmachar's Social, Cultural and Sporting Activities

It is difficult to say what institutions and organised activities there may have been in Newmachar in the medieval and early modern periods. Whatever other arrangements may have existed, the Church presumably provided the main centre for social interaction. No doubt there were sports and contests of some kind from time to time. The upper classes certainly indulged in various forms of hunting but their social inferiors had to be content with a little surreptitious poaching.

St John's Lodge of Freemasons, 1819

Apart from the Church, the first recorded organisation aiming to cater for relatively large numbers of men in the parish is the St John's Lodge of Freemasons which was set up in 1819. This foundation is interesting and important for a number of reasons.

Freemasonry may have some roots in the activities of medieval stone masons who often 'lodged' together at major building sites. However, Freemasonry in its modern form is a Scottish invention of the Renaissance period. Its main progenitor was William Schaw. The craft spread to England and other countries during the seventeenth and eighteenth centuries. 'Speculative' and 'non-operative' members, that is people who were not actually stonemasons, became more and more involved as the 'craft' spread. The Church - even the Scottish Church with its hatred of ritual - seems generally to have turned a blind eye to masonic ceremonies. This is a matter of some importance in Newmachar. The Scottish Grand Lodge had been set up in 1736. (D. Stevenson, *The First Freemasons. Scotland's Early Lodges and their Members*, Aberdeen, 1988 pp. 1-10; *The Origins of Freemasonry*, Cambridge, 1988, pp. 26-32.)

Why should a lodge have been set up in Newmachar in 1819? Although there were about ten lodges already in the region of Aberdeenshire and an important set of rules had been drawn up in the City in 1670, 1819 was not really a good time to raise the spectre of freemasonry. Spectre it had become in the eyes of many people during the late eighteenth-early nineteenth century 'Age of Revolutions.' Certainly, many people in positions of authority believed freemasonry to be a threat against order and stability. In Britain, there was some question whether the 1799 Act against Sedition made freemasonry illegal. Therefore masonic writers tried hard to prove that freemasonry was not preaching revolutionary anarchy. (For example, Alex. Laurie, *The History of Freemasonry..*, Edinburgh, 1804, pp. vii, 76, 145, 329.)

Because of suspicions about freemasonry and any kind of secret or semi-secret association, when it was proposed to set up a lodge in Newmachar, the Justices of the Peace had to give their permission. They went to the extent of adding an extra rule to the new body's regulations saying it would be dissolved if the members, entered 'into any combination for advance or regulation of wages.' This, after all, was 1819, the year of 'Peterloo' and paranoia on the part of the Tory government under Lord Liverpool at any sign of working class organised activity.

Was there any threat of revolutionary activity in Newmachar? This seems unlikely. Yet it may not be without significance that the minister, Alexander Simpson, who had expressed some mildly reformist ideas in the two statistical accounts that he wrote (see Chap. XIII), became the chaplain of the new Lodge. Moreover his son, also Alexander, described himself as 'a student of philosophy' in the list of lodge members. Perhaps William Fiddes, a surgeon, also had some advanced ideas. The Master of the Lodge was William Forbes who may have been from the laird's family in Fintray. These four men seem to have been the only members of the 90-strong lodge who would have had much education.

Whether or not Simpson had some idea of encouraging political awareness, it is quite clear that the farmers, shoemakers and the like - who made up the rest of the 90 strong membership - were certainly not revolutionary subversives; basically they were setting up a friendly society which, with the addition of some intriguing ritual, acted as a means of providing social insurance for men or their wives against sickness, incapacity or death. (*Rules and Regulations of St John's Lodge of Freemasons, Newmachar*, Aberdeen, 1819.) The Newmachar Lodge continues to exist but seems not to have published any further account of its proceedings.

Formal and Informal Games and Sports in the Earlier Twentieth Century

The one guinea entrance fee for the Masons' Lodge would have been a deterrent to most of Newmachar's inhabitants even if they had been invited to enter. Most would have to continue to depend on less organised sports and pastimes as they continued to do well into the twentieth century. Throwing an ordinary hammer, casting sticks at an 'Aunt Sally' figure, playing with clay marbles, 'Hunters Figgie' and the like are all mentioned. In a country area, naturally there was much interest in what amounted to poaching or occupations like trout guddling. Of course, as schooling became compulsory and the normal part of young life, organised sports like rounders and especially football became more and more important. A small play park with swings and roundabouts was set up near the Church in 1957. (Testimonies of Mr W. Middleton, Mr Robbie Ingram, Mr Bert Sangster; George Rennie, *Son of the Soil*, pp. 12-15; C. Imlah 'Outline', p. 33.)

Picnics were popular in the early part of the twentieth century. George V's coronation in 1910 was celebrated with a picnic in the grounds of Elrick House for the benefit of the parish children. (*Ellon Times* 'Millennium Moments', Spring 2000 p. XV.) Many remember school picnic parties being taken by special train to Cruden Bay or Newburgh. The school raised the money to pay the LNER for the train by organising a concert with the children adapting a song to 'gie us a penny to go to Cruden Bay.' Even the fierce Mr Souter did not object.

Mrs Ethel Begg remembers picnics nearer at hand in the field at Reisque where races and games were organised; local people including Andrew Cheyne at the shop donated sweets and cakes. (Testimonies of Mrs E. Walker; and of Mr Bert Sangster, Mrs Ethel Begg and Mrs M. Mitchell, as reported in *Newmachar News* Nos. 110-112, 1998.)

Organised events aimed more at adults included ploughing matches near Newmachar Inn and at Cockairns (902186) as in 1900. Indeed, it seems there was a Newmachar Ploughing Association. ('*Millennium Moments*,' p. v.) Of even more general appeal were the Newmachar Games held in the field near the Inn. They were held at the weekend nearest the traditional date for Newmachar's annual holiday - the second Thursday in August (*Aberdeen Almanac*, 1906.) The 1920 Games included the usual sports, weight throwing etc, bagpipe and dancing competitions, together with a 'fancy dress cycle parade' and a five-a-side football match. Prizes ranged from 15/- to 25/-. Mr G. Rennie of the Westside family organised the Games in that year. There were two special trains to and from Aberdeen. (*Aberdeen Journal*, 6th August 1920 reprinted in *Newmachar News 21*, 1981.) The Stoneywood Brass Band was usually in attendance. For the evening, a wooden dance floor was laid. In the 1920s and '30s it became usual to erect a marquee so that a flower show could be held; the WRI organised the industrial classes. After the Second World War, the Games died although galas were held on Andrew Cheyne's field at Reisque for a time. Today only the annual Flower Show remains, organised by the Scout and Guide Association. (C. Imlah, 'Short Outline', pp. 33-4.)

The Later Twentieth Century

With the development of organised professional sports their amateur and semi-professional counterparts began to thrive at local level. Cricket, introduced to the Northeast in 1746 did not become popular until after about 1870. The Aberdeen Grades competition became notable from the 1920s. Unlike most other Northeast towns and villages, Newmachar did not enter the Grades, but there was a team based at Kingseat which played regular fixtures against Grades teams in the 1930s and '40s. (Testimony of Mr H.G. Catto.)

Summer League 1952

Football and the Football Ground

Association Football has steadily become more and more important during the last 75 years or so. It seems that Newmachar Football Club was founded in 1920. The club began to play on a field at Reisque. This field had been bought by Andrew Wood of the Inn from the Rainnieshill Estate and it was now sold on to Andrew

Cheyne for £100. The football club itself was unable to raise such a large a sum of money and so Andrew Cheyne in effect bought the field for them and the

Newmachar FC won three cups in 1964

benefit of the community because other events like galas were also held there. Andrew Cheyne died in 1954 and part of the field was built on. Hence the ground had to be moved a little to the west on to another part of what had once been the semi-moorland rough grazing area of Reisque. (See Chap. IV.) The new field was marshy and difficult to adapt but farmers and other volunteers came with tractors and other equipment to produce a usable surface. The ground was then officially taken over by Aberdeen County Council as a public facility. The field was named after Charles Gordon, the proprietor of the village shop who was connected with the football club. (Information supplied by Mrs Sheila Bruce and Mr Archie Low.)

Newmachar Football Club continued to play only regular friendly matches until 1951 when a Newmachar and District Summer League was set up; the team now entered this League and a photograph is available showing the team in that year. The team had an extremely successful season in 1964 when they won the Cheyne, McPherson and Craigmyle cups. The manager then was Jimmie Forrest, known as 'Briggy' as he came from Bridgefoot Farm. (Testimony of Mr H.J. Barclay who also has a photograph of the successful team.) A little later, in about 1967-8, a certain degree of discord arose as some members thought Newmachar F.C. was signing too many players from outwith Newmachar; there seemed little chance for younger players to get a game. Hence Newmachar Youth F.C. was formed and played in the same Summer League; it was managed by Harry Rennie and had an extraordinarily successful season in 1970, winning not only the three cups mentioned but the Aberdeenshire Cup Winners Cup as well.

The Summer League was disbanded in the 1970s. The Youth Team now began to play in the Aberdeenshire Amateur League and gained promotion to Division 3 in 1980. But it was unable to sustain its position and was, in effect, substituted by a Colts Club which currently fields three teams. Meanwhile, Kingseat United had been formed in 1960 and also played in the Amateur League reaching Division 1 by 1980. Once more, the problem of bringing in non-local players emerged and in 1987 Newmachar United F.C. was formed. The Colts and Gordon District agreed to its using the ground at Reisque and it entered Division 8 of the League immediately, winning all of its matches and gaining promotion. NUFC now play in Division 2 East. (I am grateful to Mr Brian Wood, secretary of Newmachar United F.C., Mr H.J. Barclay, Mr A. Low and

Mr A. Robertson for providing information and to Mrs J. Robertson for letting me see a photograph of the 1970 team. See also *Newmachar News* 74, 1990.)

Newmachar's most successful footballer to date has been Neil Simpson who played for New Machar School and Newmachar F.C. before in 1978 moving on via national youth teams to Aberdeen Football Club, Newcastle and Motherwell. Mr Simpson is now an Area Coach in the Highland League and is much respected as someone interested in and helpful to school football teams.

Other Sports

A Bowls Club was set up in 1955 and continues to be a highly successful local organisation.

The most notable sporting development in the late twentieth century was the creation of a new golf course and a golf club. The project began with a public meeting in 1979, the initiative being taken by Charles Keith. Difficulties with Gordon District Council and other statutory bodies over planning permission meant a change of venue to Swailend. The land cost £120,000 and construction costs almost half a million pounds but ingenious ways of raising the money were found. A club house was built at the site of old Swailend Cottage. The club house and the course were officially opened on 28th September 1990. Since then a second course, Hawkshill, has been constructed, a pro-am shop set up and the club and its courses are now recognised as one of Scotland's premier golf venues.

The Club was put firmly on the map when their then professional, Paul Lawrie, won the Open. Perhaps the Open itself will one day be held at Newmachar.

Tennis, badminton, netball and some other sports have suffered since Kingseat's facilities ceased to be available in 1995. The presence of Kingseat, not only with its facilities but also with its staff, and sometimes patients, including people of considerable sporting skill, was of great benefit to Newmachar through most of the twentieth century, giving it advantages enjoyed by few other Aberdeenshire communities.

Two activities which have developed quite independently of Kingseat are trout fishing and horse riding. Maurice Innes has constructed ponds for trout fishing at Old Toun of Brownhills just south of the village. Beside the old path to Kingseat another fishery has been established at the pond created by the dam for the former Pinkie Mill.

The first Newmachar Horse Show was held on 19th -20th June 1983. (*Press & Journal*, 21 June 1983.) There are various small centres but the premier organisations promoting riding and associated events are the stables at Upper Tack, Lower Rainnieshill, Rosehall and, until 2001, Sessnie Equestrian to the north of the village.

Whether Chess is a sport or a cultural activity may be arguable but certainly in recent years the teams have been more than ordinarily successful under the guidance of Dave Smith. By 2001 there were 28 active graded players including Gregor Smith who has been an under-12 international playing for Scotland.

There are some notable walkers and trekkers in Newmachar. The village postie, Teresa Nicol, is a great walker both in her job and on the hills, while Elspeth Maclean cycles for charity in such places as Uganda or the Holy Lands. Two very intrepid trekkers are Rhona and Matthew Kennedy who were married on Oxen Craig and who here describe some of their walks.

Since we met in 1991 the two of us have enjoyed getting away to the hills as often as our jobs will allow us. We still regularly escape to the Cairngorms and the west coast of Scotland to explore and camp in the mountains but in October 1994 we ventured to Kathmandu and completed an independent trek to Kalar Patar above Gorak Shep (Everest Base Camp) at 5,545m to have wonderful, close views of Everest's summit. In December 1996 we climbed Mount Kilimanjaro via the Marangu route. The six-day climb from sea level via Gillman's point to Uhuru Peak at 5,896m was rewarded with stunning vistas across the African plains. Aconcagua in the Andes followed. The 6,960m mountain (the highest in the Southern Hemisphere) is on the border between Argentina and Chile. The 'El Nino' year meant heavy snowfalls, which prevented us from reaching the summit. In September 1999 we were a bit closer to home trekking through the High Atlas Mountains in Morocco and ascending Toubkal at 4,167m. In 2000 we were in Spain and also planning to visit the Torres Del Paine National Park in Patagonia, South America, to view the volcanoes and glaciers, and cross to Tierra de Fuega to look across to Antarctica. Our pipe dream is a trek to the South Pole.

Cultural and Social Activities

In the 1840s Newmachar had both a general library and a religious library. What happened to these is not clear. Whiterashes set up a library just after the Great War. There was a very active Library Committee and the organisation was run entirely by volunteers. (Information from Mr & Mrs G. Cameron.) Much more recently Newmachar began to be served by a mobile library van until in May 1985 a small purpose-built permanent library was opened. The range of books on the shelves is good, but in addition the full resources of Aberdeenshire's service are available to borrowers; for example, the small local collection can be supplemented by works from the excellent collection at the headquarters in Oldmeldrum, and books can be borrowed from other libraries as well as a proportion of the stock being changed regularly.

Music making in Newmachar was a notable feature in the earlier part of the twentieth century. Mr Knight, who took over Sittyton from the Cruickshanks (see Chap. IX), had three daughters, Mary, Marjory and Annie, who later went to live in one of the cottages near Elrick House. Annie was a music teacher who indefatigably cycled to her pupils' houses whatever the weather. (Testimony of Mrs Betty Harley.) She also organised the WRI choir for many years and a Junior Choir. Another music teacher in the parish was Miss Crombie, from the family formerly at Woodend, who became organist for the Free Church; she herself lived in Swailend Cottage. As noted in Chapter XIII, Mrs Cecilia Kerr was a talented violinist who organised the choir, and even an orchestra, for the Free Church, and conducted the WRI Choir. She co-operated with both Miss Knight and Miss Crombie. (Information from Mrs M. Nicol.)

Mrs Kerr and her musician colleagues were capable of putting on performances of Bach cantatas but there was also music and singing of a different kind in the parish. The teacher at Whiterashes, Miss Duguid, ran shows in the 1920s and '30s. Rather later, there were 'bothy nichts' with singing, recitations, playing the melodion etc. Competitions were held: Kingseat v. Newmachar could attract an audience of 500 in the Hall. Most performers had the genuine experience of living in a farm bothy. (Information from Mrs M. Mitchell.) Bothy ballads also featured in the repertoire of the Lobbans' Concert Party which gave performances over a wide area and also featured on Grampian TV. (Information from Mr & Mrs A. Hay.) Equally notable from the 1970s has been a concert party led and inspired by Margaret Mitchell, originally consisting of ladies from the WRI who had put together a show just to entertain WRI members in Newmachar and elsewhere. It was very popular in the Grampian area, entertaining a wide variety of groups, and put on about 250 shows before deciding to call it a day in 1999. (*Newmachar News* 114, 1999.)

A show of a special kind was put on in 1941 as part of an initiative to raise money for Russian children. It was organised by Mrs Birnie, wife of the builder. The children shown here include Mrs Birnie's two daughters, Ada and Lorna. Harold Barclay, Betty, Sandy and Willie Ingram and Bunty Rennie are also shown. A similar show was put on in subsequent years. (Testimony of Mrs Ada Ross née Birnie; Mr H.J. Barclay who provided the photograph.)

The early 1940s concert parties were held in the old hall. This was also the venue for a series of dramatic productions. Both Mr and Mrs Burnett-Whyte of Elrick House were keen on amateur theatre and organised several productions. They also arranged for visiting productions by Aberdeen drama groups. This was only one of the numerous activities in which Mrs Burnett-Whyte was involved. She organised events to raise funds for the League of Pity. She also regularly arranged Burns Suppers for the village. Mrs Mitchell remembers one when the speaker - perhaps one of the organiser's actor friends - became so excited that his gestures with the knife threatened those around him more than the haggis. Bert Sangster recalls another speaker who went on for nearly two hours and had to be forcibly stopped! (Testimonies of Mrs M. Mitchell and Mr B. Sangster.)

More manufactured entertainment came to the village in the 1940s and '50s in the form of a mobile cinema but once the new hall was built, the shows were put on there. (Testimony of Mr Jim Cowie.)

To mention all the clubs and societies which have existed in Newmachar in the last hundred years would be very difficult but beside the near 200-year record of the masons, there is the 100 plus years of the Church Guild which was established in 1899. Another women's organisation is the 'Rural' - the WRI. From the historian's point of view it is a model institution. Ever since the foundation of the Newmachar Institute on May 4th 1926, the records of its general and committee meetings have been meticulously kept. More important, the Institute has provided a focus of interest and an opportunity for companionship for women who otherwise might have led rather isolated lives. In addition much charitable work has been undertaken. Mrs Alexander, wife of the Kingseat Superintendent became the first Secretary under the presidency of

Mrs Quentin Irvine of Straloch. The photograph shows the committee 25 years later, when Mrs Burnett-Whyte was President. With her, standing from the left are Mrs Watson (then Miss Williamson), Mrs Rennie, Mrs Abel, Mrs Gordon, Mrs J. Irvine, Mrs Ethel Begg and (sitting) Mrs Cruickshank and Mrs King. (Information from Mrs Agnes Cran.)

The Over 50s Club is described below by Mrs Jean Emslie.

In late 1971 some people in the village met in the hotel to see about forming a Club for OAPs. It was decided to go ahead and the first meeting was held in the hall on 25th January 1972 with Mr Quirie as President and Mrs Rollo as Vice President - and pianist. The next meeting had games, cards or dominoes. That almost set the pattern - entertainment one meeting, cards or dominoes the next. Later we had a good Concert Party with Mrs Ewen as pianist. Sometimes, the school pupils entertained us. It was always very good to hear the children sing and to see faces light up when they spotted a grandparent. At the AGM in 2000, members were asked if they wanted to change the name; so it became the Newmachar Over 50s Club.   Jean Emslie

Among more recent organisations is the Thursday Club for senior citizens which was first opened in the mid-1990s by the Social Work Department, who later had to withdraw funding. The local volunteer helpers, led by Mrs Nora Whyte, agreed to try and keep the club running on a self-funding basis because it was apparent that the club was greatly appreciated by its members.

To cater for younger members of the community there was the Boys' Brigade already mentioned in Chapter XIII. In the 1950s under the leadership of John Davidson, it provided 'discipline, camaraderie and hard physical exercise' which Jim Cowie remembers as a tremendous formative influence upon him. The Scouts, as the photograph shows, were originally led as Scoutmaster by the Rev. D.R. Kerr. Latterly, Mr George Mitchell was in charge and there was a full programme of camping and  trekking. The Guides Company was originally formed by the teacher, Miss Jack, in about 1930. Later, Ethel Begg recalls weekly meetings held in a loft at Gaucyhillock Farm with Margaret MacInlay as captain. (*Newmachar News* 111, 1998.) The Guides continued to undertake full programmes of camping and training in self-reliance and various kinds of proficiency until very recently. However, it has been difficult in the last few years for both the Scouts and the Guides to find leaders.

The Aviation Gallery
Although it might be argued that Newmachar has little to offer visitors, many who come do in fact wish to see the Aviation Gallery whose inception is explained by Bruce Sutherland.

My father spent all the war years in the RAF and thereafter recounted all manner of stories to me. In addition, my pride and joy was a wooden model of an Avro York, painted silver, which was made by my uncle and taken home as a present on his demob. in 1946. My appetite for aviation was fed by attendance all the Fleet Air Arm and RAF airshow spectaculars at both Lossiemouth and Kinloss in Moray, from the early '50s to the mid-'60s, when cut backs meant a scarcity of air shows north of Leuchars.

In the early '90s I rekindled my interest and started collecting aircraft pictures and photographs yet again, especially prints with a historical connection to aviation in the north east of Scotland in the period of the Second World War. But the content of the gallery reflects aviation from the days of the 'stringbags' through the Second World War and all the other theatres of war and conflict over the past 55 years, showing how, within half a century, aircraft have developed into high speed projectiles crammed with electronics. These aircraft have been depicted by very talented artists, many being members of the Guild of Aviation Artists, some as old as 80 plus and who saw action first hand.

The gallery's visitors book has signatures from all over the world, including countries such as Sarawak, Zimbabwe, the USA, the contributors often casting their minds back to service careers which included both the tragic and amusing incidents. Historical information is often asked for by people curious to confirm events in their own memories or tracing the incidents which led to air crew being lost.

From my standpoint the project is ongoing, a history lesson in pictorial fashion of most of this past twentieth century, which has seen advances in engineering and flight from basics to space travel.

Joan Burnett's Women's Costume Collection

Mrs Joan Burnett, a notable Newmachar resident until Autumn 2000, accumulated a remarkable collection of women's apparel illustrating changes in

fashion over a century and a half. The collection has now been passed to Aberdeen City Art Galleries and Museums. Mrs Burnett here describes the nature of her collection which is illustrated by her own delightful sketches.

I have built up a collection of women's clothes dating from the early years of Queen Victoria's reign to the 1960s. Essentially it is a private and personal collection, but from early on I have been asked to show the clothes by people who became interested and intrigued by the idea of authentic examples of period costume. I was willing to do so, but clothes hanging empty, however artfully displayed, cannot convey the

circa 1860

essence of any style truly. Very soon I had willing volunteers to model for me, drawn from friends and neighbours in Newmachar, especially those with an interest in the history of costume and with slender figures!

The first shows were informal displays in private houses. The earliest organised show was for the Ladies Guild of Newmachar Church in the early '80s. Since that time we have fulfilled many engagements and travelled far and wide across North-east Scotland. Many of the shows were to raise funds for deserving charities, others were requests by various groups and organisations. In the early days we visited and were made welcome in many a village hall and school; later, grander venues provided gracious settings against which the costumes were greatly enhanced as they were displayed in castles, country houses and galleries.

circa 1905

At the end of a show, people frequently would come to me with an old suitcase or bag and bring forth relics decades old, almost apologetically explaining that they did not know what to do with these things, but the hope was that I would care for them. Some pieces were in pristine condition, others needed care and attention; I spent much time on repair and restoration as gently and sympathetically as possible.

Throughout the Victorian period and the many styles that evolved, women's dress was heavy, voluminous and tight; comfort was sacrificed to the illusion of a tiny waist and an air of feminine helplessness. The First World War divided the old order from the new in a way more cataclysmic than the date 1900 could symbolise. The more fluid fashion that developed during the '20s and the '30s gave practicality and freedom of movement at last, and reflected the emergence of women from centuries of inhibiting long skirts, long hair and short lives.

The Problem of the Hall

All the organisations mentioned and others have to a greater or lesser degree relied upon the availability of a hall in the village. Whilst Kingseat was functioning, facilities there relieved the pressure on the village hall, but the closing of the hospital has made the hall problem acute again.

As noted in Chap. XIV, the first village hall was the former parochial school building. It was sold to a board of trustees by the School Board in 1885. The trustees eventually, and reluctantly, had to give way to the local authority but a hall committee remained and remains still separate from the Parish Council and the later Community Council. Whatever arguments there may have been between competing committees, the basic problem with the old school was that it was simply too small as well as lacking in modern facilities like running water and electricity. Mrs Mitchell recalls being present at a meeting in 1938 when attempts were being made to find an alternative. The former Free Church seemed a possibility but many folk thought a new hall should be built. (Information from Mrs Mitchell; Rules for Newmachar Hall Fund Gala and Flower Show, 13 Aug 1938.) No doubt everyone was aware of the fact that, two or three miles up the road, the hamlet of Whiterashes had acquired a purpose-built public hall in 1922 which must have seemed superior to what Newmachar then had. It was renovated in the late 1990s with a four-year long programme of improvements. The War curtailed initiatives on the Newmachar problem and it was not until the mid-1950s that the campaign could resume. A series of

concerts and dances raised money in a remarkably short time to match grants, and the new hall was opened on 14th February 1955, memorable also because of the terrible storm that night. Andrew Cheyne, shown with a model of the hall, and Jimmie Forrest led the way in making the new building a reality.

The thirty-year lease of the hall given by Gordon District runs out in 2010. Even though in 1983/4 an extension and some new facilities costing over £4000 were added to the hall, it seems urgent to provide a replacement. The building is deficient by modern standards and the demands upon it from a growing population inevitably become ever greater. This is true notwithstanding the fact that, with the help of some public money, the Scout and Guide Headquarters was built in 1999. It is a very useful addition to the facilities in the village. However, neither the village hall nor the Scout Hut alone can meet all the demands which exist. There is a great need for a large, multi-purpose building in the centre of the village.

It is to be hoped that the Hall Committee, the Community Council and Aberdeenshire Council will be able to find a solution to the problem of Newmachar's hall; after 115 years it is time it was solved.

The Newmachar Self-Build Project, 1974-6

A remarkable example of what can be achieved through co-operation and hard work was the Self-Build Project. This embraced 38 houses in Burnwood Avenue, Burnwood Drive and Miller Gardens. The latter name honours Councillor Paul Miller who was the inspirer of the scheme. Acting in his private, not his local authority capacity, he wished to prove that it was possible for ordinary people to obtain for themselves pleasant and commodious houses much more cheaply than from a developer.

A firm called Caledonia Self Build bought the land in November 1974, eventually recouping the cost from the participants' mortgages. In the following Spring, work began. Those in the scheme were divided into five teams, each of which tackled a group of houses which they now proceeded to build with their own hands. Although there were two bricklayers and one joiner in the group, the majority had no building skills and had to learn as they went along. They also had to learn how to co-operate, sharing advice and skills as well as the labouring tasks. Even the roads had to be laid by the Self-Build Group; only after the scheme was completed did the Council adopt them. Mortgage companies subjected the homes to periodic inspections by architects and so nothing could be skimped.

The scheme was completed in more or less two years. Although it was a time of some strain and stress for those involved - and for their children - the end results seemed to justify the work and worry; Paul Miller's idea had been vindicated. (Based on information provided by Mrs Catherine Keith.)

Newmachar News
Another success story, and an equally notable feature of Newmachar's collective life, is the community newsletter, *Newmachar News*. It began publication in November 1977 following the setting up of the Community Council. A band of dedicated editors, Ann Boyle, Erica Watson, Steven Veitch, Christine Rance, Ethmay Dunbar and Jill Bridges, with the aid of equally dedicated contributors and deliverers, has kept the *Newmachar News* in continuous circulation ever since. Local events and developments are announced, businesses advertised and the local councillor can use it as a means of communication with his constituents. The back copies constitute now a valuable archive on the past quarter of a century in Newmachar. By the end of 2001, Issue No. 125 had appeared.

Newmachar Youth FC in 1970 when four cups were won

Chapter XXIII
The Twentieth-Century Economy: Agriculture and Farm Life
since the 1920s

Writing his account of Newmachar for the *Third Statistical Account*, Harold Ross
was able to say in December 1950 that the parish was still mainly agricultural.
(*The Third Statistical Account of Scotland: the County of Aberdeen* [hereafter 3SA]
Glasgow, 1960, p. 159.) At the end of the century, in December 2000, that
remained true in one sense: most land in the parish was still in agricultural use.
The real difference is that the majority of the population is concentrated in
Newmachar Village and does not work on the land. In the last 25 years,
Aberdeen has become an oil city and a financial centre as well as continuing in
its traditional role as a focus for fishing, farming-connected, educational and
administrative activities. Some of these activities have spilled over into the
parish area and created employment opportunities but the great majority of
Newmachar's workers have to commute into Aberdeen each day. Despite this,
for most of the twentieth century Newmachar remained a rural community and
agriculture continues important today.

Land Tenure and Land Use
The greatest organisational change in the twentieth century was the
disappearance or diminution in importance of the five or six estates which in one
guise or another had dominated Newmachar for the previous 500 years. The
largest, Parkhill, was broken up into three lots and sold in 1927. Rainnieshill
was similarly disposed of in the 1920s. Elrick changed hands from the Burnett
family to the Burnett-Whyte family in 1926 but was sold again in 1956. North
Kinmundy was left by its last proprietor to the Cruickshank Botanic Garden
Trustees. who eventually sold off the farms and in 1956 the houses. (Testimony of
Mr A. Low.) South Kinmundy was also broken up. Only Straloch has remained
as an estate which would have been recognisable to its nineteenth-century
owners. Even so, several farms on the southern part of the estate were sold in
the 1970s. Most of the estate was put up for sale in 2001 ending over 220 years
of ownership by the Ramsay/Irvine family; its future is as yet uncertain.

The situation of tenants is complicated by legislation. Under the nineteenth
century system, leases tended to be for seven or fourteen year periods - an
arrangement related to the 7 shift system of rotation. (See Chap. IX.) An Act
in 1947 gave much greater security of tenure but created difficulties for
landlords who found it difficult to realise the value of their land if they wished
to develop new initiatives. Various expedients such as partnership arrangements
between laird and tenant have been used to make the situation more flexible.
Legislation for a new system of 5 to 15 year leases is currently in prospect.

Through all these changes the general trend has been for tenant farmers to become owner-occupiers with the partial exception of Straloch. In 1896 only 8% of the land in the parish was owner-occupied; by 1966 the proportion was 63%. Larger farms have tended to swallow up small holdings. (Cowie, pp. 27-8.) There have been two consequences. First, some of the houses have been taken over for farm workers or for people unconnected with the land. In the 1950s and '60s, modern bungalows began to be built in farm areas and sometimes looked rather alien among the fields and earlier granite-built houses. Partly for this reason, a more recent trend has been to convert redundant farm steadings into luxury country dwellings. Some older cottages have been left unoccupied. The second consequence is, as the accompanying table shows, that the actual area of land in use for agricultural or connected purposes has tended to decline; many of the small farms were based on rather marginal land which it was difficult to keep in gainful use in an era of increasingly mechanised large-scale farming operations. Nevertheless, none of the Newmachar farms is inordinately large; in the 1950s there were no fewer than 134 holders of land of over 1 acre in a population of only just over 2000. Other reasons for the decline in the amount of land available for agricultural purposes in the 1990s were the introduction of forestry at Lairshill (865187) and the construction of Newmachar Golf Club's two excellent courses. (See Chap. XXII.)

Mechanisation: the Advent of the Tractor

In 1900 there may have been some steam threshing machines in use but the main sources of power on the farms were water mills, horses and large amounts of human muscle. In 1953 there were still 91 horses in the parish - how many of them working ones is not stated in the *Statistical Account*. Already, however, there were more than that number of tractors - 98 in fact. Mr Charles Ingram who took over Elrick had been a pioneer in the use of tractors as an individual farmer and as a contractor in the Newmachar area. (Testimony of Mr Alistair Ingram and see below.) Tractors could be used not only to pull ploughs with multiple shares but also drive other machines such as reapers and threshers. Later, the hire or purchase of large combine harvesters became common. Of course, the use of the internal combustion engine meant also the end of the use of horses for transport and delivery purposes.

Tractors could be adapted to provide power for other tasks on the farm such as lifting or driving circular saws. However, electrical power proved even more convenient for a great many tasks and soon it became vital to have electricity in milking parlours. For a time, many farms relied on their own generators powered by diesel engines, but use of the public supply became the norm. Mameulah Farm obtained access to mains electricity at the same time as many houses in the village which was earlier than most farms. This was presumably because a supply was needed for the pumping station nearby to bring water into the Mameulah reservoir. (Information from Mr Alexander Buchan.) However, during the second half of the twentieth century, the Hydro-Electric Board took supply cables to practically every farm and cottage. The consequence of access to new sources of power was that the water mills, which had been so important, became redundant. (See Chapter X.) Even the two meal mills at Pinkie (Boddams) and Elrick had ceased to be used by 1950. In 1986 a windmill which had operated for some time at Rainnieshill stopped working. (*Newmachar News*, May 1986.)

Another consequence of the end of the era of horse power and the way of life of which it was such a vital part was the closure of the smithies in the parish. The building on the main road in the centre of the village is the only reminder of horses and the way of life they represented. Garages took over and began to cater for the needs of the new work-horses, the 'Fergie' tractors.

Agricultural Workers
The end of the importance of the horse meant also an end to the expertise and way of life of a very important group of farm workers. (See the testimony of Mr Middleton, Chap. IX.) Horsemen had to learn other skills such as driving a tractor or leave agriculture altogether. In fact, there was a reduction in the number of workers needed on the farms. At the same time, conditions of employment generally improved; the 9-hour day had been introduced after pressure by the Aberdeenshire Branch of the Scottish Union of Farm Servants in the 1920s. It seems that in general relations between employer and employee remained good in Aberdeenshire. Even so, the drift from the land to higher paid urban jobs has continued up to 2001; farm work now demands a variety of skills, preferably some college training and continues to be a physically demanding occupation. Most farms are not only owner-occupied but also owner and family worked. In 2001, only 11 of the agricultural holdings in the parish had regular or seasonal staff as employees. In fact, only 53 individuals were recorded as agricultural workers.

Stock Rearing
During the middle decades of the twentieth century, stock rearing, especially of beef cattle, remained, as it had been since the agricultural revolution of the 1830s (Chap. IX), the principal agricultural activity in Newmachar and even increased in importance. The only hindrance to the steady increase came in the Second World War when more arable production was officially encouraged. Most livestock were being fattened on summer grass and white clover. In 1953, 2036 beef cattle were recorded as being in Newmachar. It is not clear whether this figure includes stores and calves kept only for short periods. As the table shows, there were at least a thousand such animals in December 2000. The most notable change between the middle and the end of the century as far as

cattle are concerned is the fall in the number of dairy cows from 789 to zero. In the 1940s and 50s, about 20 farms produced milk. (Testimony of Mrs Jean Emslie and see below.) But sanitary regulations plus the low prices for milk products meant a steady trend towards fewer and larger herds. By 1972 that number of dairy farms had halved. (Testimony of Mr Silver and see below.) At the end of the century there was just one dairy farm in the neighbourhood, Cairnton (863195), and even that is not in the original parish of Newmachar.

In 1953 there were 666 sheep in Newmachar and the number has continued to increase in a very marked way so that by 2000, there were over 7000. Originally confined to higher rougher land, mostly on the Straloch estate, they now occupy land on many of the farms.

Pigs had never been kept in very large numbers in Newmachar although many farms might have one or two. After the War, they became extremely important when Robert Lawson opened his factory at Dyce for pork products. At the same time, Lawson's developed Hill of Goval (889156) as a unit where the Danish Landrace breed was introduced to produce hybrid stock which would provide for the modern demands for bacon. Breeding pigs were sold to other farms. The tendency was for a small number of farms to keep large numbers of pigs as at Middle Tack which had a pig unit. (Information from Mrs Chrissie Davies.) Later, Hill of Goval was taken over by the National Pig Development Company and then by the Pig Improvement Company of Oxford. However, Lawson's closed in the 1990s and this meant effectively the end of pig farming in Newmachar. For a time, one farm, Lairshill, maintained an organic breeding herd but the land is now turned over to forestry.

As noted already, the number of working horses declined as the use of the tractor increased. In the 1990s, though, the number of horses began to rise again but this is entirely a result of leisure activities; none of the 127 horses recorded as being in Newmachar in December 2000 was used for agricultural purposes. There is an important centre for the Bavarian Warmblood breed of horses connected with Straloch estate and managed by Susan and Gerhardt Fichtner. There are also riding and livery stables at Upper Tack, Monykebbock, Rosehall and Lower Rainnieshill whilst many farmers offer grazing for horse owners from town or country.

In the early and middle decades of the century, most farmers' wives kept some chickens but widespread poultry farming was undermined by a broiler house established by the Ross Group at Fowlershill (916138) in the far south of the parish where there are well over a million birds. The broiler house is now owned by Grampian Country Foods. At one point in the 1940s there was a mink farm at Wellesley (877177) and it is said that there are descendants of escaped mink still at large.

Agriculture in Newmachar

	1791	1953	2000 Holdings	Hectares
Holdings owned	8(?)		109	2284
Holdings rented	400(?)		11	590
	Acreage	**Acreage**	**Holdings**	**Hectares**
Total arable acreage	5570 (figure for 1840)	3315	50	1401 (3460 acres)
Total grass acreage	958 (figure for 1840)	3629		1153 (2848 acres)
Total Woodland	300		24	75 (185 acres)
Other		442		123
All land	8390 (figure for 1840)	7386	115	2875 (7101 acres)
Principal Crops			**Holdings**	**Hectares**
Set aside	0	(no data)	27	248
Winter Barley	0		10	141
Spring Barley	✓		32	563
Winter Oats	0		✓	✓
Spring Oats	✓		7	42
Oilseed Rape	0		15	193
Potatoes	✓		6	25
Beans	✓		0	0
Peas	✓		0	0
Turnips	✓		7	32
Flax	5		0	0
Livestock			**Holdings**	**Number**
Horses	300	91	21	127
Oxen	64		0	0
Dairy Cattle		789	0	0
Beef Cattle		2036	25	1981
Calves & Store				1000+
All Cattle	1200			
Sheep	300	1966	15	7255
Pigs	20	2500	?	?
Poultry		30,697	16	1.2m
Ploughs	68			
Tractors		98		

Arable Crops

The general increase in the numbers of animals raised during the twentieth century meant a corresponding decrease in the acreage of land devoted to crops. In 1953 there were calculated to be 3,315 acres in tillage for crops other than grass and 3,629 acres of cultivated grass for livestock. Strains of wheat suitable for growing in Northeast Scotland were introduced after 1945 but the acreage in Newmachar has never been very large. The acreage of oats and barley declined overall although oats fell more quickly because barley was easier to harvest by mechanical means. In the 1990s the trend towards barley became even more pronounced. The now relatively small number of fields of oats to be seen is something that would puzzle an observer from the nineteenth century.

Despite the increase in livestock, the growing of turnips declined: production is hard to mechanise and it is a very labour intensive crop. Many farmers prefer to produce silage for their animals' winter feed. However, 'a neep is aye a neep, but what comes oot o' a silage pit may be onything'. (3SA p.59.) Certainly, many Newmachar farmers have continued to grow their neeps. Silage has often replaced hay for cattle. On the other hand, the growing number of horses creates an increased demand for hay once more.

Potatoes declined in importance in the middle decades of the century because they were a labour intensive crop, were subject to blight and could be more easily produced in areas with a kinder climate. Whether the end of the School tattie picking holidays in the 1960s was a cause or effect of the decline is arguable. However, both the planting and lifting of potatoes have now been mechanised; the problems of damage to the tubers have been solved and more are being grown, some of them by seed producers who rent the land.

Since the 1980s, the appearance of the countryside in Spring has been transformed by the bright yellow flowers of oilseed rape. This has now become a very important crop. By the end of the century roughly three times as great an acreage was devoted to it as to potatoes and turnips combined. None of the rape grown in Newmachar up to 2001 was of genetically-modified varieties.

Rape is a good example of a crop which it is profitable to grow because of the subsidies available for it under the European Union's Common Agricultural Policy. In fact, the modern Newmachar farmer needs not only to be abreast of all the latest technical developments in agriculture but also to be something of an expert in agricultural economics, the workings of the Brussels institutions and the latest euro/sterling exchange rate. In all these respects, it was perhaps unfortunate that the free advice service offered by the agricultural colleges came to an end in the 1990s. The amalgamation of the North of Scotland College of Agriculture in the 1990s with others also meant the end of educational services geared to local needs. All this is not to claim that the situation of the Newmachar farmer in 2001 has altered fundamentally from what it was in, say, 1851. The fatstock prices at Smithfield may have been easier to understand than CAP regulations but then, as now, the farmer had to adjust his activities to the demands of a distant market. It is ironic that the second largest crop in 2000 was 'set aside.' This is another consequence of the C.A.P.

In 2001 Newmachar was fortunate not to be directly affected by the foot and mouth outbreak, but of course it suffers the consequences of lack of markets for its livestock. Recovery will come and there will be new problems. The land will continue to be cultivated or used in one way or another. Even if the majority of the population is no longer connected directly with farming, they cannot help but be aware of its importance and its consequences for the way Newmachar's land is managed and used.

The *Third Statistical Account* volume for the County of Aberdeen and James Cowie's thesis have been the principal authorities consulted for this brief account of recent agricultural developments. Through the kind help of Mr Sandy Buchan, I was able to see Scottish Executive statistics for December 2000 on Newmachar. Mr Buchan also gave me much helpful advice on this section. He is not responsible for any mistakes which may remain. The figures shown in the table are my own adaptions from the 2000 statistics. The figures for 1791 and 1953 are derived from the first and third *Statistical Accounts*; unfortunately, the *New Statistical Account* in 1842 provided very few figures related to agriculture.

Newmachar Inn

The photograph of Newmachar Inn seems to date from the early 1900s when the building was comparatively recent. The Inn originally had a farm attached and all was part of the Rainnieshill Estate. An earlier inn building was just across the minor road to the north together with its stables (see below, under Westside). An inn at or near this site developed no doubt because it was adjacent to the common land on which fairs were held at one time and where drovers used to rest their cattle on the way to Aberdeen before road and rail transport improved.

The Strachans at Hillhead Farm (901163) and Cheesemaking

Hillhead may be identified on Thomson's map of 1826. It was of medium size and part of the Parkhill estate, having an annual rent of £75-6s-0d in 1860 when William Strachan was the tenant. He remained there into the 1880s when the tenancy was taken over by James Strachan and the rent had gone up to £90-6s-6d. Presumably the farm was bought by Mr George Strachan's father when the estate was broken up in the 1920s. George's wife, Mrs Annie Strachan, is interviewed by Peggy Findlay. (See also the reference to Granny Strachan in Chap. IX.)

The Farmer's Wife

Mrs Annie Strachan, brought up at Colliehill Farm, Inverurie, was used to 'helping at home.' Educated at Inverurie Academy, she went on to Aberdeen to qualify as a domestic science teacher, returning to Inverurie to teach for a while before marrying George. They settled in a bungalow near the 'fairm toon' and moved over to the farmhouse itself in the late '60s. Her mother-in-law was finding the farm house work a bit hard, but did not want to move as she had a beautiful big sideboard. However, it was carefully manoeuvred into the bungalow and they changed houses.

Annie loved the big Esse range in the kitchen and oatcakes, scones, pancakes, shortbread etc. were baked by the dozen. Our local sales in the Hall were always graced by Annie's cooking which was eagerly sought after as were the home-made butter and cheese which were her real speciality. The cheese was made in a big wooden chessel. 'Well,' she says, 'I had helped at home during holidays and with all the utensils necessary for cheese and butter making in the kitchen, I thought I'd have a go.' George always ensured that the cows were out to grass in early summer which enriched their milk. The milk was separated and the whey was fed to the pigs. Butter was made in a glass churn using cream from the milk.

Annie had several free-range hens until a sly fox came one night and left her with two. Other duties included providing full board for a Diploma of Agriculture student doing his practical year. And always at harvest time, a basket of 'pieces' was taken to the fields for the workers.

A dubbly fleer and clorty beats/ Oh me! Oh what a life!/ Bit there's naithing that I'd rather be, /Than be a fairmer's wife.

(Originally printed in *Newmachar News*, No. 117, 1999.)

Dairy Farming from the 1940s to 2000:
(i) The Milk Officer: Jean Emslie by Peggy Findlay
Jean was brought up in New Aberdour, went to primary school there and then on to Fraserburgh Academy. She entered for a National Diploma in Dairying. She spent six months at Marischal College, Aberdeen, three months at a Dairy School in Ayr, then three months practical work on a dairy farm in Ayrshire. The second year involved the same routine. Her college subjects included biology, book-keeping, bacteriology, veterinary hygiene and zoology. The first part of the examination was practical — making cheese and butter.

After two years in a laboratory in Glasgow, Jean moved back north and became a Milk Officer with the Public Health Department of Aberdeen County Council. She visited dairy farms as far away as Braemar and within a certain radius of Aberdeen. Jean inspected the dairy machinery, milking utensils and even viewed the cattle and byres for cleanliness. A colleague gave her a sound piece of advice: 'Always park your car ready for take off, then if you offend a farmer by pointing out his negligence of hygiene, you'll be able to make a quick getaway.'

After six and a half years, the inevitable happened — Jean married a dairy farmer. She settled with him in Newmachar and they had three boys and a girl. Jean helped on the farm when needed.

(Originally printed in *Newmachar News*, No. 114, 1999.)

(iii) Dairy Farms of c. 1950 as listed by Mrs Emslie and of 1972 by Mr Silver

1950	1972
Meadow Head	
Upper Tack	
Rosehall	
Muiryfold	
Kinmundy	Kinmundy
Moneykebbock	
Ord Farm	Ord
Highlands	
Cunninghar	Cunninghar
Whiterashes Farm	
Pitcow	
Old Town Brownhills	
Dams of Craigie	
Kingseat Farm	Kingseat
Lower Rainnieshill	
Newton Rainnieshill	
Upper Rainnieshill	Rainnieshill
Braeside of Balnakettle	
Westside	Westside
Oldmill	Oldmill
	Woodend

(ii) Dairy Farming in Newmachar in the 1940s and '50s by Jean Emslie
In the 1940s there were many dairy farms in Newmachar Parish and surrounding parishes. A few bottled and sold their own milk but most supplied dairies in Aberdeen. There were the Milk Marketing Board at Kittybrewster, the Co-operative Dairy in Berryden Road, Balgownie Dairy on George Street, and Kennerty's Dairy on Rose Street. Others were on Leadside Road and Waverley

Place. These are all gone now. The Kittybrewster dairy moved to Twin Spires at Bucksburn but that, too, has now closed.

The number of cows on a farm varied from ten to sixty. They were housed in byres, milked by machines — usually made by Alfa Laval. The milk was poured into a container and then trickled slowly over a cooler and into ten-gallon cans. The milk lorry collected these cans from 7 a.m. onwards.

Gradually, some of the farms installed milking parlours and the cattle went into courts. In the mid-1960s there was word of bulk tanks for the milk. Many people wondered what would happen if the roads were blocked with snow. Eventually, bulk tanks were installed from 1966 onwards and the tankers replaced the lorries. It was then that some of the smaller dairies ceased operations. As the farmers grew older, of the 23 dairies in Newmachar Parish and round about in the 1940s and '50s, 22 stopped production and there is now only one farm producing milk.

(iv) The Newmachar Veterinary Practice, 1972-2000 and the Decline in Dairying by C.L. Silver

In June 1972 I took over the practice from Mr Jim Martin. A few years earlier he had purchased the practice in Oldmeldrum and merged what had been two single-man practices into one. The main office and focus became based in Oldmeldrum. At that time Jim Martin had been in the Newmachar practice for about ten years. Prior to him there was a Mr Donald Bain who was there a relatively short time. Before Mr Bain had been Davie Walker and before him a vet. whose name I cannot remember but he lived in a house down Disblair Road, just past the football park on the right. [not Disblair Road; the house was 'Reezielaw' (881197) and the vet was Mr Sinclair.]

Jim Martin had a considerable task in building up the practice. When I took over in 1972, the practice was very much farm-oriented with a significant dairy bias. There were twelve dairy farms in the practice area (see above). Sad to say, only two of these farms remain in milk production today and one of these is likely to close because of the current crisis in milk prices. Similar things have happened at the Oldmeldrum end of the practice and we now serve in total only four dairy farms. The number of dairy cows has declined from approximately 2,500 to 800.

The reduction in the work load in Newmachar and district led to a decision to develop the Oldmeldrum part of the practice and build new premises suitable for small animal practice but also with a facility for large animal and equine surgery. Hence in 1982, we moved out of 41 Oldmeldrum Road in Newmachar. This brought to an end the period when there was a vet. resident in Newmachar.

A small animal clinic was run by Mrs Elspeth McLean for a time but she moved to a small animal practice at Bridge of Don.

Since 1972, the two man practice which was in Newmachar and which had 90% of its work with farm animals has become a four-person practice with about 60% of its work with small animals.

Cattle at Home Farm, Straloch (862215)

The photograph shows Jimmie Fraser in about 1955 with a crossbreed which had given birth to three sets of twins and one other calf, all in the space of no more than three years. (Information and photograph provided by Major Francis Irvine.)

Kinghorn Farm (876215) in the 1940s and 1950s.

Mr Lewis Rennie became tenant of Kinghorn in about 1923. He was one of the sons of Mr John Rennie of Westside. (See Chap. IX.) The contributions which follow are from two people who knew the farm extremely well—but from slightly different perspectives. Mrs Cecilia Penny is Mr Rennie's daughter while Mr Ian Henderson regularly worked at the farm when he was a young man in Newmachar.

(i) Kinghorn Farm as remembered by Cecilia Penny, formerly Rennie

We leave the main road behind and puff our way up the sloping way known as the 'Broon Roadie' which winds as far as you can see over to Tillygreig and other parts which were beyond my ken when I was little. There is a fine home-coming feeling as we walk towards the farmhouse and home with my father's fields all around us. The park on our right is golden with barley stubble. Look over there though, where he has marked the first feering — a brown guiding line waiting impatiently for the Autumn ploughing.

This is the field which has a roadie through it on the worst of winter days when there are long periods — sometimes weeks — when the usual side roads are blocked with snow, and only the main Aberdeen/Turriff road is kept open. It was fortunate, looking back, that we had this natural route, from one farm gate on the main road leading to another beside the farm steading, straight through the field.

We've arrived at the farm road now and turn right, leaving the Tillygreig Road to continue over the hill on its own. This one was surfaced with large stones by my father when he took over Kinghorn and remains very bumpy. Walking along this mercifully short road in high heels is impossible. Cycling down it makes your teeth rattle. Indeed, you have a carnival feeling as you leap around avoiding the worst of the stoney bumps! Today, however, we walk sedately, sensibly shod, and approach the farm itself.

First comes the cornyard full of rucks, as well finished and evenly conical as a taskmaster like my father would wish. We begin to hear the familiar sounds of the farmyard. First come the hens, clucking and curring, happy at the prospect of their evening corn feed. They escort us along in increasing numbers as we approach the farmhouse...

If you make the same journey at the present day, there are no Kinghorn Cottages to be seen, as the road has been straightened and the cottages are out of sight. The approach roads are now all tarred and surfaced smoothly. The farm has been Sympathetically Converted. There are four fine houses now. The chaumer, tool shed and hen house make one. The cart shed cum tractor shed, hay shed, laich barn and loft make a second. The byres and neep shed make a third and I know why that garden does so well. It is because it is over the fertile midden!"

(An extract from 'Sentimental Journey Home' printed in the *Heirskip*)

(ii) A Description of Kinghorn Farm to accompany the photograph
When the picture of Kinghorn Farm here appeared in *Leopard* magazine, it took some time to identify which farm it was but eventually Mrs Penny saw it and, with contributions from Ian Henderson, supplied a description.

Start at the end nearest to the house - that's the chaumer for a farm servant. Next door you see the tool shed cum coal and stick shed. Dad did most of his own repairs there. I even remember an old forge. In the corner was the hen-house where I collected many an egg and confronted clockin' hens bravely. Ian remembers muckin' out that henhouse with a 'hyow in the acrid dust of crusty guano.'

The middle row starts with the cart shed which became the shed for the Fergie. Ian was tractorman in his holiday. Next the stable and memories of big gentle Jock the Clydesdale and the corn kist where I used to sing and dunt my feet when no one was listening.

The next shed leads to the laigh barn. This contains the dusty caff hoose under the belly of the thrashing mill. The laft runs above with a handy trap door for dropping down bags of hens' feed etc.

Round the second neuk now. The big barn in the corner had a maintenance door for the huge mill wheel. Climb the stairs to the two lofts. One has a door overlooking the cornyard at cart height. Through that door sheaves were forked onto the thrashing floor and stacked. When the mill was on - the water rushing from the dam along the lade to turn the wheel - the sheaves were thrown at my father standing down below floor level. He caught them, cut the binding string and fed them into the mill. The straw spewed into the barn, the corn went up to the loft and the stewy caff to the caff shed below.

Kinghorn Farm

Then comes the big byre, handily placed next to the barn, full of cattle in winter, deserted in summer save for the cats. Continue into the sma' byre, home of pigs and caffies, and on to the neep shed at the end. There were extra sheds beside the midden where I served 'docken fish' and 'sugar sand' to imaginary customers.

(iii) Kinghorn Farm in the War
Some recollections of Mrs Penny. (See also Chap. XX.)

Pressure to bring in the harvest during the war was so great that Italian and German prisoners of war were brought in to help. There were also Poles and even members of the Palestine Police. Mr Rennie gave his instructions in broad Doric - and mime. Mrs Rennie provided lavish supplies of home baking and everyday food to which, it seems, there were varying reactions.

Germans and Italians did not get on well and had even proposed to have a duel on the issue of the quality of the mince and tatties.

Another memory is of Otto, a German POW, who cycled round the village selling his home-made rope slippers.

(iv) 'My Family and Other Animals'

Mrs Penny here echoes Gerald Durrell as she recalls animals at Kinghorn during the period of her childhood in Newmachar.

I look back on a childhood on the family farm, surrounded by animals.

There were the cattle in the byres for the winter and we shared all the work that entailed. In the days before cattle courts, our cattle, or 'nowt' as we called them, had their own stalls. They had to be fed with hay, turnips and cattle cake. They had to be mucked out regularly and bedded with fresh straw.

Cows were milked twice a day and oftener with new calves. I still remember giving the calves my fingers to suck and guiding their little heads down to the rich milk in the pail where after a few splutters they discovered the delights of feeding themselves. The pigs were next door in the next byre. The sheep were out in the field all winter, warm in their woolly coats, only brought in for shelter at the lambing time. A typical mixed farm.

Some special animals I look back on and regard with great affection. Jock the Clydesdale horse was strong but friendly and gentle. After a day in the fields, when he had pulled many loads of ripe golden sheaves to the safety of the cornyard, my father would put me on his broad back for the last journey home of that day. I would perch there, proud as Punch. With my little legs astride his broad back and holding the reins, Jock always knew when it was his final journey of the day and, instead of the usual plodding pace, would break into a happy lumbering canter looking forward to food, grooming and a good night's rest.

Daisy, the Aberdeen Angus, was the cow docile enough to let me practise on her when I was learning to milk. We became great pals. I swear she used to sigh heavily at my efforts until I mastered that steady stream of milk into the pail 'zz-zz-zz.' The cats were there behind us watching slyly, and sometimes I'd aim a stream of milk at their mouths. When I scored a direct hit and the cats enthusiastically licked their whiskers, Daisy mooed in appreciation.

Working at Kinghorn Farm and Mr Lewis Rennie

Ian Henderson, whose parents were nurses at Kingseat (and who owned the old schoolhouse from 1955), graduated from Aberdeen University and teaches history in Canada. He frequently returns to Scotland and remains deeply interested in the history, literature and heritage of the Northeast. Between 1955 and 1961 he was in the habit of working at Kinghorn during any weekends and holidays which could be spared from school and university studies.

His account shows that farm work in the 1950s remained physically arduous and needed skill — and that much depended on the character of the farmer.

The verses by Ian which follow are reprinted with permission from *Heirskip Magazine*, editor Jean McKinnon, for the Buchan Heritage Society.

Lewie an' the Loon

Fan I wiz a lad at Kinghorn ferm
Forty-some years lang syne
Aul' Lewie taught me a' he thocht
An orra loon shid ken.

Fan t' hairst and' fan t' sow
Faur t' ile the threshin' mull
Foo t' thraw a chucken's neck an'
Ca' canny wi' the bull.

Foo t' swing a sharpent scythe
Find the rhythm o' the hyow
Foo t' muck the skittery greep
An' milk a surly yow.

Foo t' kittle the Fordie up
On a caul December morn
Foo t' big a bonnie ruck
An' full a cairt wi' sharn.

I wiz a roch, ramstoorie loon
A thochtie contermacious
Nae inclint t' be telt ava
A plooky pilliedacus.

Bit Lewie rasped ma edges aff
Wi' patience, wit an' skill
He harnessed me, an' yokit me
An' bent me t' his will.

He cid be coorse an' crabbit fyles
An' mair nor a bittie morose
He telt me eence "Ah hae ma doots
That ye're worth the saut t' yer brose."

Bit maistly we got on nae bad
As we tyauved an' newsed thegither
An' the fifty years atween us
Didna muckle maitter.

Mony the strainer post we set
Mony the sheaf we oxtered
Mony the neep we ca'd in-bye
Mony the beast we doctored.

Kinghorn's no a ferm nae mair
The loon's nae langer lean
The years blawn aff like wind-teen chaff
An' Lewie's darg's lang deen.

Goval Bridge

Goval Bridge

Farming at the Greens (891196) and the effects of housing for the village: Mr John Taylor

Mr John Taylor's father, also John but known as 'Jackie', whose photograph can be seen in the picture featuring the Newmachar village smithy below, owned the Greens, a farm originally on the Rainnieshill estate (Chap. IX) of about 56 acres, with an annual value of £70 - 7s - 6d in 1895. Mr Taylor senior also looked after the farm attached to the Newmachar Inn which was part of the same estate. Mr William Wood was the proprietor of the farm and the inn, and Mrs Taylor at one time worked as housekeeper for Mr Wood.

Greens Farm itself was a mixed farm but as Newmachar village needed to expand a little in the 1950s and '60s, Mr Taylor, senior, decided to sell most of his farm for housing which was built to the west of Hillbrae Way; the field remaining to the east of the road became part of Mr Michael Ingram's farm. The present Mr Taylor felt it sensible to find a different occupation from farming.

Woodend (873207) in the later twentieth century:

During the later nineteenth century, Woodend Farm had been held by the Crombies who developed the famous shorthorn herd. It was one of the major farms on the Straloch estate valued at an annual rent of £137 - 12s - 11d in 1860. Mr Barclay's grandfather had held the lease from 1927 and then his father. In 1972 the farm was purchased from the estate when Mr Barclay began farming entirely on his own account.

When Mr Barclay retired from active farming in about 1990, he and Mrs Barclay built a bungalow near the farmhouse and let the farm to others. This is a pattern which has been followed on some other farms.

Farming at Boghead (897171): Mr George and Mrs Marie Cameron

Boghead or Bogheads was part of the estate of South Kinmundy owned by the Rev. Duncan Mearns of Disblair. Patrick Mitchell (1747-1826), whose gravestone was one of the most prominent in the Kirkyard, was an earlier tenant.

The present farmhouse appears to have been built in about the 1870s but there is a much older house on the site and a steading which has obviously been enlarged at least twice. All of it appears to be made of stone from the immediate area. Presumably it was originally a small fermtoun.

Mr Cameron and his father moved from a smaller farm in Belhelvie to Boghead in 1954, taking on the lease from the Disblair Estate. It was a 'three horse farm' of about 100 acres. Mr Cameron took over fully in 1959 after his marriage and found the farm to be a fine size for working by two people and occasional casual labour once a tractor had replaced the horses. His father had not used tractors. The farm was arable and beef cattle; no milk was produced.

For cattle feedstuff, Mr Cameron preferred silage to turnips chiefly because silage is much easier to manage with the aid of a tractor than turnips.

By the 1990s it was becoming apparent that successful farming needed now to be on a larger scale than could be managed on a 100 acre holding. The Camerons have now retired from active farming and the land is to be let.

Mrs Marie Cameron is from Bourtie but attended Whiterashes School. She and George met a dance in the new Village Hall in 1955. (See also Chap. XVIII.)

Farming at Cunninghar (882195) from 1960: the late Mr Roy Barclay
Cunninghar was presumably originally a place where rabbits were reared. (See Chap. IV.) Once a part of the Rainnieshill Estate (see Chap. IX) the farm was sold off to Andrew Wood, a horse dealer, who occupied it during the 1920s and 1930s. Mr Barclay provided this information in December 1999.

Roy Barclay arrived in Newmachar in 1960 at the time of the great snowstorm. When he occupied Cunninghar, it was a dairy farm with stalls for 18 cows and was worked by a farmer, an employee and a lady helper. The Barclays managed everything themselves initially and built up the herd to 30 Herefords, which meant enlarging the byre. The basic farm was 72 acres but to run such a herd more land needed to be rented so that the Barclays were in total running about a 100 acres. Mrs Barclay was especially responsible for several hundred chickens and so eggs and milk were the principal products.

Work was unremitting and the hours long: a day began at 5 am and work could well go on until 9 or 10 pm.

The herd was maintained by replacements reared on the farm itself. On average a cow might produce 7 calves over its working life. If you put a cow in calf too early, the milk yield falls away so the art of managing with a milk herd is to get the cow into calf at the best time. Good milk yielders had a tendency to become lame through foot rot. All the feed for the cows was grown on the farm except for some draff (barley mash) from the whisky distillers. This was needed as a supplement in July when the rapidly growing grass had less food value. Otherwise the chief bulk feed was bruised oats and barley although turnips were grown. Oats were preferred to barley in the 1960s simply because the subsidy was larger. Moreover some barleys, eg. Maja, were short and difficult to manage with the binder. Although most of the barley grown was for the cattle, occasionally it might be sold for malting for whisky. Mr Barclay never used feedstuffs containing hormones.

The rotation was a seven-year cycle of four grass and three crops. Lime was applied before ploughing and the use of cattle dung on barley stubble was normal. Silage was produced from the fields in grass.

Mr Barclay had previous experience of working with horses but he never used them at Cunninghar. A horse cost a lot to feed and keep in condition. Instead, a Ferguson tractor served him well for many years. Some of the machinery it pulled had been designed for use with horses.

Cunninghar Farm

Electricity was a great boon. It made possible the installation of new equipment in the steadings in 1966, including a milk cooler. A pipeline to take the milk from the milking parlour to the dairy meant the end of the practice of pouring buckets of milk into the cooler. All the milk produced was taken by the Milk Marketing Board at Bucksburn. Originally, it had been collected in ten-gallon churns which were manhandled by the two men with the lorry. Then the Board said that one man was all that could be afforded and so the farmer always had to be on hand to help with the carrying. Cleaning the churns was a considerable chore; a steam jet had to be used to sterilise them. A little later, tankers were introduced and farms like Cunnighar were pressed into replacing the churns with a tank which could be connected directly to the lorry's tank. Although an extra penny per gallon was offered if a farmer had a tank, no help was given with the initial capital cost.

Besides problems of these kinds, there were diseases to contend with. Brucellosis could cause cows to abort and this happened in 1964-5. The problem was surmounted and the Cunninghar herd became accredited.

Later on, and partly because of an allergy suffered by his son, Mr Barclay reduced his milking herd to four and used the milk for butter making. For a time he raised calves for selling on and eventually switched to beef cattle. This did not work too well and so the farm adapted to store cattle — usually 'forward stores' which might be kept for a few months before being sold through Aberdeen and Northern Marts. Contracts with a slaughter house for, say, twenty cattle a month could be entered into. The art in all this was to watch the market prices carefully. A lorry needed to be hired, usually from Andy Hopkins at Upper Tack, to get the cattle to market. In the mid 1980s, cattle were costing about £100 — that is, about £1 per kilo. In this situation, Mr Barclay, like many other farmers, introduced ewes and lambs instead.

The Ploughman Minister and other Memories: Mr James Imlah

When the Rev. Andrew Giles was minister of the parish, 1927-1941, the glebe land around the manse was usually let out to Greens Farm where Mr Imlah used to work. When he had to plough the glebe land, Mr Giles would come and ask to be allowed to take over for a time. Having been a countryman, Mr Giles knew how to handle horses and a plough. He said that he wanted to keep in practice.

Anvil Cottage, the Blacksmith's: an anonymous contribution

Anvil Cottage on Old Meldrum Road

Anvil Cottage was the home of Mr Forsyth the blacksmith, nicknamed 'Auld Brookie'. What are now private garages at Anvil Cottage was the blacksmith's shop where local farmers took their horses to be shod and where farm implements were repaired. The garden was famed for its 'monkey puzzle' tree. Schoolchildren going home from school in winter used to go and warm their hands at the furnace fire.

(The photograph was supplied by Mr John Taylor whose father appears in the picture on the right.)

Westside and other farms in the later twentieth century: Mr Alexander Buchan

(See also the account of the Rennies at Westside in Chap. IX.)

Mr Buchan's father, Roland Buchan, came from a line of farmers and blacksmiths living in Buchan. He married Janet Davidson (died 1991) and they came to Newmachar in 1942. From the former Rainnieshill estate, Mr Buchan senior bought Westside, Mameulah and the farm attached to the Inn although not including Newlands. In all, this was about 400 acres. (See the table with Chap. IX.) When Mr Buchan senior died, his sons Alexander and Allan continued to run all the holding as a joint enterprise but later found it convenient to farm Mameulah and Westside separately.

Westside continued to be, as it had been in the 1890s, a dairy farm with arable. For many years it had had a working mill. (See Chap. X.) The dairying came to an end in 1985.

The hotel farm is interesting in a number of ways. It had belonged to Archie Myron, whose daughter married Harold Ross, the son of Newmachar's minister. The steading for the farm which is beside the old, ruined, Inn was in fact a rather splendid set of stables for the convenience of visitors to the Inn. The hay loft was in the roof above.

Farming at Chapel of Elrick and the Introduction of Tractors: Mr Charles Ingram. (From information supplied by Mr Alexander Ingram.)

Mr Charles Ingram (1910-1993) came from a family which had farmed at Davoch near Tarland. His father had served in the South African War (1899-1902) and died in 1920. His widow and Charles secured the lease of Chapel of Elrick farm and Charles Ingram walked the 35 to 40 miles from Tarland to Newmachar together with a horse and cart and a herd of cattle; it took two days. He introduced sheep as well as cattle which was not very usual in the 1920s. In 1938 he bought a 'Case' tractor whose costs it was difficult to cover until the war came and lots of work was available at Dyce Airport which was being developed for RAF use. This tractor, then an Aston and later others, were used at Dyce by day and brought back to farms in the evening to help with ploughing the increased amount of land used for arable farming which the Ministry of Food encouraged. In this way, Mr Ingram developed a contracting scheme

Mr Ingram had begun to farm the Elrick Mains as well as Chapel and was able to buy these farms from Mr Burnett-Whyte and, eventually in 1956, most of the rest of the estate and Elrick House itself. Brokenwynd was acquired through Mrs Ingram, a Duncan. (See Chap. IX.)

Potato growing at Old Town of Brownhills: Mr Maurice Innes

One of the interesting features of present-day agriculture in Newmachar is the work of Mr Maurice Innes as a grower of seed potato varieties. Mr Innes has over 580 varieties in his collection and is listed in the Guinness Book of Records as holding the record for a joint exhibit of 525 varieties, with two fellow growers. They have won gold medals for their displays at national shows like Shrewsbury and Stockport; Mr Innes won a silver medal at Chelsea at his first attempt in 2001, and has also supplied seed potatoes to Prince Charles for growing at Highgrove.

Chapter XXIV
The Emergence of Shops and Businesses

In the medieval and early modern periods such businesses and trades as existed in Newmachar directly served the needs of agriculture and of agricultural workers. No doubt pedlars and other itinerant salesmen paid visits to the fermtouns from time to time but it was not until the nineteenth century that any number of shops and other services were established in the village of Summerhill as it began to develop after about 1840. Paradoxically, the later twentieth century has seen many such services cease to exist locally because people go into Aberdeen in their cars to shop. It is a trend which many residents now hope can be reversed as the population increases.

Trades in 1696
In Chapter VII it was noted that the 1696 Poll Tax record showed there were 37 tradesmen. Ten handloom weavers were present; their successors finally lost out to factory-produced cloths in the nineteenth century. There were a dozen souters, presumably part-time, and presumably, too, working as saddlers as well as shoemakers (which is how they are termed). There were only two tailors. A waker (a night cattle guard?), a pyper, a 'tinkar' and a 'merchant' of unspecified kind are also mentioned as well as the expected millers and smiths.

Fairs
How regularly a market was held in the parish is difficult to say though the rights to hold a fair were granted in the 1680s. According to Mr Moir, even a cattle fair was difficult to establish in the 1840s. (*NSA*, p. 1035.) Nevertheless by the 1870s there were cattle and horse fairs on the third Thursday of January, March, May and November and the second of July. (Groome, *Gazeteer*, 1884, ed.) They were held on land near the present Inn. However, another source suggests that the market had been discontinued after about 1870. (*List of Markets and Fairs*, C51872, 1890.) Whenever fairs were held, no doubt traders other than cattle and horse dealers were present.

Shops and Businesses in the Earlier Nineteenth Century
Neither the Old Statistical Account of 1791, nor the New one of 1842 precisely identify any established businesses, although Mr Stronach numbers twelve wright and millers, five blacksmiths, six shoemakers, four tailors and mentions stocking knitters, while Mr Moir was aware of the importance of carriers. (*OSA*, Revised ed. pp. 352-3; *NSA*, p. 1032.) However, there is other evidence. At least four shoemakers, two blacksmiths and a mason were present in 1819. (*Rules and Regulations of St John's Lodge*, 1819 pp. 14-16.) The 1821 Census mentions 30 people as being in retail trades or handicrafts. Surprisingly, this

figure has leapt to 87 by 1831, which suggests the criteria were different. (See Appendix.) In any case, most would probably have been weavers or stocking knitters. It is only with the 1841 census records that it begins to be possible to distinguish individuals and their particular occupations.

In 1841 Newmachar could boast a commercial traveller, William Doverty, at Elrick, while James Leslie is recorded as a merchant in the village of Summerhill - the only one apparently. There is, too, a clockmaker named James Sutherland. However, the older crafts such as shoemaker and tailor were still practised in various parts of the parish. The tendency from this period onwards seems to have been for incomers to set up businesses in Summerhill. For example, the shoemaker William Singer of Longford, mentioned in 1841, allowed his daughter to marry an incomer from Echt, John Sangster, who set up business in what is now the chip shop in Newmachar village. Possibly, Sangster was originally Singer's apprentice. In 1851 Sangster had two journeymen and an apprentice working for him, a young wife and a domestic servant. Later the 1859 Valuation Roll and 1861 Census records show that he now owned his shop and was renting some land. He was also a widower, with a small son aged nine to bring up.

The 1851 census makes it possible to take a mid-century survey of trades and businesses in the whole parish. The emphasis is still on the needs of an agricultural community. Hence there were no fewer than eight blacksmiths plus at least three apprentices, five tailors with their four journeymen and one apprentice, five mill or wheel wrights, two carpenters with two apprentices, five shoemakers with three journeymen and three apprentices. This is the first census which asked for the place of birth to be given and it shows that the majority of these craftsmen were incomers from nearby parishes in the north-east.

The Crombies and Cothal Mills

Although Cothal mills are outwith the parish, they had considerable impact on the lives of Newmachar people in the earlier nineteenth century. Moreover, James Crombie's family lived in the parish, eventually becoming considerable property owners. (See Chaps. XV and XVI.) John Crombie senior (1772-1858) had started the business of making fine woollen cloth in 1805, recruiting skilled weavers (and later, good cricketers) from Yorkshire and selling his products in London. His wife, Catherine Harvey of Monykebbock, had two sons, James (1810-1878) and John, who carried on the business with James as the leading light. When expansion of the business dictated a move, briefly to Aberdeen in 1851, and then to Grandholm, Newmachar and Cothal-based workers had to move too. James continued to live in Newmachar and became a member of the School Board as well as a J.P., a Railway director and held various other positions. John's elder son, James Edward, also became a prominent business man and eventually bought Parkhill House; another son became an M.P. (J.R. Allan, *Crombies of Grandholm and Cothal*, 1805-1960), Aberdeen, no date.)

The Expansion of Summerhill

The Valuation Rolls kept after 1858 allow houses, shops and businesses to be identified even more clearly than from the census returns and it is clear that the village was developing as an economic focus for the parish. By 1859 the Murray family were emerging there as notable tradesmen/entrepreneurs. David Murray owned the bakehouse and probably employed John Reith, a baker. David's son (or brother?) William Murray lived in another part of the bakery building, but was a carpenter and smith to trade. He employed Ross Swanson (from Keithhall) as a blacksmith and had his own carpenter's shop. This Murray also owned a house occupied by the journeyman baker, John Reith, also from Keithhall. Both Murrays were also the tenants of farms on the Rainnieshill estate. William Murray was elected as the Summerhill representative on the School Board in 1876 and again in 1879. Initially, his wife, also stood as a candidate but later withdrew before the election. (Minutes of School Board, AC 5/70/1.) The general shop and post office in 1859 was run by George Barrack who came from Fyvie.

Visiting salesmen of one trade or another like the hat renovator (see Chap. XIV) would have come to Newmachar and the village in particular. Another set of visitors were those who built the railway. Their impact was surprisingly slight. The 1861 Census lists as working on the railway 31 Highlanders, seven Irish and 24 other men living in the parish accompanied by 8 wives and 14 children; all but the three local men had disappeared by the time of the next Census. (1861 Census.)

By 1877 there were three wrights, four bakers, two blacksmiths, and three master shoemakers on the Valuation Rolls of that year for Summerhill. But perhaps the most important figure was now George Cooper. Originally from Aboyne, he was the proprietor of the general shop as well as the postmaster, a druggist, tailor and draper; in addition he was a member of the School Board, 1876-82. His only local rival would have been George Pittendrigh, who had set up a shop in Whiterashes; he was also elected to the School Board, 1873 -79, sitting beside his landlord, Ramsay of Barra, which might have been difficult. (*Worrals Directory*, Oldham, 1877; Census Returns; Valuation Rolls.)

The 1890s

In the 1890s in Summerhill itself, the principal shop was the grocery which continued to be run by George Cooper. His daughter, Mary, worked as his clerk and he had an assistant. Two van drivers almost certainly worked for him. Closely associated with him, was his nephew, Peter McAllan who was Inspector of Poor for the parish and was later to take over the shop. In Whiterashes, the shop was now William Sangster's; he employed an assistant and two apprentices.

In other parts of the parish there appear to have been general dealers and grocers mostly working on their own: Alexander Davidson at Burnside, Jane Topp at Crossroads and James Brown at the toll house at Parkhill. By 1894 there was another grocer's shop at Reisque run by Thomas Cruickshank, while in Summerhill itself, William Argo had set up a shop.

John Sangster, the shoemaker, then 67 in 1891 and still a widower, was still working with two journeymen. But his trade was probably falling away to rivals, including the saddler. Robert Jaffray, a former journeyman of John Sangster, was now working at Whiterashes, with one apprentice, while John Topp, who had come from Udny to be apprenticed with John Singer of Standryford, was living at Little Goval with one, possibly two, employees. The saddler, Alexander Brownie from Udny, was first recorded in 1881 as working in the village; by 1894 John McLeod had taken over the business. At the bakery, George Taylor, from Fetteresso, ran the business with four other bakers including one of his sons. No other bakers are recorded in the parish. A portable mill proprietor now lived at Broad Tack.

As might be expected, blacksmiths tended to be scattered over the parish. In Summerhill itself there was William Marnoch who had Adam Wildgoose as a journeyman. Four others are listed as employers or working on their own account - James Troup at Wicketwalls, William Gossip at Locheye, Alexander Murray at Swailend and James Cormack at Stonyladles. Three others were apprentices or workers, including Cormack's son who was later to move into the village.

Somewhat surprisingly, only one tailor was listed in Summerhill in 1891. This was James Rennie. Andrew McKenzie at Meadowhead and Alexander Burgess at Roadside are master tailors, or working on their own account; three other tailors are mentioned

Four masons are listed, none in Summerhill, although William Adam a contractor lived in the village in a house with yards, and presumably employed these men when necessary. The carpenter's firm in Summerhill was now run by David Murray who, like his father, was to be elected on to the School Board in the 1890s. Murray employed his brother and two other journeymen. Five more carpenters are listed in the parish; two of them - James Prosser at Longcroft and William Hutcheon at Corsehill - as employers.

In all these respects, Summerhill was not so very different as a village centre with services from what it had been thirty years before. But in other respects, changes are apparent by 1891. A watchmaker is working once more in the village; two sick nurses are named, Helen Tough and Margaret Anderson, with Jane Joss nearby at Reisque; there were three washerwomen, two dressmakers offered their services; three teachers lived in the village, plus two others who worked at Whiterashes School and two more in the south of the parish at Parkhill. There was a resident medical practitioner, Dr William Cooper, and

James Cooper, son of the grocer George Cooper, was training in medicine. A vet is established in the village; the postman and the policeman are also living there; a coal merchant lived at Newlands, by Reisque. Only one weaver was left in the parish, at Backhill of Goval. (The above analysis is based principally on the Census return for 1891 with some further information from the 1894-5 Valuation Roll. At the time of writing, the census information for 1901 had not become available.)

A comparison between the numbers and kinds of tradesmen/entrepreneurs in 1851 and 1891 shows several interesting features. The absolute number of shoemakers (eight rather than eleven), tailors (six not ten) and blacksmiths (nine not eleven) has gone down, while the number of wheelwrights/carpenters has stayed the same at nine. The explanation for this may be that by 1891 there was much more division of labour: in other words, the carpenter, for example, in 1891 was only a carpenter, not trying to be a crofter as well. To a certain extent, too, there was more centralisation on Summerhill and the growing settlement of Whiterashes to the north.

However, concentration of services in these two centres is much more obvious in the provision of grocers' and other shops. There was one grocer's shop in Summerhill in 1851, probably run by one man, who was also the postmaster, and his wife. In 1891 there was still only one (although there were soon to be two) but there were four employees working in the business. Another fairly extensive business of an employer with three employees was now established in Whiterashes and there were four other people in minor grocery enterprises in other parts of the parish. More groceries were being bought. The general point is best made, perhaps, in the bakery business. In 1851 there was one baker in Summerhill. This in itself was a sign of change: at least some people were now eating wheaten bread instead of only oatmeal and peasemeal in various forms. By 1891 the baker has four assistants to meet the demand for bread and cakes. The point about consumer demand is reinforced by the availability of extra services, like washerwomen, dressmakers, sick nurses, the doctor, and teachers all present in greater numbers and more centralised on Summerhill and to a certain extent in the growing settlement of Whiterashes. All this is despite the fact that, overall, the population of Newmachar had actually decreased between 1871 and 1891. The conclusion is inescapable that the standard of living in late Victorian Newmachar was rising.

Early and Mid-Twentieth Century Developments
The advertisements in the United Free Church's Cookery Book of about 1920 include a great many for Aberdeen businesses. This may herald the beginning of a problem for Newmachar establishments: motor and rail transport was making it easier and easier for people to get into the city to shop. Even so, there were two general merchants in Summerhill; G.C. Thomson offered grocery and draperies with 'ladies' stockings in all the latest shades,' and Peter McAllan, also

the Inspector of the Poor, now ran the Post Office and Grocery having taken over the shop formerly run by his first employer, George Cooper. The shoe shop run by Charles Leslie still claimed to be that of a maker of shoes. Frank D. Gauld was a Linen specialist who apparently did much of his business by post. (Newmachar United Free Church *Cookery Book*, n.d.) Mrs Nicol recalls Charlie Thomson's wife at the shop as being a better manager than he was. The baker,

near Mr Gauld's shop, still baked his bread on the premises in the 1920s while the butcher, Graham Dunn, had a wooden lean-to building at the side of Thomson's Grocery shop. However, Reuben Laing, a butcher based in Woodside, had a delivery van. Another visiting trader was Mr Fowler, the fishmonger, who came by train from Whitehills near Banff with his barrow and baskets of fresh fish. The photograph shows him outside the West Manse but Mrs Kerr found

that by the time he reached that part of the village, all the best and freshest fish had been sold! Today, visiting fishmongers still call at the village, but travel faster in their vans, with the fish packed in ice to preserve it for their customers. In the 1920s, there were three blacksmiths, whose work was still mainly shoeing horses; Mr McIntyre on the main road, Mr Gray at Kinmundy and a third at Disblair. The tailor was a Mr Hosie. (Testimonies of Mrs M. Nicol and Mrs Elizabeth Walker.) There was a watchmaker in Newmachar, Robert Edward Gray or 'Watchie Gray' who was also a postman. He lived in a three-room house at Woodlea (880206) just north of the village. He also rode a splendid motor bike. (Testimony of his granddaughter, Mrs Ann Hay.)

Whiterashes continued to have its own shop, the tenancy of which had been taken over in 1896 by George Davidson. His son, George A. Davidson, gives an excellent account of the shop and its place in the life of that part of the parish in the 1900-1930 period. Everything from enamel pails at 1s 6d to tailor-made suits from £3 15s was sold there. The shoemaker in Whiterashes was Mr Troup who was much interested in politics as a Liberal Party supporter. He was succeeded by James Forbes. Nearby was the tailor's shop where Mr Thomson, Mr Gray and then Tom Rearie worked. (*Memories of Whiterashes, pp. 28-29, 36-41.*)

Mr Tom Rearie

Mr Tom Rearie was the most notable of a long line of tailors in Newmachar. In fact, he had a good reputation for his skill over a much wider area; some clients from as far afield as Inverness in the north or Newcastle to the south would bring their cloth to him to have it made up into a suit. He was a traditional tailor in the sense that he worked sitting cross-legged on the 'board'. His daughter, Rita, herself served a formal apprenticeship as a tailor and worked with her father, but she was allowed to put her feet over the edge of the board on to a chair! Tom Rearie made kilts as well as suits. His tailor's shop was in the building built of pink granite just to the north of the Mace shop on Oldmeldrum Road. Much more extensive than it appears from the outside, it had a large room at the back in which Mr Rearie and his apprentices worked. Apprentices also lodged there. At one stage, Mr Rearie teamed up with his former apprentice and fellow free mason, Mr Ironside at Newburgh for making suits; the trousers were made in Newmachar and the coats at Newburgh. (Information from Mr Alec Hay.)

Born in 1896 at Tarves, Tom Rearie worked on a farm for a time. Having served in the Great War and completed his own apprenticeship as a tailor, he worked at Whiterashes then set up his own business in the village in 1931. He married a lady who was herself the daughter of a tailor. He was to continue working until he died in 1990.

Tom Rearie's equipment, such as his brass-handled shears, his irons and the special oven needed to heat them, his Singer sewing machine and needles, together with many photos, was gifted to the Heritage Centre at Alford. The display gives an excellent impression of the way in which this highly skilled man worked. In addition there is a compilation of textiles and information for a college thesis made by his granddaughter, who has inherited his and her talented mother's skills and interests.

Tom Rearie was a kindly and well-liked man and it is appropriate that Rearie Close in the village preserves his association with Newmachar. His photo is in Chapter XX. (Testimony of Mrs Rita Burr, Mr Rearie's daughter, and article by Mrs Peggy Findlay in the *Newmachar News*, 115, 1999.)

The 'Shoppie' at Reisque: Andrew Cheyne

Another well-kent and well-liked figure in Newmachar in the last century was

Andrew Cheyne. His father, James Cheyne, who had farmed at Arnage retired to Reisque and his wife ran the shop there, taking over from Miss Barnett who had presumably taken over the shop rented from the Rainnieshill estate by Thomas Cruickshank in the 1890s. Mrs Cheyne was apparently a kindly lady in the habit of giving free sweeties to children. She was the first shopkeeper in Newmachar to make and sell ice cream, and was always happy to let children come and help with the churning by turning the handle of the paddle.

Mrs Cheyne's son Andrew had been a guard on the railway before he took over the management of the shop - and the admirable habit of giving free sweeties to the children who called in. He heard much gossip in his shop but was wise enough not to pass on stories. Andrew Cheyne was one of the leaders of the campaign to get a new village hall built in 1955 and made a very generous donation to the costs but sadly died before the hall was completed. He is commemorated in the name, Cheyne Walk. (Testimony of Mrs Ada Ross and Mr Bert Sangster; upper photo from Mrs Jenny Gray.)

The later history of shops at Reisque has been given in the chapter on transport. (See Chap. XI.)

The Milkman

In the 1940s and '50s, before the days of the Milk Marketing board, many local farmers used to sell milk. One noted character was Jimmie Gray, who used his long-suffering horse and cart for deliveries, sometimes at rather unorthodox times. (Testimony of Mr Harold Barclay.)

Builders and Joiners

Mr Adam Birnie was a master builder who developed his business on a site beside the shop at Reisque from 1930, and built his own home there. As well as general contracting work around the area and in Aberdeen, he built some of the later villas and other structures at Kingseat. (Testimony of Mrs Ada Ross, his daughter.) Another prominent local builder was Alexander Low who came to Newmachar in about 1920 to take over a small builder's business previously run by his uncle, George Catto, located at the Neuk, Kinmundy cross roads. They were tenants of the North Kinmundy estate. Mr Low was essentially a mason, and successfully developed his business for about forty years taking on many important contracts for mason's work in the County of Aberdeen including several schools.   He was, for example, involved in the masonry work when New Machar School was extended in 1935. (See Chap. XVIII.)   John Mearns worked for Mr Low on many of these projects.

Mr and Mrs Low

Mr Low transferred their house and business to Roadside: the house is diagonally opposite the original builder's yard. Their son, Archie, is still at Roadside after a notable career as a technician at Aberdeen University and elsewhere. (See Chap. XVIII.) The house itself had been built in 1893. Beside it is a wooden building used by a tailor, Alexander Burgess, as his workshop for many years. (Testimony of Mr Archie Low.) Mr Archie Low now uses the tailor's room as a workshop where he is building a splendid working model of a c. 1920 Fowler's 'Showman' traction engine.

Mr Jim Cormack was a joiner but in the country, this trade includes many skills and he was also painter and decorator, millwright and undertaker. He had followed his father in the joinery trade and had a reputation for taking time and trouble to produce a pleasing result for his customers: 'Dae it richt the first time - dinna hae tae ging back on a job.' The business was located behind Ivy Cottage on Oldmeldrum Road and he used the old Free Church building as a store. The building was later bought by Mr Sandy Walker who demolished it and built his home and the shop now occupied by Carousel on the site. (Testimony of Mr Hector Urquhart, a former journeyman for Mr Cormack; *Newmachar News* 115, 1999.)

Jim Cormack and his friends, Mr Irvine the baker and Willie Reid the postmaster and shopkeeper, developed something of a reputation as practical jokers in the late 1940s and '50s. They were not above tying door knobs together and carrying out other pranks which were usually blamed on wild teenagers rather than these respectable businessmen. (Information from Mr Laurie Tinto.)

Medical Services
William Fiddes, a surgeon, was living in Newmachar in 1819, but whether practising medicine is not clear. (See Chap. XXII.) The 1851 Census records

the presence of two medical practitioners, Patrick Russell, MRCS, at Little Rainnieshill and John Christie, MRCP, at Elrick. Christie was Medical Officer to the Parochial Board. In 1891, Dr William Cooper was resident doctor in the village. He was said to be an excellent physician. He ceased work in the 1920s. (Testimony of Mrs Elizabeth Walker.) Since then, there has been no permanently resident practitioner and those having practices elsewhere came into the parish. Dr Shearer from Bucksburn was in and out of one's house so quickly that he was known as 'Dr Lightning'. (Testimony of Mrs Cecilia Penny.)

No doubt from time immemorial there were midwives in the parish. One is certainly recorded in the 1841 Census, as being based at Loanhead. The 1891 Census notes two sick nurses in the village, Margaret Anderson and Mrs Jane Joss. How far they were qualified is not clear. Later on, there were qualified district nurses on hand. Nurse Rogerson, who lodged with Mrs Scott on Disblair Road, was the first. She was followed by a fiery redhead, Nurse Minty, who knew lots of poetry. Unfortunately, she caught chicken pox and died. Mrs Macrae took over and was in post during and after the Second World War. (Information from Mrs Elizabeth Walker; Mrs M Nicol.)

The Later Twentieth Century
Mr Cormack's last apprentice was Laurie Tinto, who came from a family established at Whiterashes. He was forced by a back injury to give up active work for a time and so took advantage of Access courses at Aberdeen College and the University to retrain in Architectural Technology. From 1994 he began to run his own consultancy business. With his son as partner and two part-time employees, Laurie Tinto has seen his business thrive on the needs of residents as places like Newmachar increase their population following the building of homes for commuters. (Information supplied by Mr Laurie Tinto.)

In 1977 Bruce Sutherland started an architectural design business and was involved in many local building projects. Then he took over Mr Leith the shoemaker's shop and created also a craft, 'do-it-yourself' and hardware shop. Picture framing was added along with other services such as a copy shop and fax service. In other words, the business adapted in line with the changing needs of Newmachar as it became a commuters' residential settlement rather than the centre of a rural parish.

The building in which John Sangster had set up his shoemaker's shop continued to be used for the same purpose right up to the late 1960s. Then Mr Collie died and the shop was leased to Mr W. Lamb, another shoemaker, who eventually retired. The property was sold by roup to Mr and Mrs Middler who replaced the leaky roof and the attic rooms with the flat built on top of the shop. The shop was refitted and converted into a fish and chip shop in 1969, and still is the village 'chipper'. (Information from Mr A. Middler.)

Chalmers' Bakery is a successful and substantial Aberdeen and Northeast business with 23 retail outlets. Ronnie Chalmers, who started the firm, was from Newmachar, and so it was fitting that he should take over the old village bakery and shop in the 1980s. (*Newmachar News*, 124, 2001.)

The blacksmith's business in the village finally closed in 1961 but the old smiddy building is still there. (Cowie, p. 34.)

Adam Wildgoose's former garage, repair shop and taxi service (see Chap. XI) is now Beekie's Neuk, a public house. When the garage closed, the house was acquired by a Dutchman, named Van der Beek whose name was corrupted into the present name for the pub, Beekie's Neuk, often just referred to as Beekie's. When the present owners, Pat and Stan Reid, took over the public house in 1983, they kept the name because it had become well known in the area.

The Newmachar is much longer established, having once been beside the site of Newmachar's fairs and cattle drovers' halt. The early nineteenth century photograph (see Chap. IX) is designed to show how respectable the inn had become, with the family, including young children, posed around the front area; presumably the photo was taken when newly built after the fire in the original building. Since 1991, the inn has been owned by Linda and Grant Wright, who have built an extension so that it can function as both a major restaurant and meeting place.

Catering to different modern interests, there are two garden centres in the parish, Mr MacGillivray's Parkhill Garden Centre, and Swailend Nurseries which Harry and Michael Duncan opened in 1952.

In the village, the principal shop continued to be the Post Office, grocery and general store. In the mid 1960s it was taken over by Charlie Gordon who ran it very successfully until ill-health forced him to retire some twenty years later. The village football pitch at Reisque is named after him. The store was then taken over by the Forbuoys chain which in 2000 sold it on to Mace who have refurbished it in various ways.

Water and Electricity

In Summerhill as in other parts of the parish, inhabitants had to rely on private supplies or communal pumps until well into the twentieth century. The pump at the crossroads, near the present chip shop, was regarded as providing the most reliable supply. The need to supply water to Kingseat Hospital led to the establishment of a reservoir to the east of Kingseat but this could not provide water to the village as well; from 1926 water was taken from wells near Tillygreig to a reservoir at Mameulah. Later an electric pump took the water up to the reservoir at Westside. This meant all of the village could have water on tap by the 1940s. Newmachar's water now comes from much further north. It is taken from the River Deveron near Turriff and comes via Udny and Craigie (917194). There is a booster pumping station at Kinmundy (896179).

Electricity came to the village in 1937 although it had been available at Kingseat and nearby houses much earlier. Outwith the village, connection was sporadic; Kinmundy, for example, did not get it until the early 1960s. (Testimony of Mr A. Low, Mr A. Buchan.) Some houses produced their own supply using a donkey engine.

In 1999 the chance to have gas laid on was made available for most of the village when it was piped in for the Wimpey, Barratt and Stewart Milne housing schemes.

****

From the soutars, tailors, smiths and millers of the seventeenth century to the inns and garden centres of 2001, tradesmen and service suppliers have responded to the ever-changing needs of the population. But that population itself has been ever-changing; one clear fact that emerges from an analysis of the evolution of shops and businesses in Newmachar is that there is a constant movement of new people into the parish, mostly from other areas of the North-east. This is balanced by people, usually young, moving out of the area. The process is known as 'step migration' and continues in the twenty-first century.

James Bisset
who used to do odd jobs around Newmachar
in the 1920s and '30s

Appendix
The 1821 and 1831 Censuses, Newmachar's Population and the Extent of Newmachar Village.

Because it was felt to be an infringement of personal and property rights, detailed information from the censuses of 1801 to 1831 was not kept; only the finally resulting total population numbers were published. However, a summary of the information is available from the records gathered by the enumerator for 1821 and 1831. Since the information is not easily available, it is printed here.

From 1841 the detailed responses to the enumerators' questions were retained. One hundred years after each census, the records are made publicly available and can be readily, if not easily, consulted. They provide a wealth of information and have been drawn on for this book. As is also indicated, the census records would provide the basis for much further research.

In a work of this kind, it would be impossible to do justice to the material without drawing up immense numbers of tables and graphs. However, for convenience, as well as the 1821 and 1831 materials, the simple totals of inhabitants are provided.

The figure for 1755 is derived from the Rev Alexander Webster's survey. He asked ministers to say how many Protestants and Papists there were in each parish. Newmachar had no Papists. He assumed that one quarter of the population would be males from 18-56 and thus potentially eligible for military service - in Newmachar's case, 238. Webster's figures are conveniently printed in *Scottish Population Studies...* ed. J.G. Kyd, Edinburgh: Scottish History Society, 3rd series, XLIV, 1952, p. 54. The figures for 1782 and 1790 are provided in OSA XV, p. 352. All the other figures are the results of the official censuses. The two earliest are probably inaccurate. The loss of population between 1881 and 1891 is probably the result of the changes in parish boundaries made at the time of local government reform. The steep rise between 1901 and 1911 reflects the opening of Kingseat Hospital with its staff and patients. The rise after 1971 is the result of new housing developments. The figure for 2001 is likely to show another considerable rise for the same reason but at the time of writing the 2001 figure is not available.

It should be noted that the 1971 Census was the last to be counted directly, parish by parish. In 1981, post code areas were used for producing parish population totals. Hence the 1981 and 1991 results are calculations for Newmachar rather than direct count results. The system for 2001 is slightly different once more. Further complications are that planners now distinguish permanent residents from those who happen to have been present on Census day. As a result, rather more realistic figures can be produced for 1981 and 1991, and these are noted below the table.

The smaller map shows Summerhill Village in 1901. For comparison the larger map shows the built-up area of the village in 1999. 'A' is a housing scheme being completed in 2001; 'B' indicates areas for which planning permission has been sought but which Aberdeenshire Council has not approved.

Population of Newmachar, 1755-1991

Census	Population	Census	Population
1755	1191	1891	1397
1782	1000	1901	1393
1790	1031	1911	1882
1801	925	1921	1961
1811	923	1931	2113
1821	1133	1941	No census
1831	1246	1951	2080
1841	1262	1961	1961
1851	1298	1971	1881
1861	1511	1981	2626
1871	1483	1991	2407
1881	1505		

In 1981, 2510 were reckoned to be actually resident, and in 1991, 2424.

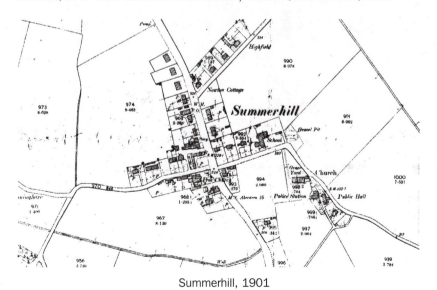

Summerhill, 1901

Form of Answers by the School Masters in Scotland to the Questions contained in the Schedule to an Act of the 1st George IV, entitled "An Act for taking an Account of the Population of Great Britain and of the Increase or Diminution thereof". - as Returned by me William Buchan School Master of the Parish, to Alexander Moir Esqr. Sheriff Depute of Aberdeen-shire, the 28th Day of June 1821.

Name & Description of Parish	Question 1st		Question 2nd	Question 3rd	Question 4th			Question 5th Persons including Children of whatever age		
Parish of New Machar in the County of Aberdeen	Inhabited Houses	By how many families occupied	Houses now building	Other Houses uninhabited	Families Chiefly Employed in Agriculture	Familes Chiefly Employed in Trade, Manufacture or Handicraft	All other Families Not comprised in the two preceding classes	Males	Females	Total of persons
Parkhill, Govil & Rosehall	59	59	0	2	34	19	6	122	161	283
Swailend	11	11	0	0	7	4	0	13	24	37
Elrick	35	35	0	1	20	15	0	69	75	144
North & South Kinmundys	47	47	0	0	25	19	3	93	109	202
Rannieshill, Boddoms & Kinghorn	55	55	0	1	32	19	4	106	115	221
Newmachar	207	207	0	4	118	76	13	403	484	887
Lands of Straloch	45	45	0	0	33	11	1	129	117	246
Totals	252	252	0	4	151	87	14	532	601	1133

Formula No 1. County of Aberdeen, Parish of New Machar containing the Population thereof, in terms of the Act of Parliament of 11th George IV entitled "An Act for taking an Account of the Population of Great Britain & of the Increase or Diminution thereof" as returned by me Willm. Buchan School master of the Parish to W. Watson Esqr. Sheriff Depute of Aberdeenshire, at Aberdeen on the 19th Day of July 1831.

	Question	In Parish of New Machar	In Lands of Straloch*	Total
1	Inhabited houses Families	199 199	44 44	243 243
2	Houses building	0	0	0
3	Houses uninhabied	0	0	0
4	Families Employed in Agriculture In Trade Manufacture All other Families	 111 24 64	 28 6 10	 138 30 74
5	Males Females	471 521	132 122	603 643
	Total population of the Parish in1831			1246
6	Males upwards of 20 years	231	73	304
7	Agricultural Occupiers 1st Class Occupiers 2nd Class Labourers in Agriculture	 42 88 50	 11 17 26	 53 105 76
8	Manufacturers	0	0	0
9	Retail Trade & Handicrafts	28	9	37
10	Wholesale & Capitalists, Clergy, Office clerks, Professional & other Educated Men	7	2	9
11	Labourers not agricultural	5	1	7
12	All other Males of 20 years	6	1	7
13	Males servants taxable upwards of 20 years under 20 years	 5 2	 6 0	 11 2
	All Female Servants Hired			77

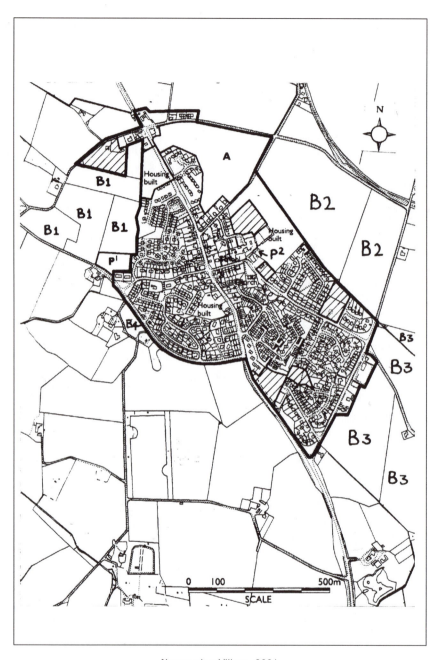

Newmachar Village, 2001

Sources

It is not the purpose of this list to show all the sources used because they have been noted in each chapter. The intention is to indicate materials which have direct reference to Newmachar.

Following the manuscript and other unpublished materials come printed primary sources. Among these, the Spalding Club editions are important; it is high time that the Club were revived.

The number of secondary works which have any direct or substantial reference to Newmachar is small. Nor is any that do exist very satisfactory for the needs of modern readers.

The manuscript or printed primary sources are the vital ones, but they are matched for the later periods by the oral testimonies and testimonies written specifically for this project. Without this testimony it would have been impossible to say anything on a great many topics and others would have been reduced to outlines. It follows that the list of the informants and contributors which follows the bibliography should be seen as equally important.

Neither a set questionnaire nor a tape recorder was used during interviews. The subjects were too varied for a fixed array of questions while a recorder can inhibit spontaneity. Generally, notes were taken during the interview and written up in a slightly more formal version afterwards.

1. BIBLIOGRAPHY

Unpublished Sources
General Register Office, Edinburgh
(i) Records of baptisms, from parish records 1676-1693, 1694-1699, 1713-1716, 1717-1854; of marriages 1676-1694, 1696-8, 1717-1793, 1798-1854; of deaths in the form of mortcloth fees records, 1738-1783, deaths 1783-1795, 1817-1854. Births, marriages and deaths after 1854 in statutory registers.
A microfilm version of the parish records is available at the Aberdeenshire Library Service Headquarters at Oldmeldrum. The parish records also contain the results of the 1821 and 1831 censuses for Newmachar.
(ii) Census Records, 1841-1891. Also available at Oldmeldrum.

Scottish Record Office
Kirk Session Records, CH2/281/1-6: Newmachar; 1665-6, 1670-6, 1676-83, 1692-1706, 1727-78, 1782-1846. The seventeenth century records tend to be fragmentary. One major blank is filled by records in Aberdeen University (see below). It is said that the patchy nature of the records is the result of losses when a session clerk's house burnt down during the eighteenth century.

University of Aberdeen Special Collections and Archives
Ms 2223 Gordon Family, Straloch 1585-1646.
Ms 2498 Notes on the Estate of Kinmundy.
Ms 2544 Newmachar Kirk Session Records, 1642-9.
Ms 2545 Kirk Session Accounts, 1667-84 concerning mainly payment of teinds.
Ms 2546 Papers concerning William Scott, 1879-83. (He was head teacher at
         Summerhill School.)
Ms 2740 Ogilvie-Forbes Papers.
Ms 2769 I/1/1-6 Stephen Family Papers 1847-80, North Kinmundy.
Ms 3652 William Shand Papers, 1816-35.

Aberdeen/Aberdeenshire Archives, Dunbar St. Old Aberdeen
Valuation Rolls 1859/60

AC 6/59/1-3 Parochial Board Minutes, 1845-95.
AC 6/59/4-5,12 Parish Council, 1895-1928.
AC 6/59/13,7,8,10 Registers of Poor, 1846-1930.
AC 6/59/9 Seperate [sic] Children's Register, 1863-1913.
AC 6/59/6 Register of Applications

AC 3/1/1- County of Aberdeen: Aberdeen District Committee Minutes,
         1894-1928.

AC 2/1/1 Sederunt Book of Trustees for Commutation Labour Roads, 1800-37.
AC 2/5/1-3 Minutes of Trustees of 6th District, 1800-66.
AC 21/1 Sederunt Book of Turnpike Trustees, 1795-1821.
AC 2/4/1 Aberdeen County Road Trustees, 1865-73.
AC 2/5/4-5 Minute Books of Aberdeen County Road Trustees, 6th District,
         1866-90.

AC 5/70/1-2 New Machar School Board Minute Book, 1873-1918.
AC 6S/G49/1/1 Log Book of Female School, 1873-86.
AC 6S/G49/1/2-3 Log Book of Summerhill School, 1873-1946.
AC 6S/G49/2/1-3 Register of Admissions, 1873-1939.
AC 6S/G49/2/4 Register of Admissions to New Machar School of Glasgow
         evacuees, mostly from Broomloan Road School, Govan, Sept 1939.

New Machar School
School Log Book, 1946-1999.

Newmachar Women's Rural Institute
Minute Books and Committee books, 1926 - 2000.

University of Aberdeen, Department of Geography
McDonald Map Collection

National Library of Scotland: Map Library
Gordon Map 32: Robert Gordon's Map of 1637.

Aberdeenshire Council
Archaeological Sites and Monuments Record.

North East Family History Society
List of inscriptions in Newmachar Churchyard compiled by Sheila Spiers.

Some unpublished Histories of Newmachar
D.R. Kerr, 'The Parish of Newmachar' n.d. [1931], 18 pp. The text of a talk
    to the WRI.
Catherine Imlah, 'A Short Outline of the History of the Parish of New Machar,'
    Typescript, n.d. [1965], 42 pp. Produced for the WRI.
Joan Burnett, a series of articles on certain aspects of Newmachar's history,
    mostly before 1800, in the Community Newsletter, intermittently
    from 7 (1979) to 99 (1995).

Unpublished Theses and Essays
James Cowie, 'The Landscape Evolution of the Parish of Newmachar,
    Aberdeenshire,' University of Aberdeen, Department of Geography
    M.A. Honours Degree Thesis, 1967.
Jill Bridges, 'School Board Membership...1873-1897' [in New Machar and Old
    Machar], Open University Essay, 1997.

Published Sources
Printed Records
Register of the Privy Council, 3rd series, 1661-1691, 16 vols, Edinburgh, 1908-
1967.

*Registrum Magni Sigilli Regum Scotorum /Register of the Great Seal of Scotland,
1306-1668*, various editors, 11 vols, Edinburgh, 1882-1914.

Spalding Club, 1841-1871, 38 vols plus six volumes uniform with the Club
series. 3(1841) contains the Straloch Papers and John Bisset's Diary; 9(1843)
includes the Description by Robert Gordon, 1662, Samuel Forbes, 1717, and

Alexander Keith, 1732; 29(1857) includes New Machar Charters (see below); in the extra series, *List of Pollable Persons 1696*, ed. John Stuart, 1844.

New Spalding Club, 1887-1924, 45 vols plus seven volumes uniform with the series. 14(1895) is *Jacobite Papers* ed. James Allardyce; 33(1907) includes the *House of Gordon* ed. John Bulloch; among the uniform works is Temple, *Thanage* (see below).

Third Spalding Club, 1929-1960, 22 vols. 3 (1932) has the Jacobite Cess Roll 1715; 4 (1933) the 1667 Valuation; 18 (1952) is Alexander's *Place Names of Aberdeenshire*.

The Statistical Accounts:

William Stronach, 'Parish of New-Machar' *The Statistical Account of Scotland*, ed. Sir John Sinclair, VI (1791), 465-476; 2nd edition, ed. D.J. Withrington & I.R. Grant, XV (1982) 349-360.

George Moir, 'Parish of New Machar,' *The New Statistical Account of Scotland*, XII (1845) 1025-1035.

Harold Ross, 'The Parish of New Machar,' *The Third Statistical Account of Scotland*, VII (1960) 156-162.

'The Parish of New Machar or Monycabock,' *Illustrations of Topography and Antiquities of the Shires of Aberdeen and Banff*, ed. Joseph Robertson, Vol. III, Spalding Club 1857, pp. 198-210. (Thirteen legal documents in Latin or English, 1405-1706.)

Geographical Collections Relating to Scotland made by Walter Macfarlane [d. 1767] ed. A. Mitchell, Scottish History Society, 1st series, 3 vols. 51-3 (1906-8). Vol. 51, 84-5 had the account of New Macar [sic].

Newspapers, Periodicals and Guides
Aberdeen Journal, 1876-1921.
Aberdeen Press and Journal, 1922-.
Aberdeen Journal, Notes and Queries, 8 vols, 1908-15.
The Aberdeen Almanac, [titles vary] 1773-1932.
Ellon Times, 1991-.
Pigot and Co's *New Commercial Directory of Scotland for 1825-6*, p. 197.
Worral's *Directory for Aberdeen and Banff*, Oldham, 1877, pp. 161-3.
F.H. Groome, *Ordnance Gazeteer of Scotland*, 6 vols, 1882-5 and later editions to 1903.
A Guide to Donside, Aberdeen, 1844.
Hew Scott, *Fasti Ecclesiae Scoticanae*, Vol. VI (1926) 65-68 covers Newmachar.
G. Reid and W. Ferguson, *Twelve Sketches of Scenery and Antiquities on the Line of the GNS Railway*, Edinburgh, 1883.

A.I. McConnochie, *Donside*, Aberdeen, 1900 2nd ed, ed. D. Withrington, 1985. The principal entry on Newmachar is pp. 32-3.

Secondary Works

Books, articles and newspaper features having major reference to Newmachar.

J.F.K. Johnstone, *A Concise Bibliography of the History, Topography and Institutions of the Shires of Aberdeen, Banff and Kincardine*, Aberdeen: Aberdeen University Studies No. 66, 1914. P. 115 specifically covers New Machar; this appears to be the only previous published bibliography for Newmachar in existence.

John Bulloch, 'Historic Scenes in Aberdéenshire' a series of articles in the *Weekly News*, 1883-5. Newmachar is featured on 13 Oct 1883. [It is a dismissive and careless piece of work.]

J. Cruickshank, 'The Palace at Bishop's Loch,' *Aberdeen University Review*, XXX (1943-4) 312-14.

George A. Davidson, *Memories of Whiterashes*, Aberdeen, 1983.

Cuthbert Graham, 'Achievement in Newmachar,' (This is my Country series) *Press and Journal*, 23 Feb. 1963.

Cuthbert Graham, 'Newmachar leaps Ahead,' *ibid*, 27 March, 1971.

J.A. Henderson, *Aberdeenshire Epitaphs and Inscriptions ... and Antiquarian Notes.*' Abedeen, 1907. New Machar is covered on pp. 441-460.

[D.R. Kerr,] *Guesses at Truth*, Aberdeen, 1913. Pp. 3-8 cover the history of the U.F.C. in Newmachar.

Kingseat Hospital, Newmachar, 1904-1979: 75 Years Commemorative Booklet, Aberdeen, 1979.

M. Munro, *Geology of the Country around Aberdeen*, Memoirs of the British Geological Survey, Sheet 77 (Scotland), 1986.

Alexander Smith, *A New History of Aberdeenshire*, 2 parts, 1875, Parish of New Machar is covered pp. 1034-1044 [in an often inaccurate account].

William Temple, *TheThanage of Fermartyn* ..., Aberdeen, 1894. pp. 287-329 deals with the parish of Newmachar and the genealogy of its proprietor families.

Website

The Genuki Website (Genealogy UK and Ireland) has pages on Newmachar consisting of a list of farm names, a slightly inaccurate statement of birth [sic] marriage and death records and the 1875 Alexander Smith text.

2.   LIST OF INFORMANTS AND CONTRIBUTORS

NB. The children from New Machar School and Dyce Academy who contributed to Chapter XIX are listed there.

Harold Barclay, (the late) Roy Barclay, Dr John Beattie, Mrs Margaret Begbie, Mrs Ethel Begg, Mrs Mhairi Bogdan, Nicholas Bogdan, Alastair Bridges, Dr John Bridges, Mrs Sheila Bruce, Alexander Buchan, Mrs Joan Burnett, Mrs Rita Burr, George Cameron, Mrs Marie Cameron, Henry G. Catto, Kenneth Chilles, James Cowie, Mrs Agnes Cran, Prof. Alistair Crawford, Mrs Chrissie Davies, Dr Margaret Deacon, Rev. Ian Dryden, Norman Duncan, Mrs Jean Emslie, Mrs Peggy Findlay, J. Douglas Flett, Mrs Jenny Gray, Mrs Betty Harley, David James Harvey, Alec Hay, Mrs Ann Edward Hay, Ian Henderson, Fergus Hood, Mrs Catherine Imlah, James Imlah, Alexander Ingram, Alistair Ingram, Donald Ingram, Robbie Ingram, Maurice Innes, Major Francis Irvine, Mrs Catherine Keith, Leslie Keith, Mrs Wendy Kelman, Matthew Kennedy, Mrs Rhona Kennedy, Dave Lee, Archie Low, Christopher MacLaughlin, John Mearns, Mr A. Middler, Mrs Evelyn Middleton, William Middleton, George Mitchell, Mrs Margaret Mitchell, Mrs Marigold Nicol, Dr Ian Olson, Mrs Frances Peace, Mrs Cecilia Penny, George Rennie, Mrs Cham Robb, Albert Robertson, Mrs Ellen Robertson, Mrs Jean Robertson, Miss Seonag Robertson, Mrs Ada Ross, Angus Ross, Bert Sangster, Ann Savours, Colin L. Silver, Mrs Dorothy Smith, Prof. David Stevenson, Mrs Annie Strachan, Bruce Sutherland, Mrs Frances Taylor, John Taylor, Mrs Ruth Taylor, Mrs Alison Thomson, Laurie Tinto, Prof. Agathe Thornton, Miss Alison Thornton, Bernard Thornton, Hector Urquhart, Mrs Elizabeth Walker, Steve Wilson, Brian Wood.